They've got
Rockies
in their heads!

**The Colorado Rockies' first season
...from the fans' point of view.**

Lew Cady

With forewords by
Patricia Calhoun,
Jim Carrier,
Norm Clarke,
Alan Dumas,
Bill Gallo,
Jack Kisling,
Dick Kreck,
David Lamb,
Greg Lopez,
J.R. Moehringer,
Mike Rosen,
and David Whitford.

Mile High Press
Denver, Colorado

December 1993
First Edition

ISBN 0-9639257-0-9

Additional copies of this book can be ordered by mail from the publisher.
Send $12 per copy (includes $2 shipping charge and tax) to Mile High Press
at the address below.

Published by Mile High Press
P.O. Box 9783
Denver, Colorado 80209
(303) 722-8357

Acknowledgements.

Numbers. They're the essence of baseball.

When someone wondered whether it really matters if Denver has major league baseball, this was the answer he got:

When it's a big league game, everything is being counted.

"Not just every at-bat and every out, but every pitch, its placement, velocity and ilk."

There are a number of people I need to thank.

This person helped by filling his pockets with peanuts and taking me as a kid to Denver Bears games at Merchants Park and, later, at Bears Stadium:

My father, H. H. Cady.

These people helped by listening to and watching the crowd instead of the game. They reported lots of good fan antics:

Jack Hidahl. Jim House. Diane Kaminsky. Dick Kreck. Peter Milstein. John Mason. Tony Trampler.

These people helped in a variety of other ways: Roger Kinney (for providing answers to some questions and pointing me toward the right answerers for others). Pat Milstein (for a lot of prooffreadingg). Mary Kisling (for research). Greg Lopez (for lots of kinds of help). Clark Secrest (for the final word on words). Lonnie Smith (for helping me with many aspects of production). Joe Mayo (for MacHelp). Joyce Meskis (for good advice). Dick Veit (for his eye). Jim McCoy (for his hand). The good people at my day job at EvansGroup (for lots of reasons). The magnificent dozen who wrote forewords (for obvious reasons). Susan Cady (for being a healthy pocket of Colorado fandom in San Francisco). Jane Cady (for driving me to Rockies games, sometimes literally).

This person helped by designing the cover and making the color pages look good:

Don Kibbe.

This person helped in many ways, with research and trips to the library—and by programming our Central City Opera functions around the Rockies' home schedule as much as possible:

Leslie Cady.

These people helped make the first season a delicious brew of observations on life, oddball statistics, silliness—and brew:

The denizens of Section 116.

Introduction.

Most of us don't play baseball on the field.

We play in the stands.

This is our story.

THEY'VE GOT ROCKIES IN THEIR HEADS is made up of capsule treatments of the 162 games the Rockies played plus a collection of comments, cracks, and criticism from fans at the 81 home games.

A glance will reveal that I didn't really write this book.

I compiled it.

It made a hunter-gatherer out of me.

I hunted for the interesting things that Rockies fans did in the stands. And the funny things. And the *strange* things.

Then I gathered all these things up and arranged them chronologically.

The book opens with forewords from a dozen people who like both baseball and words. (The original plan was to have nine forewords, one for each inning, but before I knew it we'd gone into extra innings.)

Each of the twelve forewords (twelvewords?) takes a different angle on being a fan of the Colorado Rockies and/or the great game of baseball.

Essentially, this book is by and about the best baseball fans in the history of the planet.

Is saying they're the best fans going a bit too far?

Indeed, the overly critical would point out that Rockies fans were guilty of doing the wave. Some would add that they can also be faulted for booing strategically sound maneuvers like intentional walks and repeated attempts to pick off a base runner. These acts of uncouthness in the ballpark are, indeed, disheartening. But they are small matters in light of the enormity of the support these people have given the Rockies.

Perhaps it would be more correct to designate the fans of the 1993 Rockies as the *greatest* baseball fans of all time.

Numerically, there's no denying it. In their inaugural season, the Rockies fans *were* the greatest. In numbers.

Not only were there more of them than any baseball team has ever enjoyed, they were more numerous than any team in any sport has ever known.

Yes: In the history of the planet.

Let us, then, bicker no more and recognize the Rockies' fans as the Greatest Fans In The History of Sports.

The official, final, killer number was 4,483,350 .

That, of course, includes no-shows from the astounding 28,627 season ticket base. It represents all tickets sold.

The actual, true, honest-to-Ruth turnstile number was 3,841,365. That's still far above the population of the state.

It's civic obsession on a colossal scale.

A question occurs. Does this enormous fan support make the Rockies the best-loved team in sports history...or the most-loved?

If you don't think there's a difference, ask Wade Boggs.

Of course, the Rockies could be both. Best *and* most.

Ask Steve Garvey about that.

The surprise of '93.

David Whitford

One of the first things I noticed in my travels between expansion cities in the months leading up to opening day was that you saw a hell of a lot more Rockies hats in Denver than you saw Marlins hats in Miami (or Red Sox hats in Boston, for that matter).

I only wish I'd put that in my book. Because then maybe I could claim credit for having had some inkling all along that the Rockies would draw 4,483,350 their first year in the league and destroy every attendance record known to the world of professional sports.

The truth is, alas, *I had no idea.*

Of course, I'd been told about the big crowds that used to turn out back in the '70s and '80s to watch the Bears and later the Zephyrs, not to mention the occasional big-league teams passing through on their way home from spring training. I knew how many thousands of season tickets Denver fans snapped up long before the actual awarding of the franchise. I had heard about the big show the city put on for the traveling NL expansion committee, back in the spring of '91. And I like to think I had come to appreciate—to the extent an outsider can— the depth of Denver's pent-up yearning for baseball.

But did I foresee 4,483,350? Never in 4,483,350 years.

And neither, by the way, did the Rockies executives I talked to, whose early business plans assumed 2 million tops, which struck me, skeptical reporter I am, as wildly optimistic. So here's to you, Rockies fans, for proving the experts wrong. May you demand, and receive, your money's worth in years to come. And may your devotion be rewarded.

David Whitford is the author of many articles and books about sports including Extra Innings: A Season in the Senior League *(HarperCollins) and* Playing Hardball: The High-Stakes Battle for Baseball's New Franchises *(Doubleday).*

Baseball is about losing.

J.R. Moehringer

I asked everyone.

Finally, it was a fat kid from Texas who had the answer.

Holding my notebook aloft like a candle, I meandered among the multitudes in search of the last honest fan, the one who could intelligently answer my question:

Why are you here?

From the first 78-degree day of spring training (ah, Tucson, how you shimmer in the wintry memory!) until the final home game (Eric Young's *tour de fluke*),I watched people watching the Rockies, and tried to unlock one of the baseball writer's most tantalizing mysteries:

Why do some fans rush in where even Roger Angell fears to tread?

Even when I was assigned to write about Rockies fans, I never dreamed that 4.48 million subjects would be assembled for my informal survey. How could I have known that Coloradans meant to make mincemeat of all previous fan marks, and that in counting their awesome numbers I would get a little closer to the core question, which forms the square root of all rooting:

What makes you a fan?

It's a question baseball lovers often won't brook, since being a fan is one of life's imponderables, like being Sagittarius or short. When you're a fan, you just are. It's like being a human, and picture your reaction if some gooney reporter accosted you and asked, "Pardon me, but why are you a person?

Nevertheless, I had to ask. Covering a summerlong fandango, I felt a responsibility to pose the occasional cosmic question.

I suspected that Frederick Exley had touched on the secret near the end of his great novel, *A Fan's Notes*, when he linked fanhood with fate.

"I understand, and could not bear to understand," he wrote, "that it was my destiny...to sit in the stands with most men and acclaim others. It was my fate, my destiny, my end, to be a fan."

In Denver, there was certainly that same sense of fatalism. Colorado fans described their need to cheer as one in which they had exercised no free will.

When you're a fan, they told me, something existential and inexplicable draws you to the park, and it keeps you there as surely as a dollop of super glue beneath your hindquarters.

"Every time you come," said Rich Bristol, a Littleton horticulturalist with a far-off look in his eyes that was only partly attributable to his seats in the upper deck, "you just can't wait for the next time."

Sensing a fellow seeker of truth, a real fan, I asked frantically:

Why? What makes the experience so compelling?

But he only gave me a loopy grin and returned his gaze to the field, which was the most common reaction I encountered all summer. Like interviewing a teenager in front of a mirror, you never felt that you had the Rockies fan's full attention when you interviewed him at the ballpark.

Because these weren't baseball fans. They were *Rockies* fans, in love with a team that could do no right, but one they thought could do no wrong, and when you're in love like that you just want to stare at the object of your affection without asking pesky questions.

That's unconditional love, I think, which not only has zilch to do with baseball but has a little to do with our childhood and everything to do with failure.

And, more or less, that's what the fat kid from Texas told me.

He was a likable young college freshman with a natural seatbelt around his midriff formed by too many late night or ballpark beers. After watching an inning or two with him, I pounced.

Like all the others, he didn't divert his gaze from the field. But he did throw me a learning curve.

"The game's designed for failure," he said. "That's what draws everyone out. Everyone out there"—he pointed at the field—"isn't a success."

Yes. How true. Football is an endgame of chaotic successes, with field goals providing a pathetic palliative for underachievers.

In basketball, toting up the score of even a dismal team is like tallying ill-gotten gains on Wall Street. How can a team score 98 points and lose, baseball fans ask.

But baseball is about losing, losing, losing, then learning

not only to live with losing, but somehow to love it.

When a team goes 67-95, you can look at your ticket stubs and tell yourself with the martyr's snug smugness: What a great year. I was there when they needed me most.

And there's no disgrace in it. Cubs fans, Red Sox fans, Phillies fans will understand what you're saying, while Raiders fans will edge slowly out of the room.

Which is just as well.

In baseball, there's less disgrace in losing. In fact, losing is the norm, and that's a balm for a town synonymous with oil busts, smog, and Super Bowl blowouts.

Baseball snobs have speculated recently that as the Rockies continue their losing ways, the best-ever fans will fade.

Wrongo. In 1993, Coloradans fell head-over-heels in love with losing.

It was a pleasure watching them raise "expectationless spectating" to an art form, and I predict they will repeat the feat in summers ahead.

The next real test will come when the Rockies start to win.

Cole Porter was only half right. Gibraltar may tumble, the Rockies may crumble, but are our fans here to stay?

Perhaps. But it's probably more accurate to spend this winter musing on the lyrics of John Lennon, who voiced the only real Rockies worry at the end of Season One.

Will you still need me, will you still feed me, when I'm 98-and-64?

J.R. Moehringer writes for the Rocky Mountain News. For the inaugural season, he was assigned to cover the fans of the Rockies from spring training to the first game in New York to the stands of Mile High.

The Cat owes me.

Dick Kreck

I was among thousands who trekked to Arizona in March to get a preseason look at the newly birthed Colorado Rockies.

It was a peculiar experience.

Spring training is not baseball as fans know it. The players are mostly unknowns, the strategies are often unfathomable and, ultimately, the games are meaningless, proven by the fact that the Rockies had the winningest springtime record.

Andres Galarraga, who wound up winning the National League batting championship, was struggling through spring training. He hadn't had a hit in 12 times at bat. One day, from my seat just off the on-deck circle, I shouted some coaching advice:

"HEY, ANDRES, HOW ABOUT GETTING *ONE* HIT THIS SPRING!"

I know he heard me because he turned, winked, and gave me that famous grin.

Then he stepped to the plate and drove a single to right field to score a run. When he got to first base, he looked right at me and grinned again.

In the next three games he went 5-for-11, knocking two home runs and three doubles.

After that, all he did, all season long, was hit.

And that's how I saved Andres Galarraga's career. All it took was a kind word.

I wrote about our training-camp exchange in my column in the Denver Post on March 17 and repeated it later in the season when everyone took note of his bloated numbers.

He's never denied it.

As Ol' Case would say, "You could look it up."

Dick Kreck, a columnist for The Denver Post, was a pitcher in high school who was scouted by the Chicago White Sox for two pitches. The scout thought Dick was warming up, but that was as hard as Dick could throw. Years later, Dick was struck on the chest by a fly ball hit by Dave Herman as part of the opening day festivities in a Southern California summer league.

View from a broad.

Patricia Calhoun

My career as a baseball fan began—and, until this spring, ended—with the 1968 Chicago Cubs. Not the 1969 Cubbies, who came so close to taking it all, but that slightly earlier model, noteworthy for perhaps nothing more than the team's ability to bridge the gap between adolescent boys and girls.

These were days of deep and abiding mystery; days when boys would go through puberty during a single slow dance to "MacArthur Park." You'd start out bear-hugging a short soprano, and end up clutched by some sweating behemoth sprouting whispers. And when he opened his mouth, some alien voice—half husky, half squeaky—would emerge. But it was still talking about the Cubs.

That diamond at Wrigley Field remains a bright spot in my otherwise murky memory. Our eighth-grade classes rang with discussions of the merits of various Cubs. Kenny Holtzman came in for much acclaim—most of those slow dances were at bar mitzvah parties—but other Cubs had their supporters, too. In perhaps the first and last traditional value I would ever espouse, I occasionally made a stand for Ernie Banks, arguably Chicago's greatest statesman/sportsman, if hardly a flashy fellow.

But then we moved on to high school, and forgot about baseball in order to concentrate on More Important Things. It was not until almost 25 years later—in the summer of 1993, in fact—that I realized there are no things more important than baseball. There is nothing that beats siting with a few of your close personal friends—usually people you met three minutes earlier when their kid spilled a Coke down your leg—drinking beer, basking in the sunshine, and marveling at what Major League baseball brings to a city. Among these wonders:

Truly unforgettable versions of the National Anthem. I ached along with Congressman David Skaggs as he reached for that high note...and the Bismarck, North Dakota Jazz Choir's rendition—well, as they always say, if you want to hear jazz, visit North Dakota.

Folks from Oklahoma and Wyoming catching their very first Major League game, and shouting louder than anyone else by the second inning. (If Okies can figure out how to cheer, why can't Canadians?)

The big butts of baseball. Maybe it's the uniform—designed to make even the buff-est Rocky look Dad-like. Maybe it's the beer. Maybe it's the view from the third base line, as the batter approaches and wiggles his posterior in accordance with his own inner voodoo. One female friend offered her firstborn in exchange for my first-level seat, just to watch Jerald Clark shake his booty. Again, maybe it's the beer, but there are certain unsung aesthetic bonuses to this game.

Decreased divorce rates. This could be related to all those butts in motion; I don't know. But according to the University of Denver Center for Marital Studies, which is supposed to know these things, cities with Major League teams have lower divorce rates than other towns.

The beer. Could the beer vendors at Mile High Stadium be more accommodating?

Camaraderie in the most unlikely places. After pulling every string I could think of, I managed to scalp some tickets to opening day at Shea Stadium. The weather was freezing, and the overflowing bathrooms played havoc with our beer quota, but the day was marvelous nonetheless. Getting off the subway at Grand Central Station, we ran smack into a panhandler wearing a spanking new Rockies hat.

Slurring his words but slightly, he announced: I love Colorado.

Don't we all?

Patricia Calhoun is the editor of Westword.

The sport that needs no introduction.

Jack Kisling

I hadn't really planned to go to the Rockies' home opener at Mile High Stadium this spring until I was reminded that it was a once-in-a-lifetime opportunity. So is getting married the first time, I thought. Then, out loud, I said: "OK. Let's go!"

It's never too late to learn to love baseball, so I trooped out into the fresh air, sat down among 80,226 other baseball lovers, and began anew.

It was an unusual game. There were *two* national anthems, allowing my thoughts plenty of time to drift back to the baseball of my boyhood, and to that old first-baseman's mitt that still hangs in a dark corner of my basement. It's an expensive mitt, still redolent of neat's-foot oil and dust, tinted now to a rich cordovan and dappled with the bruises of many thousands of sudden meetings with the old horsehide.

Not one of which I had anything to do with. The mitt was given to me by my uncle and as a kid I treasured it because it saved me from humiliation when sides were chosen up. With that noble mitt dangling from my belt, I had a fighting chance of being picked before they started filling in with girls. And when, after an inning or so, it was discovered that I couldn't catch a cold, I could earn my teammates' gratitude by lending my swell mitt to someone who knew which hand it went on.

In those days I was more at home with bats than with mitts. Being a switch hitter, I usually switched to something else after my first trip to the plate, and this worked so well that when I finally gave up the game, it was with the perfect record of never hitting into a double play, or anything else.

Watching those Rockies swing into action made me feel like taking my old mitt down off its peg, slipping it onto my left hand and thwacking my right fist into it a few times, for this never fails to bring tears to my eyes as I recall some of the most miserable and boring summer afternoons a red-blooded American boy ever spent.

Jack Kisling writes a column thrice-weekly for The Denver Post. Copies of his novel, The Crow Flies Crooked *(McKay), are harder to find than a beer vendor in the eighth inning.*

Growing up with a team.

Alan Dumas

Aaron Clifton-Roser is 12 years old. Though he may not fully realize it yet, the inaugural season of the Colorado Rockies will stand prominently among the most unforgettable summers of his life. This, in his own words, is his account of that experience.

It took too long for the Rockies to come, you know? They talked about it way too much. Things go faster if I forget about stuff, like in class when I look at the clock, it never moves.

The first baseball game I ever saw was a Mariners game, but I was in my mother's stomach and she doesn't remember who won. I might have seen it, though, if she opened her mouth to yawn or take in some food. If they ever do good that means I could be a Mariners fan, but if they suck I just don't say anything. I like Ken Griffey Jr., though.

The second game I ever saw was when I was 5 and it was the Royals vs. the Blue Jays. The Royals won. I don't know all the stats but I remember Bo Jackson and Brian McRae.

From the very beginning with the Rockies Eric Young was my favorite player, even before he hit the home run at the home opener. I saw him on a TV commercial and I just liked the look of him. My second favorite was Alex Cole but then it became Galarraga. I don't like Dante because he looks like a transvestite or a psycho killer in all the baseball cards I have.

I went to Opening Day and I knew they'd be fired up, except Dan Fogelberg sang the National Anthem. I hate that guy. Then EY came up and I said he's my favorite player. He cranked one out of the park and I just started screaming.

I saw 30 games this year, and my favorites were when a fan dumped beer on me and when a guy gave me a beer cup and a popcorn box and a Phillies batting helmet just to go buy him some yogurt.

And I like the retarded guy who sells pizza. I like being in there with all the vendors. It's like you can smell baseball.

I think Baylor should send Mejia back to the minor leagues. Young's a better second baseman. But the Rockies are my favorite team now. I mean that's the team I grew up with.

Alan Dumas is a writer for the Rocky Mountain News.

You didn't have to be there.

Greg Lopez

The Colorado Rockies were playing the Houston Astros at Mile High Stadium, and the men sat at the kitchen table with the radio between them, arguing about whether Andres Galarraga needs to lose weight.

The apartment is seven blocks from Mile High Stadium. The radio always is on KOA. The television blew its tube two years ago, but sometimes for a change they turn it on and listen to a couple of innings on television.

"See how long it takes for him to walk to the plate?" Nick Samuels said. "I can get up and walk to the mailbox and back faster than that. Some things you don't need to see."

"So how do you know he's fat if you never even saw him?" Al Martino said. "If he's so fat, how come we can hear everyone cheering from here? You even admitted that was almost as good as being there."

Martino is 79, Samuels is 78, and they share the apartment and the Colorado Rockies. The Rockies set the major league attendance record without them. They had to call the newspaper over whether Dante Bichette looks Italian.

"You think you know everything about baseball," Samuels said. "So how come we never agree on anything?"

"What a coincidence," Martino said. "Two old guys like us, and for both of us our favorite thing is to sit here and listen to the games and argue."

It probably isn't as much of a coincidence as they think, but enough that they will argue for two innings over whether Charlie Hayes lost a ball in the sun.

The Rockies drew 4,483,350 fans to Mile High Stadium, and two men to the kitchen in the apartment seven blocks away.

Sometimes, they can hear everyone cheering.

I was thinking the other night," Samuels said. "I never really knew I liked baseball before this."

"I wonder," Martino said. "How many other people out there were Rockies fans before this year but never even knew it?"

Greg Lopez writes for the Rocky Mountain News.

No ketchup on hot dogs.

Mike Rosen

As a kid who grew up in New York City with the Brooklyn Dodgers, the Yankees and the Giants, I've been a baseball fan all my life. I recall my ritual, first thing each morning, checking out the sports section of the New York Daily Mirror for statistical confirmation of what Mantle, Mays and Snider had done the day before. You knew it, but it wasn't really official until you saw it in the box scores.

Major League Baseball is like no other sport. It's more like a religion. We who grew up in major league cities tried to explain to Denverites who hadn't what it would be like. Now they know. It'll get even better when the Rockies are contending for a pennant.

Having said all that, there's something I've got to get off my chest. I went to 29 games this year, and there's no questioning the loyalty and enthusiasm of Rockies fans. Many, however, are rookies to MLB fandom. They need help. So, it is in the vein of constructive criticism that I make these observations and suggestions.

✓ You *don't* put ketchup on hot dogs. When God created hot dogs, he intended that they be garnished with mustard. Sauerkraut is also acceptable—in fact, I recommend it—as a complement to mustard, but ketchup is out.

✓ Home fans rise to celebrate their team in the *middle* of the seventh inning; i.e., after the last out in the top of the seventh and before the first batter in the bottom of the inning. That's why we have the community singing exercise then. If you stand right after the last out in the sixth, you're indicating your support for the Braves, Cubs, Phillies or some other enemy nine. There are visiting team fans at Rockies games, and they have every right to make their seventh-inning vertical statement, but I've seen other people in full Rockies regalia unknowingly practice premature seventh-inning stretching.

✓ There is a way to yell at the players and umpires, and a way *not* to yell at them. Virtually anything can be shouted at an umpire. He not need be referred to by name. "Hey, you bum, what game are ya watchin?," for example, is perfectly acceptable. Conversely, when you approve of a ruling, something like: "Nice call, blue," connotes approbation and adds an insider's touch with the congenial appellation " blue."

Players, on the other hand, should always be referred to by name. You can generally find those names displayed on the backs of their jerseys or in the program next to their number. Avoid remarks like: "Hey! No. 29, you throw like a girl!" Certainly *never* say anything like: "Hey! batter, batter, batter." You'll embarrass the whole stadium. That's for kids in the Little League. Something on the order of: "Furillo, you stink!" is an old standby that you can't go wrong with. Substitute another name if necessary.

✓ One last note, and this is a longstanding, personal pet peeve. I was at a game at Mile High that went into the 10th inning, at which point several thousand people got up to leave. (Many of these same people didn't get to the game until the third inning.) It was 4 o'clock on a Sunday afternoon. Where the heck did they have to go? How can you watch three hours of baseball building to an extra-innings climax, and leave before it's resolved? If you're going to arrive late and leave early, why come?

Such people are not true baseball fans. I bet they put ketchup on their hot dogs, too.

Mike Rosen is a well-known Denver personality. He's a KOA talk show host and a regular columnist in the Denver Post.

The authentic fan.

Bill Gallo

In the century-long preamble to the arrival of Major League Baseball in this city, baseball has always been present, and it's always been appreciated—at least by those who hold The Game itself more valuable than the dream of a big league pennant or the Second Coming of Barry Bonds.

Before Colorado Rockies fans gathered in Chinese-army numbers at Mile High Stadium (or in U.S.-army numbers at Coors Field) they gathered at Merchants Park, at Jack Carberry Field, at Bears Stadium, or the sandlots of neighborhood legend, to witness the timeless drama and the persistent comedy that is baseball. They did so without paying $3.75 for a cup of beer, enduring the temper tantrums of twenty-four-year-old multi-millionaires, or feeling the undeniable urge to perform The Wave in mid-inning.

Baseball fans—true baseball fans—came not for the hype, not for the thrill of feeling Major League at last, but for the simple thrill of the double play turned at twilight, the spiked shoe hooked into third an instant before the sweep tag, the smile illuminating a kid's face upon finally snagging a fly ball to left.

These are the eternal attractions of baseball, and they have little to do with the presence of ESPN's cameras, the negotiation of multi-year contracts that would shock a sheikh, or the instincts of owners who stuff extra seats into a new ballpark and greedily crow about the sales of officially licensed caps, bats and bottles.

The beauties of the Major League game may be grander than those of the Little Leaguer or the Denver Bear, but the authentic fan always remembers a couple of things out at the ballyard, wherever it may be. This is the game that made us. Those are boys out there. Let's hope they'd play for pleasure.

For better or worse, the Bigs have nothing to do with it.

Bill Gallo writes about sports for Westword.

The disease of the incurable fan.

David Lamb

A few years ago, while writing a book on minor league baseball, I had occasion to spend a week in Denver with the Zephyrs. Mile High Stadium was cavernous and mostly empty in those days, and by the time I got to Denver, the season was nearly over. The city's thoughts were turning to football.

During the four months I had been on the road, rattling through minor league towns in my RV, I had tried to remain more an observer than a fan, keeping a certain distance between myself and the players and idolatry that is part of the baseball landscape.

But my last day with the Zephyrs, standing at the batting cage and talking with Lamar Johnson, the Milwaukee Brewers' roving batting instructor, an unexpected fantasy overcame me, as though I suddenly understood that a secret mission had brought me to Denver: I was the forty-nine-year-old writer who had come to save the pennant for the Zephyrs. My feet remained planted in dirt but my mind raced across the grass, and from the deserted stands behind me the crowd's roar grew.

The catches I made were miraculous. Every ball—a liner to left, a towering drive into the alleyway between center and right—found its way into my glove after a long run, and soon the Zephyrs put down their bats and stepped away from the cage to watch. My arm was a cannon, not at all like the chicken wing that had strained in grammar school to get the ball from short to first, and the strikes I fired from right field struck the catcher's mitt with a loud pop, arriving on the fly, a foot off the ground.

Johnson waved me in and I took my place in the cage. I felt loose and strong and invincible. The bat was light as a broom handle and the first pitch I drove high over the outfield fence. I set my feet again. Bugles sounded "Charge!" and in the press box Frank Haraway, who had covered Denver baseball for nearly sixty years, reached out, ready to clang his old bell. The pitches came in machine-gun-fire succession, and each one thundered off my bat and hurtled toward the clouds. The Zephyrs had found their Hurricane Bob Hazel and together we would rope the stars and conquer the heavens.

I carried the fantasy with me on the way out of Denver, plotting the story of the mysterious stranger whose astonishing skills had been hidden for half his life. My summer journey had broken the chains of journalism and freed my imagination. Now, bound for Salt Lake, home of the Pioneer League Trappers, slipping through the Eisenhower Tunnel and climbing the Continental Divide, I knew I had been afflicted with the dream disease of the incurable fan. It is, in fact, our ability to lose ourselves in dreams that explains the hold baseball had on our lives and as I drove west on Route 40, a voice asked again, "If someone is to be chosen for stardom, am I the one?"

And the answer came back: "Why not?"

David Lamb has traveled the world as a correspondent for the Los Angeles Times. He is the author of The Arabs *and* The Africans *and* Sense of Place *and* Stolen Season: A Journey Through America and Baseball's Minor Leagues *(Random House).*

The first game I never saw.

Norm Clarke

Mom and Dad were on the telephone. They were in New York City for something called the World Series. I was nine, a kid from Montana who had never seen a minor league game, let alone anything of the magnitude of the Yankees and Dodgers.

But even for that young age, I sensed this was something big. It had been a main dinner table topic for weeks. The way townfolk reacted, not too many people actually got to see a World Series.

This was October, 1951. Television was still several years away from reaching isolated Eastern Montana. Gunsmoke and the Game of the Week were not words in our vocabulary. Imagine the excitement in tiny Terry, Montana when the World Series finally arrived, beamed through our snow-flecked, black and white TV screens.

When my parents came home from their World Series trip, they brought gifts for the kids, my sister Nancy and little brother Newell. Mine was a silver replica of the Empire State Building. Kept it in a drawer for years, treating it as some treasured artifact. My mother had another souvenir: a matchbook. On the cover was a black-and-white photo of her, my father and the Hickeys at a New York City restaurant.

When my father died little more than a year after the 1951 World Series, that matchbook was, for many years, the most vivid memory of Dad.

When I was older I often wondered if the World Series trip was one of Dad's final wishes.

That thought overwhelmed me in October 1976, when I entered Yankee Stadium for the first time and stood near the batting cage. I was there as a sportswriter for the Associated Press, covering the World Series between the Yankees and Cincinnati's Big Red Machine. Dad would have loved that, every bit as much as I enjoyed the idea that he was there in 1951, watching Joe DiMaggio take his final swings before retirement and two rookie outfielders named Mickey Mantle and Willie Mays.

As Pete Rose, Johnny Bench and Tony Perez took turns

in the batting cage, I temporarily forgot the assignment at hand and indulged in a moment of personal nostalgia. I found myself scanning the cavernous ballpark. Where did my parents sit? Were their World Series tickets somewhere among our family keepsakes? If only I could find those tickets.

Someday I would like to take a child to Yankee Stadium and watch a game from my parents' seats. It would be a nice way to complete the circle. Because that's where it began for me, that lifelong connection with baseball.

The 1951 World Series. Yankee Stadium. DiMaggio, Mantle and Mays.

Norm Clarke, a sports columnist for the Rocky Mountain News, is the author of High Hard Ones, Denver's Road to the Rockies from Inside the Newspaper War, *which chronicles the city's efforts to win a National League franchise in the midst of a fierce newspaper war.*

True purple fans.

Jim Carrier

Baseball rising over the Rockies has sent the howlin' coyote packing in artsy Santa Fe.

In Kansas, the Rockies are pushing the Royals toward the Missouri.

And in Wolf Point, Mont., a long fly ball from Canada, where baseball is heard on the Northern Ag Network, "CR" caps are replacing "Banvel" (a herbicide) and "United Grain."

We're talking regional ball here.

From Hobbs, N.M., to Coolidge, Ariz. to Conway, Ark., to Bend, Ore., to Belle Fourche, S.D., to Garden City, Kan., the Rockies have quickly snared a fan base that may be the largest in the country in terms of square miles.

So far, 11 percent of the season tickets have come from outside Colorado. The true-purplest fans are driving three hours from Wyoming and Nebraska.

The Rockies games are being heard on 60 radio stations in 11 states, including 11 in Wyoming, seven in Montana, six in Utah, five in New Mexico and three each in South Dakota, Nebraska and Kansas.

The televised games are being seen on eight stations in seven states.

For my sports money, nothing beats a game fading and crackling on radio from some distant place. Long before the Rush Limbaughs trashed up the dial, the night belonged to baseball.

"We had a fellow call from Gallup, N.M., 250 miles from our transmitter, wanting to know if we could increase our power during the games," said Lance Armer, manager of KBOM in Santa Fe. "We've even had people ask how far they'd have to drive to hear the Rockies."

Jim Carrier covers the West for the Denver Post.

Dedicated to the guy Jim Armstrong spotted
in Tucson during Spring Training
who was carrying one of those home-made cardboard signs.

Instead of "Will work for food,"
this guy's sign said, "Why lie? I need a beer."

"Whoever heard of the Rockies before this year?"
– Danny Glover

"The Rockies may be the first team in history to draw four
million fans and give up four million runs."
– Woody Paige

"Isn't it about time Major League Baseball finally awarded
a franchise to Denver?"

"Nah. Every year it'll be the same thing—win the pennant,
lose the World Series. Win the pennant, lose the World Series.
Win the pennant, lose the World Series."
– Inside Sports

"You must recognize baseball for the piddly, inconsequential
goings-on that it is."
– Holling Vincouer
on
Northern Exposure

Entrepreneurs. Some call 'em RockHats. Some call 'em Rocky Mountain Mohawks. It's a CR Helmet with a mini mountain range on top. A brainstorm of Mike Barrowman (front) and his pals, Mark and Matt, RockHats are the ultimate in strange CR headgear. A business venture was also launched by Bert Matthews (below). When he wasn't it jail, he sold the Homestand Flyer, a mini-program-plus-scorecard, outside the ballpark for a buck. It became a popular alternative to the official three-dollar program of the Rockies.

Changing affiliations. With the arrival of the Rockies in Denver, Regis Groff, formerly a very large fan of the Cubs, now supports them with lowered enthusiasm. *Substantially* lowered. As you can see. Groff admits that he enjoys it when the Rockies sock it to 'em.

Scorekeeping. A grand activity that enriches one's enjoyment of The Game. The how-to aspect is oft passed from one generation to the next.

The first road win in history so delighted this South Denver homeowner that he put a sign on his front door for all to see the next morning.

Beer. Lots of companies bought blocks of tickets and enjoyed afternoons at the old ballpark. EvansGroup, the ad agency, was one. Don Kibbe rejoins his Evans-Group pals after making a run to the concession stand. As you can see, his trip wasn't without incident. He's carrying some beer. And wearing the rest.

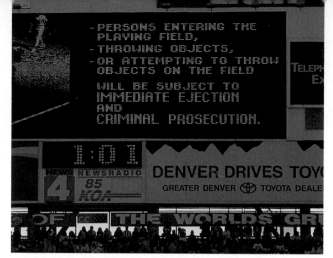

Ballpark Law. Unlike other ballparks, Mile High Stadium has a rule against throwing the opposing team's home run balls back.

Foul balls are another matter. The prize of prizes was taken home by hundreds of Rockies fans this season, including Brendan Giles (left), who caught his in the seventh inning of the second game of the doubleheader on August 21.

Monday, April 5: New York 3, Colorado 0
The first game ever.

2:10 at Shea Stadium
The National Anthem: Glenn Close
The first ball: Fay Vincent (first time in a ballpark since fired as Commissioner)
The starting pitchers: Nied (0-0) vs. Gooden (0-0)
The W-L pitchers: Gooden (1-0) and Nied (0-1)
The attendance: 53,127 announced, later revised to 53,134 (either would be an Opening Day record for Shea Stadium)
The Post headline: Starting without a bang
The News headline: At long last, the Rockies play ball
The New York Times Headline:
For Openers, Gooden and Key Close Down the Batters
The New York Daily News Headline:
RUNNIN' ANDRES A ROCKIE HORROR

The First 25-Man Roster:
Pitchers: Scott Aldred (32), Andy Ashby (43), Willie Blair (19), Butch Henry (27), Darren Holmes (40), David Nied (17), Jeff Parrett (38), Steve Reed (39), Bruce Ruffin (18), Bryn Smith (28), Gary Wayne (53). **Catchers:** Danny Sheaffer (60), Joe Girardi (7). **Infielders:** Freddie Benavides (12), Pedro Castellano (15), Vinny Castilla (9), Andres Galarraga (14), Charlie Hayes (13), Jim Tatum (20), Eric Young (21). **Outfielders:** Dante Bichette (10), Daryl Boston (6), Jerald Clark (24), Alex Cole (5), Gerald Young (2).

The First Ever Starting Lineup:
Eric Young 2b
Alex Cole cf
Dante Bichette rf
Andres Galarraga 1b
Jerald Clark lf
Charlie Hayes 3b
Joe Girardi c
Freddie Benavides ss
David Nied p

On the field: Just before the game, Charlie Jones says it's The Opening Day of History.

Bob Kravitz calls it Opening Opening Day.

And then, at 12:17 or 12:18 MDT (there are conflicting reports), the first pitch leaves Dwight Gooden's fingertips and heads toward home plate. There stands Eric Young. It's a strike. The Rockies' leadoff man tries to use The First Plate Appearance Ever to bunt himself onto base. But he is thrown out. The First Out Ever.

Gooden is vintage Gooden. He four-hits the Rockies— Young, Bichette, and Galarraga (two)—and gives the fans from The Mile High City very little to cheer about in The First Game Ever.

David Nied, the Rockies' poster boy, puts in five innings, but allows six hits, six walks—and two runs.

The first of which, in the fourth, is scored by Gooden, himself. It's the first run ever scored against the Rockies in regular season play. (It comes at 1:43 MDT.)

Although that was all the Mets needed, their fans stop booing long enough to enjoy a bonus run—a Bobby Bonilla home run in the fifth.

In the next inning, New York tacks on an insurance run.

Doc Gooden uses just 101 pitches to deliver unto the newborn team its first L.

The critical moment is in the third when the Rockies have the bases loaded and a 3-2 count on their cleanup hitter, Andres Galarraga. This, everyone knew, could be *it*.

It turns out to be a fastball that Galarraga swings hard at, but misses. (The first time three Rox are stranded on base comes at 1:13 MDT.)

From then on, it's Gooden In Charge. All the way. And it's Gooden's first shutout in nearly two years. It is also only the second Opening Day shutout of an expansion team. The other was in '77 when California's Tanana beat Seattle, 7-0.

The 4-0 score could have been worse. New York left 13 runners on base.

Colorado does not go entirely quiet into the late afternoon. In the ninth, with one out and a runner on first, the Rocks are thinking rally. With one out and one on, Galarraga knocks a single to right field, but he tries to stretch it into a double and is thrown out easily. Groans are many because Rockies fans are many in the stands.

4

Naturally, there are firsts. Almost everything is a first.

Some of the ones that need to be marked down in The Book of Things:

Dante Bichette is the first Rocky to foul off a pitch into the stands (12:22 MDT). Nied's first pitch—at 12:25 to Vince Coleman—is a ball. Two minutes later, the Mets' leadoff man has become the Rockies' first strikeout victim. (Which, to be technical, gives Girardi the first putout.) Galarraga gets the Rockies' first hit (in the second inning at 12:38) and is the only Rocky to get two. Bichette is the first Rock to be hit by a pitch (1:05). Eric Young is the first to steal a base (also at 1:05). Alex Cole is the first to draw a walk. Galarraga is the first to be left on base—and to strike out (1:12). Butch Henry is the Rocks' first relief pitcher. At 2:34, former Met Daryl Boston is the Rockies' first pinch-hitter, but to no avail. Harry Wendelstedt is the first ump to call balls and strikes for and against the Rocks.

It is the Rockies' first game that lasts two hours and 39 minutes.

But the Rockies' first run, first extra-base hit, first RBI and first save are still to come. (Come to think of it, so are the first error, first balk and first wild pitch.)

Well, as Woody Paige says, "You can't win 'em all. How about 161-1?"

In the stands: There are some empty seats in sold-out Shea. How else is a dealer or collector of pristine, unused tickets to historical games going to obtain same? But it brings up some ethical issues. It is right to leave a seat empty at an event of this magnitude? Perverse is a good word.

Cagey operators scrounge for today's ticket stubs. They're not worth nearly as much as unused ducats, but they're still *worth*.

And buying a program is impossible. Very early birds bought them all up at $2 per for resale at another place—and another price. The worms.

"No programs?" a Denver fan complained. "I came all this way for the historic game and I can't even take home a program? That really furs my duck!" Indeed.

In the absence of either programs or scorecards, dedicated fans improvised. Some fashioned scorecards out of those cardboard carriers the concession stands give you for transporting multiple beers and dogs.

From Section 34 in the Upper Level, a Rockies fan watches the tiny players *way down there.* "I feel like I'm watching TV from two rooms away."

Indeed, many wound up with LaGuardia level seats, but at least they were there for the historic First Thisses and Thats.

The CR caps on the DEN-to-N.Y. planes were abundant.

And many Mile Highers met at a brew pub in Manhattan, Zip City, the day before The Day.

Among the many prominent Denverites in attendance: The Wynkoop's John Hickenlooper. Bonnie Brae Liquors' Joe Scanlan. Duffy's Gary Bloom. And Westword's Patty Calhoun.

In Currigan Hall: It's a baseball open house and it attracts about 3,000 zealots to watch the Opening Day game on large screen TVs. It's something called "Rockiesfest." This is day one of three. There are vendors. There are $3.75 beers to buy. But first, there's $5 to pay to get in the door.

The Rockies are now 0-1 for the season and are tied for last place of the NL West with Houston and Los Angeles. Colorado is one game behind the division leaders, Atlanta and Cincinnati. In the NL East, the Marlins, Mets and Phillies share the lead. (In Florida's first game, they stuffed the Dodgers, 6-3.)

Wednesday, April 7: New York 6, Colorado 1
The game in which the Rockies scored their first run.

1:40 at Shea Stadium
The starting pitchers: Ruffin (0-0) vs. Saberhagen (0-0)
The W-L pitchers: Saberhagen (1-0) and Ruffin (0-1)
The attendance: 27,290
The Post headline: Rockies suffer expansion-itis
The News headline: Defense rests in Rockies' 6-1 defeat

On the field: Yesterday, the Rocks were able to amass only a quartet of hits. Today, there were but *two.*

But there *were* a bunch of firsts: Error (Hayes). Pinch-hit (Tatum). Home run, run scored, and RBI (Bichette).

While Saberhagen had the Rockies shut down, the Mets methodically put runs on the board in each of the first four innings. They lead, 6-0, until Bichette smashes a long homer into the wind in the seventh to avoid the shutout, score the first run in Rockies history, etc., etc.

Until then, the Rockies' scoring history consisted of 15 innings of nothingness. (The '62 Mets, oft-cited as the very embodiment of futility, opened with 11 scoreless innings. And they didn't win their first game until their tenth outing.)

In the stands: Yesterday, there were quite a few CR caps scattered amongst the Mets fans. By now, most have returned with their owners to The Time Zone With One Team. But a couple of Rockies fans remain so they can say, "You saw Game One? That's nice. *But I saw Game Two.*"

A New Yorker gives a Denverite some inside info: "The best knishes in New York are sold right here at Shea on level two." Suggestion tastily taken.

Today's Milestones: Freddie Benavides' birthday (1966) and Mark Thompson's birthday (1971)

The Rockies have now lost both (all) of their games and are in next to last place in the NL West, a half game ahead of 0-3 Houston.

Thursday, April 8:

The LET'S PLAY Ball.
Months ago, the Colorado Symphony Orchestra began planning a joint celebration of The First Home Game Ever with the Rockies.

It was to be called The LET'S PLAY Ball and it was scheduled for the night before the home opener.

Plans included an elegant dinner and an auction offering all sorts of good baseball/symphony things like a base jointly signed by the Rockies' firstbaseman and by the principal bass player of the Symphony.

Then there'd be a baseball-oriented concert, with the conductor conducting not from a podium, but from a *mound*.

The Colorado Symphony Chorus and the Colorado Children's Chorale would all be there.

The Symphony conducted a Rockies song contest and got nearly a hundred entries. The winner would be premiered at this concert.

And everybody in attendance would get baseball caps. In Rockies colors, but with CSO instead of CR.

The plan was to have the program *end* with the National Anthem. To point to the historic tomorrow to follow.

It would be a salute to the team. Players, coaches, manager and management would all be there. And it would be fun. And it would raise funds for two good causes: The Colorado Rockies Foundation and the Colorado Symphony's educational program.

And at $150 per, it was going to raise serious dollars.

Suddenly, the Rockies pulled out of the deal. We can't have our guys out the night before the big game, they said.

The Symphony scrambled to return the $150 checks and the Rox kicked in with free game tickets to assuage the disappointed fans of baseball and Beethoven.

Time for pre-opener goosebumps.

A fan composed the following the day before the first game in Denver. It makes mention of every Rocky on the Opening Day roster plus all the coaches.

It even notes the events in Shea leading up to the big home opener.

The night before baseball

'Twas the night before baseball, when all through the state
Everybody was saying, "Won't it be GREAT!!!"

The bats were all stacked in the dugout with care
'cause Baylor and company soon would be there.

The children were nestled all snug in their beds,
while visions of autographs danced in their heads.

And Mamma and I in our CR caps
Had just settled down for night-before naps.

We dreamt of a season—our first for that matter,
When we'd love every pitcher, adore every batter.
The former would hurl the ball like a flash,
The latter would rack up smash after smash.

The sun shined bright on a Mile High Day
As the team of our dreams took the field of play.

How wonderful this gang of Gebhard's and Baylor's...
With pitchers like Nied backed by eight great players.

With a crafty, sly manager, a man on the move
I knew in a moment it had to be Groove.

More rapid than eagles his runners they came
And he whistled and shouted and called them by name:

"Now, Dante! Now, Alex! Now, Freddie and Andres!
On, Darren! On, Jerald! On, Joey and Hayes!

When you get to first base, keep your eye on the ball!
Now, dash away! Dash away! Dash away, all!"

As we dream, so dreams an entire time zone
Of players that're ours, soon to be nationally known,
Like Jeff and Bruce and Butch and Reed
And Blair and Andy and Daryl for speed.
For Gary, Scott and Vinny we'll yell out our lungs
Same for Danny and Jim and both of the Youngs.

I hear the crack of Dale's bat, a beautiful sound,
And out of the dugout Baylor comes with a bound.
He wears purple pinstripes from his head to his foot.
And he has an assistant who he happily put
In charge of the bench and he yelled, "Hey, Zimmer!
Look at old Bryn—he's starting to simmer!"

Smith's eyes—how they twinkle!
'cause he's learned well from Larry!
Bear's plan is simple: the Expos to bury!
They'll come up to bat, and down they will go...
Like the beard on Smith's chin they'd be as gone as the snow.

The lump of a chaw Zimmer holds tight in his cheek,
As he, too, has mischief on Montreal to wreak.
Zim has a broad face and a round little belly

9

That asks that old question: "Which way to the deli?"

With coaches like Zim, Ron, Jerry and Amos
You know our Rockies soon will be famous.

Baylor's confident look told me I had nothing to fear
So I leaned back in my seat and had a cold beer.

He spoke not a word though he knew a lotta good lines.
And he filled all the bases, then flashed 'em some signs.
And laying his finger aside of his nose,
He gave 'em a nod, and up the standings they rose.

Then I awoke and remembered we'd dropped a pair to the Mets
But the home opener's here; this is as good as it gets!
Sure it'll be tough. Yeah, we'll take our knocks,

But the dream's coming true! Hooray for the Rox!!!

Friday, April 9: Colorado 11, Montreal 4
The first home game—and the first win—ever.

3:05 at Mile High Stadium
The National Anthem (Canadian): Gisele Quiniou
The National Anthem (U.S.): Dan Fogelberg
The first balls: Connie Sidas, Edgar Flores, and Nathan
       Jecminek (students)
The starting pitchers: Smith (0-0) vs. Bottenfield (0-0)
The W-L pitchers: Smith (1-0) and Bottenfield (0-1)
The attendance: 80,227
The Post headline: How's That for Openers?
The News headline: Baseball, victory barge into Denver

Days before the game: The battle for tickets is fierce. The season ticket people are covered, of course. But some of them have relatives. Friends, even.

    So both papers are heavy with classifieds that nearly wear out the word, "WANTED." Other oft-seen phrases are "top dollar paid" and "Will pay $125–$225 each."

Although some scalpers got up to $150 for $4 tickets, most tickets went for $35–$100.

Hours before the game: Lots of TV equipment is deployed. The game will be broadcast live on NHK-TV in Tokyo. All told, six million people in 48 countries will receive the game.

Nobel Sysco delivers all-beef hot dogs by truckload.

Coors trucks roll out the barrels, a thousand of them. By the end of the 7th inning, when beer sales are cut off at Mile High, the equivalent of 165,000 cans of beer will be sold.

Operators of parking lots near the stadium put up their $15 signs. They're pretty sure the traffic will bear it. Literally.

Just before the game: There is a moment of silence for two of Denver's best and most beloved sports journalists who, as the P.A. announcer says, "left us before this dream came true."

Indeed, Bob Martin and Dick Connor would have loved it.

(A seat in the press box is left vacant in Connor's honor. The veteran sportswriter died of cancer last December 30.)

On the field: The Show has come to Denver. At last. And it turns out to be an amazing one, indeed.

3:08—Bryn Smith, a former hurler for the Denver Bears, throws the first big league pitch in the history of The Time Zone. To Mike Lansing. It is low and outside. (Unlike the the 80,227 fans in attendance.)

In the first inning, all three outs are made on grounders to secondbaseman Eric Young.

It is Young who then steps to the plate as the first Colorado Rocky to bat in Colorado.

At 3:17, Eric Young leads off Colorado's end of the first with a home run. The crowd goes absolutely berserk. (Young's home run ball is caught by a fan from Greeley, Ron Miller, who turns down an instant offer of $5,000 for it.)

In the third base coaching box stands Don Zimmer. His comment: "I'm a 62-year-old man who has been in this game for 44 years, and when he hit that home run I had chills running up and down my spine."

A fan: "Think of it! Ruth hit the first in Yankee Stadium and Young hit the first here!"

Six minutes later, still in the first, Charlie Hayes hits a two-run shot. Delirium.

At the end of one, the Rockies have a 4-0 lead.

When Montreal's starter, Kent Bottenfield, leaves after four innings, the Rockies' margin has grown to 7-0.

In total, the Rocks put together 18 hits of offense. Meanwhile, veteran Bryn Smith throws seven shutout innings. The shutout is preserved by Willie Blair in the eight, but relinquished by Steve Reed in the ninth. That's when the Expos' offense comes alive. It consists primarily of Mike Lansing's three-run blast. But it's OK. Lansing's from Casper, Wyoming.

The game ends at 5:48 when Moises Alou flies out to Dale Murphy. The region's first date with its new team went well. It seems destined to bloom into a love affair of Broncomaniacal proportions. At least.

Firsts Dept.: First Rocky to steal second and third on consecutive pitches—Alex Cole, in the first. First double—Jerald Clark. First error—Freddie Benavides. First sacrifice fly—Bichette. First future Hall of Famer to take the field for the Rockies—Dale Murphy in the seventh. First Rocky to go 4-for-4—Eric Young. First TV station to miss the pregame ceremonies of the most historic game they'll ever televise and damn near miss the opening pitch—KWGN-TV.

Echoes of the past dept.: First Rocky who played in the last Zephyr's game in Mile High—Jim Tatum. First former manager of the Denver Bears to lose to the Rockies—Felipe Alou, the popular skipper of the 1981 Bears. (Ironically, Bryn Smith was Alou's starter in the first game he managed in Denver. They lost, 8-6.)

After three games, two Rocks are batting .417 (Young and Galarraga) and one is batting 1.000 (Dale Murphy, who went 1-for-1 today).

At the Rodgers C445 double-manual organ: Chuck Shockney, entertaining the throng with the kind of music that was played here when the Denver Bears had an organist back in the fifties. Which is good. In real life, Shockney sells organs and plays one for Bear Creek Evangelical Presbyterian Church.

In the stands: There are 1,555 more humans on hand than filled the Coliseum to witness the West Coast debut of the Dodgers on April 18, 1958.

Among them: Todd Thomas of Knoxville, Tennessee, who flew in for the game. And Clarence Reich of Lake Geneva,

Wisconsin, who drove over. And John Elway of Denver, who lives here. He is seen in the company of a Coors Light.

And there are 300,000 programs on hand. Each with a soundchip in it that plays "Take Me Out To The Ballgame."

For those who'd made the trip to New York to see the First Away Game Ever, it is great to be in Mile High where you can actually *buy* a program—even if it does cost five bucks a pop. Shea had sold out of its $2 models nearly two hours before game time.

While basking in Mile High's pregame wonderment, John Mason observed that "You can tell by the umpires we're in the major leagues. They look well fed."

"But who," John wonders, "is that lady singing 'O Canada?'"

Sounds like a job for the Fans' Ombudsman. He looks into it and reports that Ms. Quiniou sings the Canadian national anthem for the Montreal Canadiens. And she sang it at the closing ceremonies of the Winter Olympics in Calgary.

Mason also notices that, for the first time in memory, the grounds crew had installed coaches' boxes. Throughout their Triple A history, Denver hadn't bothered to install same on the grounds that the coaches never bothered to stay inside them.

And he engages those around him in a discussion of who the Rockies should've gotten to throw out the first ball. Most agree: It ought to be Fay Vincent, Bill White, Bob Howsam or Bill Clinton. After all, this *is* a day of days.

Best of all, beer is once again being sold in the stands.

Upon seeing vendors up and down the aisle, Mason thinks back to the article in the Post about vendors' serving underage fans a few years ago—the article that resulted in the discontinuance of beer sales in the stands during Zephyrs games. And Mason makes this pronouncement: "Woody Paige is dead."

Ballpark beer also leads to the discovery of the difference between men and women: To buy beer at Mile High, men have to show their IDs. Women *get* to.

Women also seem more transfixed by Jerald Clark's, uh, swivelhipped stance at the plate.

Some noteworthy firsts that may not have been chronicled elsewhere:

3:05—first beer spilled at a Rockies home game. (By and on Ray Jones.)

3:23—first foul ball hit into the stands. (Section 110.)

3:40—first pitcher to bat in Mile High Stadium in many years. (Montreal's Bottenfield.)

3:50—first overconfident Rockies fan heard from. (Dick Veit: "I don't see how the Rockies can lose—let's go home.")

4:25—first successful wave is executed. In the News, Randy Holtz noted with perhaps a soupçon of disdain that "the Rockies now have more waves in one home game than the Chicago Cubs have in more than 100 years."

4:26—first anti-wave movement launched.

5:13—first seventh-inning stretch.

5:16—first idiot jumps the wall and dives into second base.

Other than the gaucheries at 4:25 and 5:16, the entire game was your basic highlight film from Eric's blast to the East Stands' total rejection of opposition home run balls.

Some fans dined at Mexico Lindo to celebrate. And chose Number 28 (green chili and tortillas) in honor of winning pitcher Bryn Smith.

The Time Zone is happier'n a cowboy on Saturday night.

In the TV booth: Charlie Jones and Duane Kuiper are agog at Eric Young's Homeric feat, the stuff of instant legend.

Especially Kuiper, who hit but one home run during his 1,057-game career in the bigs.

In all fairness: Today's crowd may rank as the largest ever to see an opening day game and the largest for a regular season National League game, but an exhibition game between the Dodgers and Yankees in L.A. Coliseum on May 7, 1959 drew more. It was Roy Campanella Night, a year after the car wreck that ended Campy's career. The numbers: 93,103. Given the capacity, of course, today's game at Mile High would've drawn well over 100 thou.

Ungood Friday.

One of the classified ads begging for tickets to the opener began thusly: "ATTENTION: GOOD CATHOLICS. We want 4 of your opening day Rockies tickets."

In the opinion of the Archdiocese of Denver, the Opening Day game was very ill-timed. After all, it was scheduled for Good Friday. Which is why Catholics were urged not to attend the home opener.

Bob Feeney, spokesman for the Archdiocese: "For any Christian, it's an inappropriate day to be going out and cheering loudly when we're remembering the passionate death of Christ."

And: "Good Friday is a day of fasting and abstinence. No meat—like a hot dog. And you certainly shouldn't be sitting around drinking beer on Good Friday."

The Denver Catholic Register: "We suggest that Catholics don't root, root, root for Colorado's home team on opening day."

Serious stuff. And Woody Paige agrees. Although he does point out that major league baseball has been playing games on Good Friday for decades, he concludes that boycotters should go to church on Good Friday.

And get rid of their tickets.

By sending them to him.

N.B.: The Bob Feeney mentioned above is the same Bob Feeney who bet several of his friends ten bucks each that the Rockies wouldn't even match the Mets' 1962 ineptitude.

Why didn't the Rockies open at home?

Because they didn't want to.

It's true. The Rockies *asked* the schedule-makers to arrange an away opener to set them up with the financially rich weekend series that they're enjoying. Few know this. Most think this is just a scheduling oddity, not a request.

Those who *do* know about this think that it was cruel that the fans of Denver, as long-suffering and much-deserving as they are numerous, were being denied the opportunity to see The First Rockies Game Ever.

Bob S.: "I think they would've sold out that first one even if they'd had it on Tuesday at four in the morning."

"It's weird. No, it's cruel," says Mehl Goforth, "Those New Yorkers got to see the historic game instead of *us*."

Us had to settle for The First Rockies *Home* Game Ever.

The Rockies are now 1-2 for the season, are two games out of first, and are tied for third (and fourth) place with the Padres. The Marlins are 1-3.

The game that gives the Rockies their first .500 record.

1:05 at Mile High Stadium
The National Anthem: Nitty Gritty Dirt Band
The first balls: Roy Romer and Mike Sullivan
The starting pitchers: Nied (0-1) vs. Martinez (0-1)
The W-L pitchers: Nied (1-1) and Martinez (0-2)
The attendance: 65,261
The Post headline: Rockies enjoy second helping
The News headline: Rockies feeling right at home

Outside the ballpark, fans had wondered what they were going to use as scorecards.

Not another five-dollar program, that's for sure. Just in the nick, they encounter the First Bootleg Scorecards Ever.

Two kinds, the *Homestand Flyer* and *Colorado Stat Sheet* are being sold outside the stadium. For a buck, they provide player info and a place to score.

(Later in the week, these guys would be largely put out of business by the cops and/or the Rockies. Too bad.)

On the field: Once again, the Rockies open with a first-inning four-master, this time by Galarraga.

A four-run explosion in the 7th (helped along by a couple of errors) puts it away.

Girardi's triple in the fifth is the first three-bagger by a Rocky. In the next inning, Cole matches the feat.

Nied allows four runs in seven innings, and the Rocks lead by just one when, in the bottom of the seventh, the Rockies combine a couple of hits, a walk, some stolen bases and some timely Expo errors to add a four-run cushion to their lead.

In two games on the road, the Rockies scored one run. In two games at home, they've scored 20 runs.

In the stands: Saturday was lovely and once again so are the Rox.

They go .500 for the first time in their history.

Then, as our boys bash out runs (against perfecto pitcher Martinez, no less), fans realize something is missing. The bell that Frank Haraway used to mark the Bears and Z's scoring at the end of each inning.

So the Section 116ers make do. "DING!" they yell for each run at the end of each stanza. The nearby crowd joins in.

A soft drink vendor walks by calling out "Soda!" An easterner, obviously. Regis Groff, a westerner, calls to him thusly: "Pop!" And a sale is consummated.

After a Rockies miscue, Diane Kaminsky grumbled, "That's the kind of play you can expect in a stadium where they try to do the wave."

And, when the crowd of 65,261 was announced, she commented, "I would've settled for three or four fewer if I could've chosen who they were."

In general, though, giddiness was rampant throughout the stadium.

Although the wave is attempted over and over, it fails every time—to the credit of the sophisticated fans on the first base side.

Meanwhile, in Section 116, fans puzzle over this one: If Snow White married David Cone, what would her name be?

An idea is run up the flagpole, but Bernie doesn't salute.

A fan had an idea. Maybe a pretty good idea. So he passed it on to Rockies exec, Bernie Mullin.

Victory Flags. Every time the Rockies win a game, right after the last out, a big purple flag is hoisted where passers-by on I-25 can see it. And know that their Rox are winners.

A new Victory Flag would be flown for each win. The date of the game and the score would be noted on each flag.

These flags would have appeal to collectors and could be given as special gifts or used as auction items for fund-raisers.

Nothing came of the idea. Too bad. The best traditions are traditions that begin with Game One.

The Rockies have now won two in a row for the first time, have a 2-2 record, are one game behind, and are tied for second (and third) place.

Sunday, April 11 (Easter): Montreal 19, Colorado 9

The first home loss ever.

1:05 at Mile High Stadium
The National Anthem: Up With People
The first ball: Walt Disney Kids (2)
The starting pitchers: Henry (0-0) vs. Jones (0-0)
The W-L pitchers: Jones (1-0) and Henry (0-1)
The attendance: 66,987
The Post headline: 19-9: A major dose of reality
The News headline: Rockies bullpen fails test

On the field: The wretched New York Mets didn't give up 19 runs to an opponent until their 12th season. See how far the Rockies are ahead of the Mets!

The Expos scored in every inning but the eighth—and made up for that by erupting for seven in the ninth.

The Rox relievers are pretty scary. Holmes is remarkable in that, in 1/3 inning, he gives up *seven* runs.

In the stands: Nobody knew it would turn out that way, of course. Or how embarrassing it would be.

Many fans were so confident that we'd sweep on Sunday that they smuggled in brooms to taunt the Expos with. A couple of guys had them stuck down the backs of their pants. (Perhaps the no-sticks-or-poles in Mile High Stadium rule should be suspended whenever a sweep of a series is in the offing.)

One superstitious 116er who had worn his tuxedo to Friday's home opener (which we won) and again on Saturday (which we won) was still wearing it today.

John Mason to the tuxedoed fan early on when another Rockies victory was in the offing: "I hope you're not renting it."

This was the day Mason was betting people $100 that women will be playing in the major leagues by the time his four-year-old daughter, Casey, is 21.

After the pregame show by Up With People, Diane K. joked, "Are they going to do this at halftime, too?"

Speaking of football fans, the wave once again sputtered out against the stalwarts along first base.

And Bill Koerber looked out at that tent in the parking lot past right field and wondered what the new airport was doing here.

1:12—first time the Rockies had been behind in a home game. Ever. (As they say.) And it goes quickly downhill from there.

"Some of the earned run averages," says Bill Gallo, "are starting to look like bowling scores."

The Rockies and Expos wind up drawing 212,475, an all-time major league record for a three-game series. The previous mark, set by a visit to Cleveland by the Yankees in 1948, was 188,081.

The All-Time Free Baseball Day

Kerry Maloney, a 29-year-old designer and computer wizard, tells about his all-time free baseball day (as he tells the story, he uses the word, "free," ten times):

"Oh, it was a great day. First of all, me'n this buddy of mine decided to go to the game and we didn't have tickets so we went down to Old Chicago's where we heard there was a free shuttle that would take us to the stadium to buy tickets. We ended up entering in a drawing and after the first ten people were called and didn't pick up the tickets, finally my name was picked and we won two free tickets to the game. So we were pretty happy about that. We went into the bar and we were telling the bartender about it so he loads us up with two free shots of tequila which we thought was pretty good. And then we hopped on the free shuttle, went over to the stadium, and realized that the seats that we'd just won were out in the boondocks so we looked around and found two free seats that were between first and home about thirty rows off the field so we had great seats. As it turned out, my friend knew somebody in the public relations office and when we went and saw him during the seventh-inning stretch we ended up getting free programs, free hats and a free baseball card holder so that was pretty neat. And then, after the game, we took the free shuttle back to old Chicago's and ate free pizza that they were going to throw out so all in all it was a great day."

Who won?

"The Expos won. It was quite bad, actually."

The Rockies now have a record of 2-3, are two games behind first and are tied for fifth place.

Monday, April 12: Colorado and New York (rain)

The first rainout ever.

7:05 at Mile High Stadium
The Post headline: It's another first: Rockies, ppd.
The News headline: Rockies, Mets take rain check

In the stands: There is some grumbling about not getting to hear Lannie Garrett sing the National Anthem. And many fans remember that the Cubs' first night game was rained out, too.

On the way to the bank: During the rain delay, four thousand people bought tickets. And $70,000 worth of Rockiestuff was sold.

In the spirit of entrepreneurship: A rare highlight is the vendor encountered on the way in who was yelling: "Getcher program today and say you got it Friday!"

Tuesday, April 13: New York 8, Colorado 4

The first night game ever.

7:05 at Mile High Stadium
The National Anthem: Zion Baptist Choir
The first ball: Ben Nighthorse Campbell
The starting pitchers: Ashby (0-0) vs. Saberhagen (1-0)
The W-L pitchers: Saberhagen (2-0) and Holmes (0-1)
The attendance: 52,087
The Post headline: Mets walk over Rockies 8-4
The News headline: Rockies get little relief, lose to Mets

On the field: With too much help from the Rockies' pitching staff (12 free rides), the Mets take a heartbreaker from the Rockies.

In the sixth, New York gets three straight walks from Darren Holmes (two with the bases loaded).

Still, going into the eighth, the Rockies are clinging to a 4-2 lead. Then Willie Blair comes in. Soon, he allows the go-ahead run on a WP. Then, to make the situation even more bleak, he issues a walk and permits a triple (that Bichette actually should've caught).

The Mets leave 15 runners on base, a club record.

Tonight's firsts: The first save opportunity. And the first blown save. And Holmes' ERA is now 60.75.

In the stands: 7:05—first snowflake to fall on a Rockies game.

7:21—first time the Rockies have led the Mets.

Everybody notices the new sign in right field announcing the elevation of Mile High Stadium.

Then there's the subtle evolution of the cotton candy.

"It used to be pink," Pat Milstein observes. "But now it's becoming purple. But then what isn't?"

Purple or not, Pat has a problem with the stuff. "Cotton candy and beer just don't make it."

John Ashton's recommendation: "Dunk it."

It was at this game that fans began to tire of the toot-TOOT-toot-toot fanfare that leads up to CHARGE!

The consensus: It's a little on the footbally side. And, instead, organist Chuck Shockney should be introducing each Rocky with a bar or two of theme music as he comes to bat.

For Eric, a few bars of "Young Love." For the Big Cat, perhaps a little something from "Cats" or a bit of the Pink Panther theme. And for Alex, "Workin' In A Cole Mine." Yes, they take liberties.

Daryl Boston? Maybe a bit of the old song about being lost on the M.T.A.

When Hayes comes to bat, perhaps some "Yankee Doodle" to twit the New York team that whined when they lost their thirdbaseman to us.

Back to the game on the field: A fan pulls out his pocket calculator and punched in those 12 bases on balls the Rockies issued. Let's see, at 90 feet per, that means that Colorado let the Mets walk *over two-tenths of a mile!*

The Rockies have now lost two in a row, have a 2-4 record, and are tied for fifth (and sixth) place in the NL West with San Diego. The Marlins, at 2-6, are in last place in the Eastern Division.

The first home game played while the Nuggets were also playing at home.

7:05 at Mile High Stadium
The National Anthem: Lee Greenwood
The first ball: Wyoming's Dick Cheney, former
      Secretary of Defense
The starting pitchers: Smith (1-0) vs. Fernandez (0-0)
The W-L pitchers: Fernandez (1-0) and Smith (1-1)
The attendance: 57,489
The Post headline: Rockies go 0-for-4 against the Mets
The News headline: Rockies' bats go cold in 6-3 defeat

Before the game: 1,200 enlistees in the U.S. armed forces were sworn in.

On the field: There was considerable swearing as the Mets once again crush the Rocks.

    The New Yorkers put up single runs in the first and second innings. Mets' starter Fernandez faces the minimum through four, then leaves with shoulder stiffness—and a 2-0 lead.

    The Mets add another run in the fifth and then, in the eighth, each team scores three.

    Galarraga remains a bright spot in the Rockies lineup, still batting well over .400.

    Today's first: The first mid-inning double switch.

In the stands: Not a pretty episode in the Rockies' young life except for Young Love's triple in the 8th. (Which was caused, incidentally, by Peter Groff's wearing of a rally cap.)

    And there's a Great Breakthrough in the world of beer.

    This was the day the Fans' Ombudsman measured the Commemorative Cup of beer sold on the concourse for $3.50 and reported that they are 20-oz. cups that contain about 19 ounces by the time you've spilled your way to your seat. Then the old pocket calculator compared it to the 12-oz. cans sold in the stands for $2.75 (or $3 when you tip a quarter).

    Findings: On the concourse, you pay 18¢ per ounce. In the stands, it's 23¢ (or 25¢ when you tip a quarter).

An insight from Bill Hook: "In general, you don't boo in baseball. It's not good form. You applaud great works from our team and from the opposition. The exception is Bobby Bonilla. When you boo him it makes him feel at home."

In a related observation, Allan Singer offers this definition of a Met: "A dead superhero."

When yet another wave is attempted, Alton Dillard yells out: "A. This isn't football season. B. We're landlocked. C. *Sit down.*"

And when additional unpleasantness is created by bases on balls, Dillard comes up with a new name for our team: The Colorado Walkies.

Which might become a name for the fans, too, if $15 parking becomes standard.

In tomorrow's Post, it will be reported that Fernandez had a perfect game going when he left.

Woody mentions it. Armstrong says so. Irv does, too. Give the broadsheet three errors on one play.

Fact is that Dante Bichette worked the Met hurler for a walk in the second inning. Although Bichette was erased while attempting to steal, his appearance on base instantly rendered Fernandez' perfecto imperfect.

Today's Milestones: Roberto Mejia's birthday (1972)

The Rockies are now 2-5, in fifth place, 2.5 games out of first.

Thursday, April 15: Colorado 5, New York 3
The first complete game victory.

1:05 at Mile High Stadium
The National Anthem: Nacho Men
The first ball: Byron Johnson (Negro League great)
The starting pitchers: Nied (1-1) vs. Gooden (1-1)
The W-L pitchers: Nied (2-1) and Gooden (1-2)
The attendance: 52,608
The Post headline: No Nied for relief this time
The News headline: Nied, Rockies slide past Mets

On the field: A rematch of the season opener, but this time the kid prevails. In fact, he goes the distance, distributing a sixpack of hits in a relatively harmless manner. The Rockies' ace also whiffs six.

The Mets open the top of the first with a pair of runs, but the Rockies answer with a mix of walks, steals and singles that adds up to a four-run response. The rest of the game is an edge-of-the-chair waiting game to see if the Rox' lead would hold up.

There is a trade of single runs late in the game, but, ultimately, The Color Purple prevails.

Danny Sheaffer starts his first game of the season. And singles in his first ML at-bat since '89. Gerald Young also makes his first start of the year. He walks twice and scores once.

In the stands: As you enter Parking Lot G, you're met by the cheeriest parking attendant on the planet.

"Howdy howdy howdy howdy!" he says. Must have his taxes done.

Then to our seats to employ the New Knowledge about beer. Problem: *Nary a single beer vendor comes by the entire game.* Tim Wirth should launch an investigation immediately.

Beerless, a fan notes some of the game's special—at least to him—moments.

His report:

1:05—game begins.

1:08—Mets lead.

1:16—Dwight Gooden takes the mound in Mile High Stadium for the first time.

1:18—Dwight Gooden makes his first pitch in Mile High Stadium.

The Rockies employ a suicide squeeze to good effect in the seventh. Eric Young is the squeezer and Freddie Benavides the squeezee. Which brings a suggestion from Diane K. for a new code for those keeping score—GBB. For Good Baylor Ball.

Indeed, this was a game among games. First victory over the Mets and Doc Gooden. First complete game. And the first home game with no attempted wave. Ever. Delicious.

A deliciousness enjoyed by many. The attendance for this, the Rockies first home stand, is 374,659. This exceeds the 306,763 the Oakland A's drew for the entire 1979 season.

As the game unfolds, fans come to a realization: Although our victories have been few, they've been extraordinarily sweet. And our losses, while they hurt, only hurt a little.

Could this be because it is better to be visited and beaten

by Coleman, Murray, Bonilla, Saberhagen, Gooden & Co. than to be in Buffalo, Orlando, Washington, or Tampa/St. Pete where they never come calling?

Yes.

As the Rockies go on the road, fans wish them Godspeed. Especially on the basepaths. And in right field.

And there's a plan to bring one of those call bells (three or four bucks at Office Depot or Bizmart) to the next home stand.

The Rockies are now 3-5, 2 games behind first, tied for fourth.

Friday, April 16: Montreal 3, Colorado 2
The first game played outside of the U.S. of A.

6:05 at Exhibition Stadium
The starting pitchers: Henry (0-1) vs. Bottenfield (0-1)
The W-L pitchers: Bottenfield (1-1) and Henry (0-2)
The attendance: 17,483
The Post headline: On the road again...
The News headline: Henry improves, but Rockies fall

On the field: Once again, for the fourth time in the last five games, the other guys score at least one run in the first inning. Tonight, it's two, and the Rocks never catch up. Montreal's pitcher, Bottenfield, is the same guy the Rockies rocked in their home opener. This time, though, he gets 26 of the 27 outs with little difficulty.

This is the Rockies' first one-run game.

Only three players have started all of the Rockies' first nine games: The first, second, and third basemen. Galarraga, Young, and Hayes.

Today's milestone: KWGN-TV signs five-year contract to televise Rockies games (1992)

The Rockies are now 3-6, 3 games out of first, in fifth place.

Saturday, April 17: Colorado 9, Montreal 1

The first road win.

11:35 at Exhibition Stadium
The starting pitchers: Ruffin (0-1) vs. Martinez (0-2)
The W-L pitchers: Ruffin (1-1) and Martinez (0-3)
The attendance: 23,166
The Post headline: Rockies, Ruffin rough up Expos
The News headline: Rockies road warriors for a day

On the field: There are many firsts: Not only is this the Rox' first road win, it is their first dome win, first artificial turf win and the first time a Rocky pitcher gets a hit (Parrett).

And, as Baylor says, it's "our first laughter."

Galarraga jump-starts the Rockies with a two-run double in the first.

The Rockies are now 4-6, two games out of first, in fifth place.

A thought for the First Road Trip Ever.

The Rockies opened on the road, so it wasn't actually the team's first road trip. Now is. And now that the season—and this account of same—is well under way, it is time that readers be issued a warning.

Warning:
This is Rocky reading.

Some say Darren Holmes is a Rockie.

Some say Darren Holmes is a Rocky.

We need to find out which and we need to do it soon. Before the wrong one becomes standard usage.

Here are nine arguments in favor of Rocky and one in favor of Rockie.

• **The Logic Says So Argument.** Clearly, the team was named for the Rocky Mountains. Also known as the Rockies. Which certainly seems to suggest that a single mountain is a Rocky.

• **The Everybody's Doing It Argument.** The Denver phone book contains 602 Rocky Mountain somethings and nary a Rockie anything

• **The That's The Way Words Work Argument.** Many

words that end in -y become -ies in their plural form. And many with -ies plurals convert to -y in their singular form.

Examples:

Batteries/Battery
Skies/Sky
Flunkies/Flunky
Studies/Study
French fries/French fry

• **The Sylvester Stallone Argument.** Sly was Rocky, Rocky II and a lot of other Rockies. But never a Rockie. (And, given a chance, who'd want to be?)

• **The Be Strong Like Bull Argument.** Sports teams need tough names. Rocky is stronger than Rockie

• **The Don't Be A Weenie Argument.** Words that end in -ie tend to be dear little words. Weenie words. Like birdie. Cutie. Sweetie. Twinkie.

Woody Paige wouldn't want to be Woodie Paige. Would he?

• **The "Rocky" Is A Great Sports Word Argument.** To wit: Rocky Marciano, Rocky Graziano, and Rocky Colavito.

• **The "Rockie" Is Too Close To "Rookie" Argument.** Let us not go on forever one letter away from "Rookie."

The solitary argument supporting the -ie ending is that it may work better with certain suffixes. Is Rockiemania better than Rockymania? Maybe. But Rockiesmania just might be better than either.

The News' Charles Roos uses the term, "Rockyball," and it is clearly superior to Rockieball.

The which-is-better question was posed to some of Denver's better writer types. This elicited a (mountain) range of response.

Jean Otto of the Rocky (not Rockie) Mountain News says the singulars Bronco and Dodger come easier than either Rocky or Rockie. "It's a judgment call," she says. "There is no right or wrong here."

She also notes that "Rocky of the Week" has an unstable sound. (Indeed, one of the definitions of "Rocky" is "unsteady." But another definition of the same word is "rocklike, steadfast.")

Patricia Calhoun, editor of Westword, says "I'll go with the -y. The Rocky Mountains argument is the best one. Besides, "Rockie" *is* too close to twinkie."

Bill Gallo, also of Westword, says "Common sense tells

me to spell it with a y in the singular. It's far superior." He also states his preference for Rox (as in Sox) as the casual way to refer to the team in the plural.

The Rocky Mountain News' Alan Dumas is neither wishy nor washy. "Both grammar and manhood require we call a Rockies player a Rocky and anyone who does otherwise is sadly misguided."

J.R. Moehringer, who covered Rockies' fans from spring training to the last game for the News, writes: "The argument is sillie, and only a bunch of marketing dummys could fail to realize that Rocky is the only answer possible."

Another Rocky writer of note, Bill Husted, writes: "I like Rocky, but I am worried that people will, if only subconsciously, think of Rocky the Flying Squirrel. And then there's Sly Stallone. And Nelson Rockefeller. Still, I vote for Rocky even though the Rockie Mountain News style book says otherwise. We stick to Rockies and Broncos."

Trouble is, the writers at the Rocky *don't* stick to Rockies and have frequently inflicted the wimpy -ie word on their sensitive readers.

Mike Rosen of the Denver Post and talk radio says that he believes Rocky should be the preferred spelling.

Post columnist Jack Kisling agrees. His argument is simple: "Plural: panties. Singular: panty. Plural: Rockies. Singular: Rocky."

Let us now turn to some writers from afar. When queried, David Lamb, Los Angeles Times writer and author of *Stolen Season* responded thusly:

"Without a doubt, the preferred singular spelling should be Rocky. I base that on common sense and what looks right to the eye. If you use Rockie in a baseball context, the eye/mind stumbles, and tends to translate the word as "rookie."

The New Yorker's Roger Angell disagrees, saying that "rocky" suggests the adjective, as in "feeling rocky." He says: "'Rockie' has the proper connotation, that the individual player is part of the whole, one of the Rockies." Angell goes on to state that "the problem has no clear solution, I suspect. It's like the singular of Red Sox. Is Roger Clemens a Red Sock?"

David Whitford, author of *Playing Hardball*, takes a completely different—and very strange—position. "How do we refer to a single mountain in the Rocky Mountains? We never say Rocky Elbert *or* Rockie Elbert. We say *Mt*. Elbert. So why not Mt. Charlie Hayes, Mt. Andres Galarraga, etc.?"

George Will was out of the country, but his assistant, Michael Andolina, had this response: "Had the Rocky series ended after the second film, or even perhaps the third, I would have contended that Rocky is an admirable figure and would certainly be worthy to serve as the namesake for a Colorado baseball player. However, the utter silliness of the final two Rocky movies leads me to believe that no baseball player deserves this connection."

And now, let us hear the judgment of James J. Kilpatrick, syndicated writer of the Writer's Art column, the all-about-word-usage feature that appears in the Rocky every Sunday.

"The problem with Rockies is that it is but one vowel removed from rookie…it would be uncomfortable to live with. The trouble with Rocky is that it carries unpleasant connotations—a rocky road, a rocky time of it. Put to a hard choice, I suppose I would have to vote for Rocky instead of Rockie, but it's a close call. "

Dave Barry, the humor writer for the Miami Herald (his column appears in the Post on Sundays), had a breakthrough idea:

"I think the singular should be just Rock."

Since the majority of our panel of experts supports Rocky over Rockie, that's the word that is employed here. One quickly gets very comfortable with it, and finds the -ie word to be rather irritating.

In addition, the Rox variation is employed from time to time. As is Dave Barry's singularly brilliant suggestion for the singular—Rock.

Sunday, April 18: Montreal 4, Colorado 2

The first time Alex Cole is thrown out trying to steal.

11:35 at Exhibition Stadium
The starting pitchers: Ashby (0-0) vs. Hill (1-0)
The W-L pitchers: Hill (2-0) and Wayne (0-1)
The attendance: 25,034
The Post headline: Bullpen fails team again
The News headline: Rockies let another get away

On the field: The Rockies restrict their scoring to the fourth inning, when a Hayes double brings in two. As the game progresses, it even looks like it might be enough. Indeed, after six, they lead, 2-1.

In the bottom of the seventh, Blair takes over for starter Ashby and things begin to unravel. By the time the third out is achieved, the Expos have nicked three Rockies relievers for as many runs and lead, 4-2. 'Twas the final score.

Young steals his seventh base. Cole steals his sixth and seventh, but he's nailed once. This is the first time either has been caught this season.

The Rockies are now 4-7, tied for fifth, three games out.

April 19 is an off day, so it is spent in contemplation of Andres Galarraga, who is now batting .422. Is he The Big Cat, the Big Cat, The Cat, the Cat, or just Cat?

Baylor simply calls him "Cat."

Another thing to contemplate: Four of the eight home runs the Rockies have smacked were off pitches by the Expos' Kent Bottenfield.

Tuesday, April 20: St. Louis 5, Colorado 0

The first meeting with the Cardinals.

7:35 at Busch Stadium
The starting pitchers: Smith (1-1) vs. Arocha (2-0)
The W-L pitchers: Arocha (3-0) and Smith (1-2)
The attendance: 30,516
The Post headline: Win-chill in St. Louis: zero
The News headline: Cards give Smith rude welcome back

On the field: The Cards shut out the Rockies on five hits off Rene Arocha, who goes 5 2/3 innings. Then Omar Olivares comes in to stifle the Rox the rest of the way.

Struggling Bryn Smith lasts just four innings, during which St. Louis victimizes him for five runs on seven hits.

The Rockies have now won 4, lost 8, and are in sixth place, four games out of first.

The first road win in the U.S.

7:35 at Busch Stadium
The starting pitchers: Nied (2-1) vs. Magrane (0-1)
The W-L pitchers: Nied (3-1) and Magrane (0-2)
The attendance: 25,434
The Post headline: Rockies go to bat for Nied, rip Cards
The News headline: Into the swing of things

On the field: The Rockies' first road win (last Saturday) was in Montreal. Now the boys with the purple buttons on their caps have won one on the road here in the U.S. of A.

It is also the first win over the Cards, the first night game win, and the first time a Rocky pitcher scores a run (Nied).

Nied goes eight innings, giving up two runs on six hits. Winning his third in a row, Nied had a shutout going into the eighth. Parrett comes in and finishes off the Cards in the ninth.

Meanwhile, the Rockies are nicely offensive. They turn 14 hits into 11 runs. Bichette's three-run shot in the eighth is the Rockies' first three-run homer.

850 on our AM dial.

Since everybody in Colorado was at the home opener, or watched it on the tube, one assumes that nobody heard the Jeff Kingery and Wayne Hagin account of Eric Young's historic blast on KOA.

Hagan has it memorized: "Here's the payoff pitch. He hits it to deep centerfield. That ball is hit way back, way back. And...kiss it goodbye! Eric Young! The first man to bat for the Colorado Rockies in Mile High Stadium hits a home run...and has brought this crowd to its feet. And the snow on Pikes Peak is falling off with the decibel level of Mile High Stadium!"

The Ombudsman asks Hagin about his and Kingery's' feelings about The Wave. "I don't think it's an announcer's job to tell the fans what to do. Jeff would say that The Wave is wrong. I don't know who made him God."

The Rockies are now 5-8, three games behind first, tied for fifth place.

Thursday, April 22: St. Louis 5, Colorado 2

The loss that gives the Cards their first win of a series with the Rockies.

12:35 at Busch Stadium
The starting pitchers: Henry (0-2) and Cormier (1-1)
The W-L pitchers: Perez (2-1) and Wayne (0-2)
The attendance: 34,218
The Post headline: Traveling down a beaten path again
The News headline: Rockies pay for gaffes on base paths

On the field: Henry pitches a strong 6+ innings, giving up just five hits and two runs and the Rocks cruise into the eighth knotted with the Cardinals, two-all.

Along the way, the Rockies' base running misfired and costs them a couple of runs.

Once again, the relief pitchers provide none.

Wayne lets Lankford lead off with a "triple" (Bichette misplayed it) and is replaced by Parrett, who quickly permits a flurry of singles. When the dust clears, St. Louis leads by the final score, 5-2.

Galarraga: .414.

The Rockies now have a 5-9 record, which puts them in sixth place, four games out of first and a half game ahead of last-place Cincinnati. The Marlins are in last place in the NL East with a 5-10 record.

Friday, April 23: Colorado 5, Florida 4

The Rockies' first game against —and first victory over— that other expansion team.

6:05 vs. Marlins at Mile High Stadium
The National Anthem: Elvis Impersonator Charles Kelly

The first ball: Kevin Flannery, junior high student from Colorado Springs.

The starting pitchers: Ruffin (1-1) vs. Hammond (0-2)
The W-L pitchers: Reed (1-0) and Hammond (0-3)

The attendance: 57,784
The Post headline: Bullpen finally rescues Rockies
The News headline: Victory a huge relief for Rockies

On the field: In the first game ever between the expansion teams, the Rocks get off to a nice start with a four-run first fueled by a three-run shot by Charlie Hayes.

Ultimately, the Marlins tie it up, but the Rockies take a 5-4 lead on Jerald Clark's leadoff homer in the fourth and tonight there is no more scoring by either team the rest of the way.

Benavides boots a couple and falls out of favor. Jerald Clark leads off the fourth with a homer. Starter Ruffin and reliever Parrett do well. Closer Holmes (who enters the game with an ERA of 60.75) has some more scary moments, but ultimately prevails and gets his—and the Rockies—first save.

"I'm the happiest man in Colorado," he says, "I guarantee you that."

A bunch of firsts: It's the first game the Rockies have won by one. And the first game—after nine successful attempts—in which Eric Young got caught stealing. And the first time Steve Reed has batted in the bigs (ground out). And the first time the Rockies' bullpen has gotten a win.

In the stands: The new homestand brings a new look to HOMESTAND FLYER, the bootleg one-buck scorecard. It now lists each player's salary. A fine touch.

Another: Much has been made of the outfielders' tendency to lose the ball in the crowded-to-the-fifth-level Mile High Stadium, so a group of fans devises a plan to befuddle the opposing outfielders: We get everyone with seats in the upper decks to wear dark green shirts when the good guys are in the field. To make a nice background. Then, to make fielding extra befuddling for the opposition, all will slip into shirts rampant with big polka dots. How big? Oh, about 3" in diameter.

Indeed, the conditions that make right field a living hell for Dante can—and should—be turned to the Rockies' advantage.

Speaking of hell, Gary Bloom has an idea. "Instead of throwing the opposition's home runs back on the field, they ought to be passed down to some central place where there is an incinerator or maybe a bucket of acid to throw them into."

There is substantial anti-Marlins sentiment displayed in the stands today. The Men of Teal are subjected to numerous signs and shouts of SQUISH THE FISH!

Diane K.: "I was hoping the Marlins would be wearing pants that color, too, so I could call them Buns of Teal."

And there is talk about 90-minute Marlinizing. Everyone thinks it's a funny concept though nobody knows what the hell it means.

In the third, the East Stands tries to start a wave, but it never makes the jump to the South Stands. In the sixth, the wave makes it past the East Stands and it even breaks through the stalwarts along first base who can usually be counted on to snuff it out.

Dick K., after an E-6: "Freddie makes up for not hitting by not fielding."

And: "I predict that Jason Bates will be shortstop before the end of the season."

A new, and highly disgusting, vendor's combo: "Iced coffee and cherry Slurpees!"

Today, on the radio, fans hear Jerald Clark refer to "Andre" Galarraga. Hmm. One wonders if, perhaps, the s is silent.

Pete T. has an idea about the singing of Take Me Out To The Ballgame during the seventh inning stretch: "The first time through, we sing it. Then the organist ought to play it a second time and everybody should whistle it. Could be very neat. And it would be *ours*."

Quoteworthy:

"You know what I'm waiting for? The first game with no firsts. Of course, *that* would be a first."

On the way home, fans note that the Burger King on Alameda announces that one can get "RKY MUGS HERE."

The abbreviation of the team's name ends in "Y." This is good.

A random thought: Two reasons to be glad that Don Baylor is in a Rockies uniform:

1. He's a helluva smart manager.
2. The sweaters he wore before the season were godawful.

The idea that the Rockies rejected for an ad to herald the first Mile High encounter with the Marlins: *Us vs. Them.*

Today's milestone: The Blue Jays' Nelson Liriano spoils a Nolan Ryan no-hitter with a ninth-inning triple (1989)

The Rockies now have a 6-9 record, which ties them with the Padres for fourth (and fifth) place in the NL West. They're three games out of first. Florida is 5-11.

Saturday, April 24: Florida 2, Colorado 1

The Rockies' first loss to that other expansion team.

11:15 vs. Marlins at Mile High Stadium
The National Anthem: Great Plains
The first ball: Mel Engbar
The starting pitchers: Ashby (0-0) vs. Aquino (0-1)
The W-L pitchers: Aquino (1-1) and Ashby (0-1)
The attendance: 58,263
The Post headline: Blunder ball strikes Rockies
The News headline: Rockies run into trouble

On the way to the park: The Safeway at 26th and Federal has a truck in its parking lot which is selling food at "snactacular" savings. As the sign says, buy your ballpark provisions here and "AVOID STADIUM PRICES."

On the field: Rain. And snow. And a delay of an hour and eleven minutes before ball is, indeed, played. Very embarrassing because this is the Rockies' first national TV game. The first time the Big Eye of CBS has looked at the two expansion teams.

Finally, the tarps came off and The First Pitchers' Duel Ever ensues.

Andy Ashby throws a nice game, fanning five and giving up just four hits and one run in seven innings. Then Parrett comes in and permits another run in the eighth. That ends the Marlins' scoring, but those two runs turn out to be enough.

Through eight, the Rockies have scored naught, largely due to baserunning blunders.

They do manage to score in the bottom of the ninth, but just once. Their mini-rally is snuffed when Cole flies out with

Bichette on second.

Ashby's single in the third is the second hit by a Rockies pitcher.

Galarraga drops -gasp- below .400.

In the stands: Fans spontaneously break into a chant for Joe Girardi: "LET'S GO, JOE!" And Girardi answers with the most hits he's ever gotten in a major league game (he goes 4-for-4), scores the Rockies' only run, and steals his first base in the bigs since 1990. Another first: This is the first game the Rockies have lost by one run.

Observation: The guys who fly the banners over the stadium promoting (mostly) strip joints must love having 80 or so baseball games to fly over. Before the Rockies came to town, all they had was a couple of dozen Broncos and CU games.

Rumor: The Bonnie Brae Tavern, famous for its pizza, has reprinted its menu—in purple.

Fantalk: "I hope Freddie didn't buy a home."

Susan L.: "I miss the breaking glass sound."The CRASH! we heard for years of Z's games when a foul ball bonked off one of the windows in the press level. Guess somebody thought it was Too Minor League."

The Rockies now have a 6-10 record and are in fifth place, four games behind the leader, Houston. Every team in baseball has six or more wins except for the A's and O's, who have five.

Sunday, April 25: Florida 11, Colorado 1
The first embarrassing loss before a crowd of over 70,000.

> **1:05 at Mile High Stadium**
> **The National Anthem:** Stephen West
> **The first ball:** Eric Scanniello, 9
> **The starting pitchers:** Smith (1-2) vs. Bowen (1-1)
> **The W-L pitchers:** Bowen (2-1) and Smith (1-3)
> **The attendance:** 71,192
> **The Post headline:** It's a black Sunday for Rockies
> **The News headline:** Rockies try, and fail, before crowd
>   of 71,192

In today's Post, letter-to-the-editor-writer John Donohue is steamed. He wonders if the Rockies are trying to make up the $95 million entry fee in their first month of operation.

"I wanted just a scorecard but you can't buy just a scorecard," Donohue says, "you must buy a $5 program and they won't even give you a stinking pencil with it. You have to go to the novelties stand and buy one for 50 cents. Maybe the name should be changed from Rockies to Gougie$."

At Brooklyn's: Before the game, the Denver chapter of the Society of American Baseball Research names the chapter after Frank Haraway, the official scorer of the Bears, Zephyrs and Rockies. An excellent selection.

On the way in: The price of parking at the lot near Federal on Dick Connor Drive is a good barometer of how big a draw a game is. A really big game brings out the $10 sign. Like tonight's.

On the field: Starter Bryn Smith goes into the fourth. His reliever, Scott Aldred, gives up—among other things—a grand slam to Junior Felix. It's the first slam in the history of The Fish. It's all part of the Marlins' stunning eight-run fourth inning. [It will turn out to be Aldred's last appearance as a Rocky.]

Galarraga's .382 puts him in third place in the NL batting race behind Barry Bonds and Don Slaught.

Today's firsts: After starting every game for the Rockies in the lead-off spot, Eric Young is switched with Alex Cole and dropped to the second spot. And Bryn Smith is credited with the first stolen base of his 11-year career in the third, but injures himself while pitching in the fourth and is placed on the 15-day DL.

But frankly, we don't give a dome.

Fans are all too aware of -ug- The Astrodome, The Superdome, The Kingdome, and The Metrodome. And when we refer to any of them, the first name is "The." But not so with the facility in Toronto. Broadcasters always call it "Superdome," never "The Superdome."

The question is this: How come?

Perhaps we should call our ballpark The Mile High Stadium.

In the stands: It is the second largest gathering of Rockies fans of the season.

It's your basic sellout crowd.

And it is, perhaps, the largest crowd the Marlins will play before. Ever.

A fan explains why so many humans have gathered at Mile High today: "It is better to see the Rockies play the Marlins by day than see the Rockies play the Cubbies by night."

Which leads to: "The worst day game is better than the best night game." A good thing, too, considering what's happening on the field.

The musical question is how come Mile High's music maven played Billy Joel's "Pressure" when Aldred came into the game? That's the song that's supposed to be played when the *other* team brings in a new pitcher in a tight situation.

Castilla has replaced the struggling Freddie Benavides at short. Which brings forth numerous smartass comments. Such as this exchange in the second inning after Castilla slightly muffs a ground ball, but still throws out the man at first by a couple of steps.

"Freddie would've fielded it cleanly."

"Freddie would've thrown him out by *three* steps."

Then, after a pause: "Freddie would've *struck him out!*"

Another interesting exchange follows the playing of a bit of a song by the resident organist:

"It's nice that we've got a traditional organ."

"*Who's* got a traditional organ?"

A fan looks over his scorecard and makes this observation about the Marlins: "Many of them are former major leaguers." A good comment, but maybe better suited to another day.

In light of the horror unfolding on the field, one fan pretty much sums things up thusly:

"It's a beautiful day at the ballpark," he says, "if you don't look at the game."

Today's milestone: Darren Holmes' birthday (1966)

The Rockies are now 6-11 on the season, four games out of first, in fifth place.

Monday, April 26: Chicago 6, Colorado 3

The first encounter with the Cubs (and the first loss to same).

7:05 at Mile High Stadium
The National Anthem: The Bismarck Jazz Choir
The first ball: Henry Schimberg (Coca-Cola)
The starting pitchers: Nied (3-1) vs. Harkey (2-0)
The W-L pitchers: Harkey (3-0) and Nied (3-2)
The attendance: 48,768
The Post headline: Nothing changes for Rockies
The News headline: Rockies fall behind, can't get up

Before the game: It's the Cubbies' first regular season visit to Denver (they've played here before in exhibition games), and much excitement surrounds the encounter.

This afternoon, KOA's Ancel Martinez interviews a Cubs fan at Brooklyn's. Ancel's question: "What's so special about Wrigley Field?" Her response: "We can drink beer anywhere the hell we want!"

On the field: Rockies make many (16) hits, including a pair of triples by Castilla, but can only turn them into a trio of runs. One reason: Jerald Clark hits into three inning-ending double plays. (He also lets a fly ball ploop off his glove for a three-base error.)

Meanwhile, the Cubs convert 10 hits into a sixpack of runs.

It looks good for the Rocks when they've got a 3-1 lead in the sixth, but then the Cubs put four of their hits together to go ahead 4-3.

The finishing touches are put on the Cubbie win when Dwight Smith hits a home run into the South Stands. It's the first homer anyone's hit there in Denver's short history in the big leagues—and it may well be the first time a home run ball off a visitor's bat is not thrown back by the fans. In spite of tremendous pressure from the entire ballpark, Smith's home run ball becomes a collectible instead of a rejectable.

Turns out the guy who caught it is a Cubs fan. No wonder he wanted the souvenir.

Mike Rosen has an idea he believes to be better than

throwing the balls back. "I say find a Cubs fan and throw *him* onto the field. A human sacrifice might discourage the practice."

Another first: Nied gets his first hit as a Rocky and the first RBI of his ML career. It is also the first ribbie for a member of Colorado's pitching staff.

On the way from Colorado Springs: Scott Fredrickson becomes the answer to a trivia question. Who was the first player the Rockies ever called up from the minors?

On the scoreboard: More errors than on the field. The singers of the National Anthem are billed as "THE BIZMARCK JAZZ CHOIR." Obviously, the scoreboard operator has been exposed to too many Bizmart ads. During the singing, the Z turns into an S and and sigh of relief goes up from the crowd.

Later, a scoreboard ad for a summer resort suggests that it's a good place to "Ejoy golf." There is precedent for all this, of course: The first couple of games saw this spelling: "Sacrafice."

Fans wonder if the scoreboard operator was involved in the multiple gaffes in the calendar given out two days ago: Its embarrassing solecisms included: "Veteran's Day." "Baseball Hero's" "Kid's Cap" And, yes, "Calender."

In the stands: For the first time, there are fewer than 50 thou on hand. Quite a surprise considering it's Game One with the Cubs. Still, the Rockies have now beaten the Denver Bears' all-time attendance mark for a season (565,214, set in 1980). And it took the Rocks just ten games.

It is a difficult day for many of those on hand. Lots of Cubs fans in the Denver area and they're going through a transformation. Regis Groff, a long time Cubbie rooter, is wearing a Cubs label pin tonight. It is his last salute to his former favorite team. (Tomorrow, he says, he'll be at the ball-park for the second Cubs game, but his lapel pin won't.)

Bill Koerber thinks that converted Cubs fans will make excellent Rockies fans. "We know how to lose gracefully."

Still, there is this thought: Wouldn't it be great if the game pitted Chicago against *Denver* rather than against the whole state?

A FEW KEY MOMENTS:

7:06—First Chicago Cub in the history of the planet (Dwight Smith) steps to the plate in Denver in an actual major league ball game.

7:07—First Chicago Cub-caused foul ball goes into the stands (Section 115).

7:08—First Chicago Cub base runner. (Smith on a walk.)

After that, things go pretty much downhill and the only other moment of note is in the bottom of the first (at 7:28) when women fans become upset by Jerald Clark. For the first time all season, he doesn't do his signature bottom-wiggle in the batters' box. And he pays dearly for this oversight: He hits into a rally-ending DP.

By the third inning, Andres Galarraga is once again batting .400+.

To the fans, the scoreboard operator is not only a lousy speller, he is also a chicken. Early on, the umpires came down hard on the Rockies' practice of replaying controversial plays on the DiamondVision. The Big Show frowns upon those little shows. So what do the Rockies show the fans? The beginning of the great fielding plays—then they cut it off before the actual put-out.

The photos of Our Heroes that are flashed on the scoreboard are very passportesque. Especially the one of Dante Bichette. He either had his eyes closed when they shot the picture or Bichette is of Far Eastern extraction.

Upon seeing Bichette pictured on the DiamondVision, Diane Kaminsky breaks out in a rousing chorus of "Wake Up, Little Dante!"

Then, in the 9th, when Dante makes a great catch and he acknowledges the crowd's appreciative applause with a bow, a fan says, "See! He *is* Oriental!"

The big flap: WGN broadcasted this Cubs-Rockies series throughout the nation—but not in the Denver area. People blame the Rockies management for trying to force attendance up through this selfish maneuver, but people are wrong.

Fact is, Todd Phipers reports in the Post, it's the fault of the FCC. Says there's a federal reg that prohibits superstations carrying a game from airing it within 35 miles of a team's home game if that game isn't being provided by an over-the-air telecast locally.

(Several days later, Phipers dismissed the above as misinformation that came from a major league baseball source. The fact is, he says, all televised games could be shown if the Rockies gave permission, but the team opted to invoke the blackout. The FCC lets the club make the call, and the Rockies have chosen to protect their gate.)

The little flap: Although the crowd pleads with Harry Caray to sing "Take Me Out, etc.," he refuses. As he did a couple of days ago, he conducts the crowd from his radio booth during the seventh-inning stretch—but no singing.

It is his policy, he says, to sing only at Wrigley and Ho Ho Kam Fields. Nowhere else.

But that may just be the beer talking. Fans with memories recall that he did, indeed, sing the song at Mile High Stadium during a preseason exhibition game a few years back.

The generous offer: AAA Colorado is on hand after tonight's game—and after all Rockies games—to help those who have car trouble. And not just the first 20,000 fans, either.

Today's milestone: Amos Otis' birthday (1947)

The Rockies have now lost three in a row, have a 6-12 record, and are in next-to-last place a half game behind the Reds and ahead of the Dodgers. The Marlins are 7-12 and in last place in the NL East.

Tuesday, April 27: Colorado 11, Chicago 2
The first victory over the Cubs.

> **7:05 at Mile High Stadium**
> **The National Anthem:** La Tanya Hall (Miss Colorado)
> **The first ball:** John Suder (Channel 2)
> **The starting pitchers:** Henry (0-2) vs. Morgan (1-3)
> **The W-L pitchers:** Henry (1-2) and Morgan (1-4)
> **The attendance:** 48,328
> **The Post headline:** Rockies roll over Cubs in 11-2 win
> **The News headline:** Bats boom as Rockies crush Cubs

On the field: Butch Henry goes the distance as the Rockies (who couldn't make more than three runs out of 16 hits yesterday) turn eleven hits into as many runs today. The Rox start fast with four in the first. The Cubs answer with a pair of dingers in the second, but that was pretty much it for them. The

Rocks add six more in the fourth, highlighted by a 464-foot blast over the center field wall by A. Galarraga. [It turns out to be the longest circuit clout of the season.]

Firsts: First victory over the Cubs in Rockies history. And first ejection of anybody from the field of play during a Rockies game. It was Cubs manager Jim Lefebvre for arguing strikes and balls with the plate ump.

Seconds: Second complete game in Rockies history. Second RBI for a Rockies pitcher (Henry).

On the way in: Three middle-aged matronly type fans have their shopping bags checked for cans or bottles by an Andy Frain operative. They protest that the search is unnecessary as their bags contain just blankets and coats. Andy Frain guy to matrons: "Chill ass."

In the stands: A fan discovers she left her lighter in her car. She searches the concourse for a source of matches. Finding none, she asks Joan and Joyce, the nice Coors Light vendors she has befriended (this early in the season!) if they have a pack of matches. Joan: "Here, take my lighter. I only smoke when I play bingo."

Cotton candy monitors note that, tonight, it is no longer purple. It is pink or blue, your choice.

After the Rockies explode for a sixpack of runs in the fourth, a fan brings out one of those call bells (the kind they have in hotels to summon a bellhop) and replicates the ancient tradition of the Bears and Zephyrs.

The bell: DING!
The crowd: "ONE!"
The bell: DING!
The crowd: "TWO!"
And so on, up to "SIX!"

On the way out: Highlights on KOA's account of the game just played are played for the amusement and pleasure of the crowd making its way to the parking lots.

It's a nice touch, but an even nicer one would be to carry KOA live in the restrooms during the game so that fans don't have to lose track of what's happening while they're away from their seats.

Many stadiums have this and fans like it because it lets

them keep up with the game. Plus it reduces resentment among those who have to wait in line to use the john.

Good idea. The Fans' Ombudsman finds out why Mile High doesn't offer this amenity.

The Rockies' Kevin Carlon: "It would be cost prohibitive to install a totally separate P.A. system in the concourse to broadcast the game." Oh.

Radio in the restrooms won't be happening in Denver, it appears, but even that wouldn't be good enough for Jack Hidahl. "Let's have *TV* in the restrooms."

Then he thinks about it. "Hmm. For gender equality, they'd have to put one in every stall in the ladies' rest room."

The Rockies now have a 7-12 record. This puts them in fifth place, four games out of first. Florida is 8-12.

Wednesday, April 28: St. Louis 7, Colorado 6
The first visit by the Cards.

7:05 at Mile High Stadium
The National Anthem: The Poor Boys
The first ball: Dealin' Doug
The starting pitchers: Ruffin (1-1) vs. Osborne (1-0)
The W-L pitchers: Murphy (1-1) and Holmes (0-2)
The attendance: 49,765
The Post headline: Rockies gift-wrap victory for Cards
The News headline: Holmes lets win get away

On the field: When the Rockies take a one-run lead into the ninth inning, scary things have been happening of late. And it happens again. First, Holmes walks three batters in a row. Then Jerald Clark fails to make the catch on a pop fly to left. Then Rod Brewer singles in the go-ahead run which—after Lee Smith comes in to pitch the ninth inning and collect his 364th career save—turns out to be the winner.

This is Holmes' third blown save in three chances.

Gerald Young gets his first hit as a Rocky, a single. [It will turn out to be his only.]

Galarraga starts the game batting under .400, goes above, goes back under, goes above—and winds up right at four-oh-oh.

Hayes had gone to the plate 79 times in a row without

fanning—the longest stretch in the majors—until tonight. When he did it *twice*.

In the stands: The first visit of the Cardinals is an emotional and historic evening. There are many St. Louis fans in Denver. Indeed, a couple of years ago, prodded by the Post, Denver adopted the Cards as its major league team. (Not a good choice; they were lousy that year.)

A kid is spotted on the concourse wearing a CR cap *and* a Cards' cap.

Another guy took it a step further and cut his two caps in half and had them sewn into a two-sided cap.

John Ashton said it for hundreds or maybe thousands in attendance today: "Well, today's my day to go out to the ballpark and say goodbye to my old team and say hello to my new team."

Marking the moments: At 7:17, Ozzie Smith takes his place at shortstop. At 7:42, the Oz makes the first play in his career above 5,000 feet (he starts a 6-4-3 DP in the second).

A fan query: "If Ozzie Smith married the Cardinals' pitcher, Donovan Osborne, would his name be Ozzie Ozzie?"

"Yes. And if he then went on to marry Ozzy Osbourne, he'd be Ozzie Ozzie Ozzy. Or maybe even Ozzie Ozzie Ozzy Ozzie."

A fan to a friend: *"Mi cerveza es su cerveza."*

A fan sensitive to nuance: "Why do they say that a player was recalled from the Sky Sox when he's never been to the bigs before? They ought to just say that he was called up from the Sky Sox."

The scoreboard misfires again: THE FIRST 20,000 ADULTS THORGH THE GATES GET FREE CAPS.

Fantalk: "Freddie hasn't made an error in *three* days!" Or played.

And this important argument: "If we lost Bichette, wouldn't we be unDanted." "No, we'd be Danteless."

There's something new on the scoreboard. The board now tells what a batsman did earlier in the same. Example: "1 FOR 1 (DOUBLE)." This is good, since few keep score these days and fewer still remember what every player did earlier in the game.

The DiamondVision is not showing head shots of the Rockies as much as they used to. "Maybe," Peter M. says, "they're ashamed of their pictures." Or of their pitchers.

Especially the left-handed ones.

Cotton candy is purple again, much to the delight of those who have been watching it rise and fall like The Cat's batting average.

A scorecard is entrusted to Jackie Brown while a beer run is made. Jackie claims she knows how to keep score. Upon his return, the scorecard's owner finds a rather unlikely entry: 2-7.

Rally caps bring home a run in the seventh, but are ineffective in the penultimate and ultimate innings.

Today's Westword contains a letter from JD McWilliams who, apparently, is responsible for at least one of the scoreboard's misspellings. But he stridently denies that the scoreboard still displays "sacrafice."

Today's milestone: The Blue Jays' Nelson Liriano doubles in the ninth inning to spoil a Kirk McCaskill no-hitter (1989)

The Rockies now have a 7-13 record and are in last place, five games out of first and half a game out of next-to-last. The Marlins are 9-12. The Mets are 8-11.

Thursday, April 29: St. Louis 5, Colorado 2
The loss that gave the Cards the distinction of being the first to sweep the Rox at home.

1:05 at Mile High Stadium
The National Anthem: Donna Pierce
The first ball: Lee Larson (KOA)
The starting pitchers: Ashby (0-1) vs. Tewksbury (0-3)
The W-L pitchers: Tewksbury (1-3) and Ashby (0-2)
The attendance: 57,472
The Post headline: Victory wasn't in the cards
The News headline: Rockies bats go cold in loss

On the field: Cards' starter Bob Tewksbury gets his first two hits of the season, one with the bases loaded for two RBIs (all last year, he got only three!). The only highlights for the Rockies are Charlie Hayes' homer in the fourth and Scott Fredrickson's ML debut. He retires all six of the Cards he faces.

St. Louis is the first visiting nine to sweep the Rocks at home ever—though it is just a two-game series—and gives the Rockies a 7-14 record which drops them into uncontested possession of last place in the NL West for the first time ever.

They call up pitcher Armando Reynoso from the Springs.

To clear a spot for him, they ask waivers on Scott Aldred. Unfortunately, the Expos claimed the 24-year-old hurler.

The Galarraga Watch: Andres enters the game batting .400 and, during the course of the contest, finds himself batting .395, .390, .398, and, at the conclusion of the contest: .405.

In the stands: Peter Groff takes charge of rally cap protocol for Section 116. He decides when it's time to turn the CR cap around for good luck.

When a plane pulling a sign proclaiming FREE BUFFET AT DIAMOND CABARET flies by, a fan comments "I didn't know Jimmy was being held against his will there."

After making a beer run: "I missed an entire inning out of my life!"

Woman: "I could almost be Dale Murphy's mother."

Man: "Are you talking about an age thing or about not being invited to that party?"

And, finally, "I hate this homestand. I can't wait for it to be over. And I can't wait 'til the next one."

The Rockies have now lost two in a row, have a record of 7-14, and are in last place, six games out of first and a half game behind the sixth-place Dodgers.

The Marlins are 10-12.

Friday, April 30: Colorado 6, Florida 2
The first game the Rockies have played in Florida. And their first win.

5:35 pm at Joe Robbie Stadium
The starting pitchers: Reynoso (0-0) vs. Bowen (2-1)
The W-L pitchers: Reynoso (1-0) and Bowen (2-2)
The attendance: 42,535
The Post headline: Friday night fish fry in Florida
The News headline: Reynoso goes the distance

The Game: Armando Reynoso, called up from Colorado Springs on Thursday, debuts with a six-hit complete game victory powered by Galarraga's first-inning three-run homer over the 434' sign in the deepest part of Joe Robbie Stadium.(Following which, The Big Cat is walked intentionally three of his next four at-bats.)

The Fish fried up a couple of runs in the second, but it wasn't enough.

Cat is now up to .412.

It's been announced that the Rockies' Double-A team will be in New Haven next season. They're a lock to be the Eastern League champions.

In today's Post, Todd Phipers calls the Marlins' home "The Teal Deal." Phipers also gives today's game a rating of ✓✓✓ and says "Add one ✓ if the Rockies don't have to go to their bullpen."

Tempest in a hardware store: The Belcaro Ace hardware store displays a cup filled with bat-shaped cookie cutters with this sign: "ROCKIES COOKIE CUTTERS 59¢." But a close look reveals that someone took out a ballpoint pen and added two words after the first word on the sign—"or Yankees."

Today's milestone: Ryan Hawblitzel's birthday (1971)

The Rockies now have a record of 8-14. This ties them with the Reds for fifth (and sixth) place in the NL West. Two teams have worse records, the Mets and the Indians.

The Rockies' first April: 8 wins, 14 losses.

Saturday, May 1: Florida 7, Colorado 6 (12 innings)
The Rockies' first extra inning game.

> **5:05 pm at Joe Robbie Stadium**
> **The starting pitchers:** Nied (3-2) vs. Harvey (0-1)
> **The W-L pitchers:** Harvey (1-1) and Reed (1-1)
> **The attendance:** 43,583
> **The Post headline:** Rockies fall short in a time of Nied
> **The News headline:** Rockies lose last battle, then lose
> game

The game: It's 24-year-old Nied against 45-year-old Charlie Hough (the opening day pitchers for the two expansion teams).

Although the kid is staked to a three-run lead in the first, he allows six runs in five innings. Neither starter is around four hours and fifteen minutes later when this 12-inning battle (the first extra-inning contest in the Rockies' brief history) concludes on Renteria's game-winning hit off Reed. After fouling off seven pitches.

A record for both teams: The 4-hour, 15-minute contest is by far the longest.

A first: The first grand slam a Rockies pitcher has allowed—Conine off Nied in the Marlins' four-run fifth. It's also Conine's first ML home run.

A first you don't tell the grandkids about: In the eighth inning, Eric Young is charged with being caught stealing twice in the same inning. The first time, he escapes actually being put out by a Marlin throwing error. Moments later, he does get thrown out attempting to steal. Only five other players have suffered thus in the history of the game.

One of them is Don Baylor.

The Marlins' mascot: "Billy" the Marlin is prominent in the TV coverage of the game. Which reminds many fans in Denver how nice it is not to have a corny, irrelevant distraction like that flopping around Mile High Stadium.

In today's News: Ken Kreutzer wrote in to ask "What happened to the bell at the Bears and Zephyrs games that they used to ring at the end of each inning to show how many runs the team got? I thought it was a great tradition to continue in Denver."

The response of Mike Swanson, the Rockies PR chief: "That bell belongs to the Zephyrs...and they took it with them."

Let's see, bells like that cost what—thirty bucks?

Today's milestone: Armando Reynoso's birthday (1966)

The Rockies now have a record of 8-15, which ties them with the Cleveland Indians for the worst record in the majors. The Rockies are in last place, seven games behind the first-place Astros and a half game behind the next-to-last-place Dodgers. The Marlins are 11-13. The Mets are 8-14.

The game that gave the Rockies their first series victory on the road.

6:05 pm at Joe Robbie Stadium
The starting pitchers: Henry (1-2) vs. Armstrong (2-2)
The W-L pitchers: Henry (2-2) and Armstrong (2-3)
The attendance: 41,370
The Post headline: Rockies breathe a sigh of relief
The News headline: Defense rescues Rockies

On the field: What we have here is the second game the Rockies have ever come from behind to win. And the second time they've won a series. And the first time they've won a series on the road. They've even climbed back out of the cellar.

Doesn't look good most of the way, though. In the eighth, with two outs, the Rox trail, 1-0.

Then Clark and Young single, Young steals second, and Alex Cole singles in both Rockies' runs.

The Marlins claim they wuz robbed. Indeed, in their portion of the eighth, the replays on ESPN *do* reveal that Magadan's long fly actually went over the wall, then bounced back. The umps say the ball never left the park and was still in play and Magadan ends up on second and proceeds no farther.

The next—and last—excitement comes when Eric Young throws out Weiss at home for the game's final out. There's a Weiss-Girardi collision at the plate, but the Rock stands fast.

Henry notches eight strikeouts, a career high. Also a franchise record.

Andres Galarraga enters the game batting a nifty .411. But in the course of the evening, he goes 0-4 and sinks into the .300s, maybe forever.

On ESPN: During tonight's national broadcast of the Rockies-Marlins contest, ESPN's Jon Miller says that he wishes that these teams were named after their cities rather than their states. Furthermore, he predicts that someday, they'll become the Denver Rockies and the Miami Marlins. What a concept!

On the bum: In the News, Norm Clarke says that "as great as this Rockies season has been, imagine the joy if the seats were a few inches wider."

In a letter in today's Post, Jon Karuschkat writes an impassioned letter opposing the practice of throwing back the opposition's home run balls.

"To the best of my knowledge this is only done in one other ballpark...Chicago fans by no means hold the key to absolute truth. This is Denver, not Chicago. We should not be governed by the bleacher bums at Wrigley."

Karuschkat then points out that getting a souvenir ball is something that kids and adults both dream about.

And says that "I for one will keep any and all balls that come my way no matter who hits them."

A visit to Arlington, Texas, will reveal to Mr. Karuschkat that the fans in at least one other ballpark reject the visitors' home run balls.

Perhaps a ballpark survey is in order.

Perhaps someone should ask the kid who is going to all the ballparks this summer.

The Rockies now have a 9-15 record, which puts them in a tie with Cincinnati for fifth (and sixth) place, seven games behind the first-place Giants and half a game ahead of the last-place Dodgers. The bottom two teams in the NL East are Florida (11-14) and New York (9-14).

May 3 is an off day, but a good time to sit down with some nice stats. We see that Barry Bonds leads the NL in BA with .425. The Cat is next with .394. The Cat leads the league in hits with 37 and is second in RBI with 26 (Bonds has 28).

Tuesday, May 4: Colorado 14, Chicago 13 (11 innings)
The Rockies' first visit to the Friendly Confines. And first win there.

> **6:05 pm at Wrigley Field**
> **The starting pitchers:** Ashby (0-3) vs. Guzman (3-2)
> **The W-L pitchers:** Blair (1-0) and McElroy (1-1)
> **The attendance:** 32,199
> **The Post headline:** Rocky Rockies wriggle out of Wrigley
> **The News headline:** Rockies outlast Cubs 14-13

On the field: Our boys' first visit to Wrigley Field, former home of Girardi and Zimmer. Too bad it has to be under the lights. Of course, there *are* a lot of fireworks. The Rocks get 17 hits and the Cubs get 21.

In the 5th, Girardi and Clark get homers off Jose Guzman on consecutive pitches.

Later, Jim Tatum (who got a homer in the last game as a minor leaguer in Denver) puts up a lot of firsts: His first ML homer which is the Rockies first pinch-hit homer which is also the Rockies first grand slam.

Because the fans at Wrigley reject the home run balls of opponents, Tatum gets the ball back, a fine souvenir. At the time (the eighth inning), it put the Rox ahead, 10-5, and everyone in The Time Zone thinks all is well.

Nope. In the bottom of the ninth, with two outs, Sammy Sosa ties it up with a three-run homer.

After a zero-filled tenth, the Rocks score four times in the 11th and, once again, think they can breathe easy.

Wrongo.

Blair lets the Cubbies get three of them back with the help of Sosa's second homer. But that leaves the Cubs a run short and the Rox take Game One at Wrigley.

Girardi calls this "the craziest game of my life."

Galarraga goes 3-for-6 and winds up back at .400.

In today's News, Gene Amole laments the passing of the days when he felt less like a mountain goat up there in Section 413 and more of a fan.

What he misses most about minor league ball, Gene says, is David Flaming, "the best peanut vendor I have ever seen." Amole goes on to describe how Flaming knew hundreds of fans by name and invited them to his home to watch the World Series from bleachers rigged in his living room.

Flaming is now back east.

And Amole is up high. And wishing that "we can retain that sense of fun now that we are in the big show."

The Rockies have now won two straight for the first time since games three and four, have a record of 10-15, and are in fifth place in the National League West, six games out of first and one game out of fourth. Trailing the Rox are L.A. (10-16) and Cincinnati (9-16).

The first game played at Wrigley during the day as God intended.

1:20 pm at Wrigley Field
The starting pitchers: Reynoso (1-0) vs. Hibbard (1-2)
The W-L pitchers: Hibbard (2-2) and Reynoso (1-1)
The attendance: 20,266
The Post headline: Daydreams: Rockies' bats fall asleep
The News headline: Reynoso's good effort lost on Cubs

On the field: After yesterday's slugfest, this contest is mighty peaceful. Colorado has two one-run innings and Chicago has three. Simple as that.

Reynoso, making his second start, goes seven innings and Chicago's Hibbard goes eight.

Galarraga gets but one hit in four trips to the plate, drops to .394.

And the Rockies now have a 5-8 record at home. Same as on the road.

On the TV: We are forced to hear Duane Kuiper, a Television Sports Professional, repeatedly speak of the Cubbies' "Ryan" Sandberg.

On the way to Colorado Springs: Darren Holmes. For a tuneup in the hope that he can become the closer that everybody thought he was going to be. Holmes is the first Rock to be sent from the bigs to the littles.

On the way from the Springs: Pitcher Mark Knudson. He's 3-1 with the Sky Sox with a 2.25 ERA.

On Channel 4: Larry Green mentions the numbers on the Rockies' jerseys. Jerseys? Maybe he needs a little more seasoning in the Springs, too.

The Rockies now have a 10-16 record, same as Cincinnati, and the two teams are tied for last place in the NL West, seven games out of first and a half game behind the Dodgers. Florida has a 12-15 record, putting them ahead of the 9-16 Mets.

Thursday, May 6: Atlanta 13, Colorado 3

The game Knudson would most like to forget (but probably can't).

7:05 at Mile High Stadium
The National Anthem: Steve Watts (saxophone)
The first balls: Sage Robinson and Dennis Paresa (Little
  Sister and Little Brother)
The starting pitchers: Nied (3-2) vs. Smoltz (2-3)
The W-L pitchers: Smoltz (3-3) and Nied (3-3)
The attendance: 50,618
The Post headline: Braves batter Nied, Knudson
The News headline: Braves batter Rockies 13-3

On the field: It is the much-heralded first-ever match-up between Nied and his former teammates. The tone is set early when Justice tags the kid for a two-run homer in the first. Soon the former Brave has been touched for five runs in six innings.

When Mark Knudson comes in, the scenario is strictly fairy tale:

Knudson's a local product. He lives here. His wife is expecting triplets any day. He's been toiling in the Springs pining away for the call from Denver. When the Rockies sent ineffective closer Darren Holmes down, they called up Knudson.

So here's Knudson, summoned to the big team earlier this very day. At precisely 9:01, he is sent out to the mound in the 7th to stifle the Braves (who led at the time, 5-2).

His first pitch is, indeed, a strike. Then, all of a sudden, the ball game is out of control. Knudson is quickly shelled for eight runs and leaves the game with a heavy heart—and a hefty 72.00 ERA.

On Dick Kreck's desk: A package arrives containing a T-shirt. NO WAVES IN MILE HIGH STADIUM, it says.

Stockbroker Art Kaufman starting a campaign. Many hope he'll sells thousands of them to the people in the reserved general admissions, sections AA to EE.

Or, as they're more popularly known, the South Stands.

The cruel Jim Armstrong quote: "The only thing the Braves did wrong was miss the extra point."

In the stands: It is noted that this was a game of many firsts:

First meeting with the Braves. First meeting with a team in the NL West. First blackout of Turner's superstation in Denver. Before the evening was over, it also became the first appearance for new Rockies Mark Knudson and Nelson Liriano.

(Odd Liriano factoid: In 1988, he was the Blue Jays secondbaseman in two exhibition games against the Twins in Mile High Stadium.)

As the fans settle into their seats to soak up all this firstness and welcome the Rockies back from their first-ever winning road trip, they discover that the cost of soaking up beer appears to have gone up while the Rocks were out of town.

A fan attempted to explain: "They raise the beer prices when a higher caliber team comes in."

An analysis by The Fans' Ombudsman reveals that, ounce for ounce, the price of beer has actually gone *down*.

The 20-ounce Commemorative Cup is gone from the concourse beer sales stands. In its place: A $3.75 cup of beer said to contain 24 ounces. Analysis reveals that it holds 22 ounces tops. Which brings it in at 17¢ an ounce. Also new: A so-called 16-ouncer that may actually contain a bonus half ounce. At $2.50, that works out to just *15¢* an ounce.

Justice's first-inning homer off Nied is the first home run ball not thrown back by the East Stands.

Knudson faced eleven batters. In order, here is what happened: Single, triple, single, homer, ground out, walk, fielder's choice, homer, walk, walk, homer.

Which led a fan to cry out: "Whatever happened to good old Darren Holmes?"

Speaking of which, there's this: "It's wrong to say Holmes was sent down to the Springs. Colorado Springs is *higher* than Denver."

It is announced that tomorrow "The first 20,000 people will receive a baseball cap." Guess they'll have to share it.

And, once again, the scoreboard commits a misspelling. This time, assistance was put up as "assitance."

Speaking of questionable orthography, the fans haven't forgotten Will Scalzitti. Scalzitti, the guy who whomped the game-winning grand slam in the first Bend Rockies game.

And they wonder what became of the first hero in Rockies history. (Catching and DHing for Class A Central Valley.)

The Rockies have now lost two in a row which gives them a 10-17 record and drops them into the cellar of the NL West. Plop. Maybe forever. Or, at least, for the rest of this season.

The Rocks are a game behind Cincinnati and L.A.

Friday, May 7: Atlanta 13, Colorado 5
The third game in four days wherein the Rox gave up 13 runs.

7:05 at Mile High Stadium
The National Anthem: Tommy Williams (Calvary Temple)
The first ball: Dan Hesser (Invesco)
The starting pitchers: Henry (2-2) vs. Avery (1-2)
The W-L pitchers: Freeman (1-0) and Parrett (0-1)
The attendance: 65,429
The Post headline: Dice land on unlucky 13 again
The News headline: Blauser helps Braves bash Rockies again

On the field: The Rockies jump off to a 3-1 lead after the initial inning, but it quickly vanishes.

For the third time in the last four days, the Rockies let the opposition score 13 runs. (A Rockies Pitcher's Dozen?) Or more. Incredibly, we won one of the three. Today isn't the one.

With the Braves leading by a run, Parrett comes in to pitch. When he leaves, their lead has grown to five.

This is the first game of the season that Eric Young isn't in the lineup. Liriano, in for Young at second, gets his first ML hit since May of 1991 when he was with Kansas City.

In the stands: Behind home plate sit Ted Turner and Jane Fonda. But nobody notices.

Except, perhaps, for people sensitive to proper ballpark headgear. Ted's hat is sized, a real baseball cap. Jane's isn't; it is a *souvenir* cap.

Speaking of caps, tonight is Invesco Hat Night. "They gave away 20,000 caps," says Jim Z. "We were 20,001, 20,002, 20,003 and 20,004."

We may have a record here: At 7:10, Rob buys a purple cotton candy. At 7:14, Rob finishes his purple cotton candy.

You can't tell the players without an illegal scorecard.

The bootleg scorecards being sold around the ballpark for a buck are unauthorized, underground, and unofficial. But they are gently referred to as "non-sanctioned baseball newsletters" and "alternative publications" in newspaper stories.

The most prominent of these, Homestand Flyer, has had a couple of scrapes with the law. Is a vendor's license required to sell it? Is it covered by the First Amendment. Exactly *where* can and can't it be sold?

It all came to a head on April 28 when its publisher (and hawker) Bert Matthews was arrested and jailed.

In the Post, Matthews described the irony of the incident: "I'm sitting on the ground near McNichols Arena, handcuffed,and I could hear them singing the national anthem."

With a little *pro bono* work from Holland & Hart's Bob Crouch, and a series of meetings with the Denver city attorney's office, Matthews now has the green light to sell the Homestand Flyer from sidewalks near the stadium.

Now that he hassle is gone, it'll be interesting to see if Kal Rucker's Colorado Stat Sheet will reappear.

Today's milestone: Purple announced as official primary color of Denver's new National League baseball team (1991)

The Rockies have now lost three in a row, have a 10-18 record, and are in last place, a game behind L.A. The Marlins have won two more and lost two fewer.

Saturday, May 8: Atlanta 8, Colorado 7

The game that made us hate Mile High Stadium.

> **1:05 at Mile High Stadium**
> **The National Anthem:** Peach Fuzz (done as a round)
> **The first ball:** John Villarreal (Colorado Springs 7-11)
> **The starting pitchers:** Ruffin (1-1) vs. Smith (2-2)
> **The W-L pitchers:** Mercker (2-0) and Fredrickson (0-1)
> **The attendance:** 64,614
> **The Post headline:** Rockies fall 8-7 as Baylor bolts
> **The News headline:** Rockies die with their boots on

On the field: The Rox are looking good going into the eighth. They're leading, 6-zip, on Bruce Ruffin's three-hitter.

Then comes the Braves' six-run eighth fueled by three Rockies errors.

That's when pinch hitter Sid Bream caps off the scoring when he flicks a Blair offering over the left field wall for an opposite-field grand slam.

On we go into the final stanza. Tied.

Then they get two and we get but one.

Atlanta manager Bobby Cox: "A lead is never safe in this place. There's just nothing safe here—absolutely nothing."

Tell us, Bobby.

Wasted efforts: Clark's two-run homer in the first and Galarraga's three-hit, three-RBI day.

Scott Fredrickson takes the loss. [It turns out to be his only decision of the season.]

In the stands: John Ashton has a lot of admiration for the guy from 7-11 who threw out the first ball this afternoon. "He faces death every day."

A number crunchy fan points out that today, after just 16 home games, the Rockies have surpassed the Mets' initial year numbers.

Maybe they should change its name to Almost Mile High Stadium.

Bob Gustafson is a cartographer by trade and has mapped out a life for himself that is ruled by baseball. Naturally, he viewed the new, Baylor-inspired signage on the wall behind Bichette with a critical eye.

"Elevation 5,280 feet" it says.

After poring over a few maps and following a few contour lines, he proclaimed the sign off by 75 feet.

"Actually," Gus says, "it's about 5,205 feet."

Don't tell the opposing players who Baylor is trying to psych out.

The Rockies have now lost four in a row for the first time ever. The team's 10-19 record is identical to that of the unspeakably awful 1962 Mets after 29 games. Needless to say, the Rox dwell in last place. They're two games behind the tied-for-next-to-last Reds and Dodgers.

Sunday, May 9: Atlanta 12, Colorado 7

The game we went over the one-million mark.

1:05 at Mile High Stadium
The National Anthem: Littleton H.S. Troubadours
The first ball: Steven Green, 9 and Chris Pellant, 16
The starting pitchers: Ashby (0-2) vs. Glavine (4-0)
The W-L pitchers: McMichael (1-1) and Reed (1-2)
The attendance: 70,786
The Post headline: Same song, fourth verse
The News headline: Rockies swept deeper into cellar

On the field: The Rox eschew the black uniform tops that have caused so much heartbreak. In their stead, their regular home pinstripes are the garb for today's encounter.

At first, it seems to work. The Rox get off to a good start. Shut down the Atlantas until the fifth. And had nicked Glavine for six hits and had a nice 4-0 lead. The fifth. That's when the Braves get a couple of walks and three hits—one a Ron Justice homer—and go ahead, 5-4.

The Rockies fight back, regaining the lead when they score twice in the fifth and once in the sixth, but a five-run Atlanta explosion in the seventh—featuring another Justice homer—puts the game away.

Scary: Galarraga leaves the game after aggravating a strained hamstring running from second to third. A standing ovation for the Rocks' top Rock, who is currently batting .395

When is your first sweep not your first sweep?

On Mothers' Day 1993, it became very clear that the Rockies and the National League Champion Atlanta Braves have very little in common.

They have pitching and hitting.

We have proof that a pitcher is worth 1,000 hits.

As a result, the first four-game meeting between the haves and the don'ts resulted in a sweep for the Braves. True, the Rocks had been swept in two two-game series earlier in the season, but two games hardly a series makes.

This, then, will stand as the first true sweep in the history of the Colorado Rockies.

In the stands: "You know how some ballparks have nicknames? We oughta call Mile High Stadium 'The Spa.'"

How come? "Because teams come here to get well."

Today, just the 17th home date, is the day that the Rockies fans hit the one-million mark. Heretofore, the record was held by Toronto. They set it last year, but it took them 21 dates.

The designated one-millionth fan is Lydia McKee.

Surprise of surprises, McKee is a mother. This, of course, *is* Mothers' Day. She gets all sorts of good goodies, the best of which are tix to the All-Star game at Camden.

The Rox' millionth fan says she is a big fan of Charlie Hayes, Eric Young, and, as she puts it, "Andre Scalarraga."

On people's heads: Strange hats with miniature mountain ranges on top. The ultimate CR cap. To order one, send $17.95 to RockHATS, P.O.Box 5602, Arvada CO 80005.

In the News: Mark Wolf reveals that the $3 bag of peanuts he bought at the ballpark contained 94 peanuts—and recommends smuggling in your own.

The Rockies have now lost five in a row (for the first time ever) and have a 10-20 record. This puts them in last place of the NL West, 8.5 games behind the first-place giants and two games behind the sixth-place Reds. Florida has a 14-16 record. The Mets are 10-18.

Monday, May 10: Colorado 7, San Francisco 4

The first game against—and the first victory over—the Giants.

7:05 at Mile High Stadium
The National Anthem: Timothy P and Rural Route 3
The first ball: Mark Murphy (Bronco Billy's)
The starting pitchers: Reynoso (1-1) vs. Wilson (0-2)
The W-L pitchers: Reynoso (2-1) and Wilson (0-3)
The attendance: 50,705
The Post headline: Reynoso, Rockies cut Giants down to size
The News headline: Reynoso cuts Giants down to size

On the field: When you beat the division leader, you reduce your games-behind number by one.

And after the dust settles, that's what the Rockies do.

Bichette's three-run homer stakes Armando Reynoso to a 3-1 lead after one inning is played, and the rook never trails from that point on as he rolls on to a complete-game victory.

But there are some bumps in the road along the way. Bonds opens the sixth with a triple and scores. Williams opens the Giants' eighth with a homer on Reynoso's first pitch. Benzinger opens their ninth with a pinch hit triple and scores.

Meanwhile, the purple pinstripers are methodically putting up a run here and a run there. The big blast? Reynoso's first major league hit—which is a home run. And it's the first homer by a Rockies pitcher.

Yesterday's injury of Galarraga causes him to miss his first start at first base for the Rocks.

In his place: Tatum, making his first start as a Rocky and his first start at first base in the bigs. In the sixth, when Rockies' thirdbaseman Hayes is tossed from the game, Tatum shifts over to third and catcher Sheaffer becomes a firstbaseman.

Hayes' ejection is historical. He's the first Rocky to be given the heave-ho.

Seems Charlie took exception to plate umpire Don Hohn's bouncing of the ball to Reynoso. When third-base ump Davidson told Hayes to stick to playing third and leave the umpiring to the umps, Charlie said The Bad Word. The next word: Adios.

And so, after 30 games that began and ended with Galarraga and Hayes playing first and third, this one ends with neither playing either.

More history is made today. Don Baylor and Dusty Baker are the first black managers to meet in a regular-season National League game.

Baker didn't make it through the entire contest, however. In the eighth, he argued a checked-swing strike and was tossed. It was the first tossage of Baker's career.

In the stands: The Rockies have been let down so many times by their relievers of late that when Blair started warming up, the crowd chanted "NO BULLPEN! NO BULLPEN!"

At the top of the eighth with the Rockies leading 5-2 and the Giants coming to bat: "Are you ready to have your heart broken? It starts now."

And: "Maybe we ought to move all the pitchers to Castle Rock to keep them handy."

And a fan explains why he's now buying 24-ounce beers instead of 16-ouncers. "I went up to the bigs."

In the mouth: According to the Post's Bill Briggs, wearers of braces (the orthodontic variety) are opting for elastic ties in, as Briggs puts it, "the team's contusion-like colors," purple, black and gray.

The Rockies now have an 11-20 record and are in last place, eight games behind the Astros. Only one team in the majors has fewer wins—Oakland, with 10.

Tuesday, May 11: San Francisco 5, Colorado 3
The Rockies' first loss to the Giants.

> **7:05 at Mile High Stadium**
> **The National Anthem:** The Sidekicks
> **The first ball:** Fred Emich (Dodge dealer)
> **The starting pitchers:** Nied (3-3) vs. Swift (3-1)
> **The W-L pitchers:** Swift (4-1) and Nied (3-4)
> **The attendance:** 49,072
> **The Post headline:** Rockies suffer a Swift loss
> **The News headline:** Little Giants do damage, beat
>   Rockies

On the field: David Nied isn't a Giant killer today, but he isn't shelled, either.

He goes seven innings, allowing but three runs. Strangely, they are delivered not by the meat of the Giants' lineup, but by the bottom of the order.

Meanwhile, Nied's teammates muster just one run off Bill Swift until the ninth. That came in the first inning on an error.

In the ninth, Bichette hammers a Swift pitch for a two-run home run, but the rally wasn't big enough to overcome the Giants.

The Rocks have now lost six of their last seven games.

The injured Galarraga is forced to miss today's game, too. So Jerald Clark makes his first start at first.

In the stands: "The Giants have come to Colorado to take the cure" a fan mutters. "Years ago, people came here to heal their TB. Now it's their BA."

A fan explains why he's not yet marking his All-Star ballot: "First, I need to hear the debate."

A season ticket holder: "I think it would be nice if we could leave our peanuts and stuff here under the seat instead of having to haul them back and forth to home." Maybe a locker.

In an editorial in the News, the Rockies policy of blacking out cable broadcasts of their games "is dumb so long as fan support is so high...the Rockies are playing ugly, in more than one way."

How to pack 150,000 into Mile High Stadium.

There is much chatter in the stands about the Rockies' attempt to increase the capacity of Coors Field.

Fans who know why a smallish baseball stadium is desirable (intimate, encourages season ticket sales, not like Cleveland, etc.) are scratching their heads.

They hope that jamming bigger numbers into Coors Field isn't realized through the old let's-just-make-'em-smaller trick.

When a couple of couples from Denver were in Tokyo, they took in a Nippon Ham Fighters game and noticed that the seats were, well, unamerican in their dimensions.

"I know an easy way to expand Mile High's capacity to 150,000," one of them said. "Just replace the seats that are there now with seats this size."

Indeed, the seats in Mile High are smaller and less comfortable than those at many or most baseball parks, but when you only have to sit in them eight or so times a year for football, they suffice. For enjoying baseball day after day, one really needs more room.

Most modern baseball parks put their most comfortable seats down low where they'll be used on a regular basis. Upstairs, where the seats are only used for Big Games, they jam in smaller ones. The idea, of course, is those people will be so darn glad just to *get* seats they won't mind. Or notice.

Those who know that stadium seats come in different sizes hope that Rockies fans will not be sold short. Or narrow.

The Rockies now have a record of 11-21 and are in last place. A couple of teams have won as few, but none has lost so many.

Wednesday, May 12: San Francisco 8, Colorado 2

The game from which Barry and Bobby Bonds were both ejected.

7:05 at Mile High Stadium
The National Anthem: Trumpeter Joe Collier (former
    member of James Brown Band)
The first ball: Ken Haddad (Lakewood Fordland)
The starting pitchers: Henry (2-2) vs. Black (2-0)
The W-L pitchers: Black (3-0) and Henry (2-3)
The attendance: 50,105
The Post headline: Giants win game; fight ends in draw
The News headline: Giants bats punish Rockies again

On the field: Scrambling to make something good happen on
the mound, the Rocks make a couple of moves. They activate
Bryn Smith from the disabled list and send Steve Reed down to
the Springs.

Today, the Rock have a 2-1 lead after a couple of innings,
but the Giants peck away at rocky Rocky pitching the rest of
the way. Remarkably, they get their leadoff man on base in
every inning but the second. Henry gives up a two-run shot
(Carreon) in the sixth and a three-runner (Williams) in the
seventh.

Meanwhile, Bud Black has the locals well in control,
permitting only one hit after the first stanza.

And there was that melee in the ninth—the first bench-
clearing incident amid a Rockies game ever. After he's hit by a
pitch from Giants' closer Mike Jackson (the second time he's
been hit in the game), Jerald Clark walks toward the mound.
Clark is walking slowly, but he's headed for the pitcher, so both
benches empty instantly. Whereupon nothing happens for a
while, just a lot of benign blatherskite and milling around until
Barry Bonds and Henry begin to push and shove and, ultimately, swing. This gets the melee going.

After about 10 minutes, the umps get the game going
again. But not before the Bonds duo, both father and son, are
thrown out. As are Clark and the Rockies' first base coach Ron
Hassey.

The first time father and son are tossed together? No.
That honor goes to Cal Ripken Sr. and Billy Ripken. The pair of

Orioles were banished from a game in 1990.

Galarraga and his .395 batting average miss their third game in a row.

In the stands: A vision comes to a fan. He explains: "The Rockies caps would be niftier if they had purple bills, right?"

Yeah. Maybe..

"So I predict that next season the players' caps will be just like this year's caps except that they'll have purple bills."

Go on.

"Which will mean that next year the Rockies will sell *another* 88 billion CR caps. I know *I'll* have to have the latest version."

So this whole thing is a plot to separate each and every one of us from another seven bucks—or 25 bucks for the sized version?

"Absolutely. It's like when they design a car. They already *know* what changes they're going to make to it next year to make it even spiffier."

We'll see.

In the Post Office: It is late afternoon. A customer walks into Terminal Annex to mail a package. Sitting there on the counter is a ticket to tonight's game. The postal clerk notices the customer eyeballing the ducat.

The clerk explains: "Want to go to the Rockies tonight?"

"What's the deal?"

"One of our customers had an extra ticket for tonight's game and couldn't use it, so he left it here for us to find a good home for it."

Turns out that the U.S. Postal service is *not* involved in a promotion with the Rockies after all. Unlike virtually every other enterprise in the Rocky Mountain Region.

In the Brown Palace's Ship Tavern: Although the game isn't on the tube tonight, the gang sitting at the storied old bar keeps an eye on the ESPN account of the Rangers-A's game because, from time to time, the score of the Rockies-Giants game is flashed on screen.

With each flashing, the plight of the Rox becomes more bleak. And a patron mumbles a song fragment: "The Rockies may crumble..."

Watching baseball in a bar can cause a heart attack.

Here's the scenario:

You're watching your team on TV in a bar. And watching is what you have to do since you can't hear the commentators. The TV sound is off and Billy Ray Cyrus is on.

No problem. You can enjoy the game, the music, and the beer all at the same time.

Then the cruelest of cruelties is inflicted upon you:

As an opposition batter comes to the plate, they rerun an earlier appearance when he hit a homer. You think, "Oh, no! He did it again!" spill your beer, grab your chest, and topple to the floor.

An FCC regulation should require that they put a super on the screen for people watching TV sans sound. It could say "LAST AT-BAT" or "IN THE THIRD INNING" or "EARLIER" or "REPLAY."

Or maybe put the replay in a little box in the corner.

Anything to let viewers know not to have a heart attack at this time.

The Rockies have now lost two straight, are 11-22 on the season and in last place, 2.5 games behind the Padres. Florida is 16-18.

Thursday, May 13: San Francisco 13, Colorado 8
The everything-went-wrong game.

3:05 at Mile High Stadium
The National Anthem: Grafton H.S. Marching Band
The first ball: Steve Katich
The starting pitchers: Ruffin (1-1) vs. Burkett (5-0)
The W-L pitchers: Burkett (6-0) and Ruffin (1-2)
The attendance: 58,833
The Post headline: Bumbling Rockies a lost cause at
        home
The News headline: Rockies bumble, stumble again

On the field: It was as if the Rockies wanted to demonstrate the multifarious ways you can lose a ball game. Horrible starting pitching (Ruffin). Lousy relief pitching (Blair and Smith and Parrett and Fredrickson). Two errors on the same play

(Hayes). A dropped fly ball (Bichette). Getting picked off base (Young). Turning a fly into a double (Cole). Hitting the batter (Parrett). Outfield nonchalance (Boston). Wild pitch (Parrett). Throwing the ball to the wrong base (Cole).

And the killer: A ninth inning wherein the Rockies gave up four runs, all unearned, on just one hit and *three* errors.

Thus is concluded an 8-game homestand in which the Rox won one.

In other (bad) news, the Rockies have put Galarraga on the DL. They say it'll be ten days before he returns to the lineup. So the team calls up Jay Gainer from the Sky Sox.

The good news: Bryn Smith is back. And healthy.

In the stands: It is noted that today's game is the first played by the Rocks in Mile High in 80°+ weather.

Talk about wishful thinking. The P.A. guy announces "Dante Galarraga."

A discussion of the no-alcohol "Family Section" produces this insight: "If it weren't for alcohol, there wouldn't be nearly as many families."

After witnessing enough blunders to stock an Abbott & Costello movie: "Do the Rockies get one practice season?"

Wistfully: "I have no control over baseball, but baseball has control over me."

Collectors of truly arcane firsts note that, in the fourth inning, the first Rocky pitcher is replaced by a reliever with a 0-3 count on the batter. (Ruffin, Blair, and Manwaring.)

And DIRTBALL is being played.

In Section 120, Row 29, four guys pass around a plastic Pinehurst Country Club coffee cup that stockbroker Bruce Devore brought to the game. They take turns holding the cup—a half inning per person, then on to the next. As each person gets the cup, he gets to decide how much all four of them have to contribute—a dime or a quarter. Each time the third out is made, all eight eyes focus on the ball.

The player who winds up with the ball that made the third out almost always tosses the ball toward the mound on his way to the dugout.

Usually, the ball winds up on the grass, but when it does come to a rest on the mound, the guy holding the cup gets its contents. Tonight, the first payoff—$2.75—is won by Bob

Murphy, the dentist. The second cupload of money is won by Jim House. That's a nice $8.50 winner. And the woman sitting next to them says, "I wanna get in!"

It should be noted that this group counts edgers (when the ball is sitting on dirt but resting against grass) as dirtballs.

Purists would blanch. And have bigger pots.

We assume Elias is keeping stats on all the players and their accuracy in tossing the third out ball toward the mound.

The Rockies have now lost three in a row and are in last place with a 11-23 record, 10.5 games out of first and 2.5 games behind sixth-place San Diego. No other team has won so few games.

Friday, May 14: Cincinnati 13, Colorado 5
The game in which Jay Gainer got a homer on his first ML pitch.

> **5:35 at Riverfront Stadium**
> **The starting pitchers:** Ashby (0-2) vs. Pugh (2-3)
> **The W-L pitchers:** Pugh (3-3) and Ashby (0-3)
> **The attendance:** 48,352
> **The Post headline:** Rockies are left Red-faced
> **The News headline:** Reds pound Rockies for 13-5
>   victory

On the field: It may be the team's first visit to Riverfront Stadium and their first meeting with the Reds, but they didn't make much of a celebration out of it. Once again, the Rocks' pitching staff gives up thirteen runs. They've done it *five* times in their last eleven games.

This time, they get off to an especially rocky start when Ashby surrenders five in the first. This is the season's new high/low for the Rox. Knudson replaces the Ashman, but he gives up five runs in 2 1/3 innings. Not a good outing for either.

Reds manager Tony Perez likes it, though. It's a good 51st birthday present for him.

Only one item for the highlight film today: Jay Gainer, just up from the Springs where he was tearing up PCL pitching, takes over first for the injured Galarraga. Leading off in the second inning, Gainer does something only eleven others have done in The History of the Game—he hits the first major league pitch he is thrown over the fence.

Out of all the players who have played in the big leagues—over ten thousand—only 66 homered in their first at-bats. That's rare enough. But to homer on the first *pitch*...

In the stands are 7,000 Cincy-area kids who got straight A's. Is it just a coincidence that the Rockies' starting pitcher is Andy Ashby? We think not.

The Rockies have now lost four in a row, have a record of 11-24, and are in last place, 3.5 games behind the teams that are tied for next-to-last, the Dodgers and the Padres.

Saturday, May 15: Cincinnati 5, Colorado 3
The first game with no firsts.

5:05 at Riverfront Stadium
The starting pitchers: Reynoso (2-1) vs. Browning (3-2)
The W-L pitchers: Hill (3-0) and Reynoso (2-2)
The attendance: 49,697
The Post headline: Rockies fall, but it's not a total loss
The News headline: Mitchell, Reds keep Rockies reeling

On the field: At this point, Reynoso is the closest thing we have to an ace. But even he can't stop the Reds and their heavy heavy hitter, Kevin, The Mitchellin Man.

The Rocks get off to a pretty good start, putting up three in the third and lead 3-0 at the halfway point. Then Reynoso weakens. The result is a two-run inning for the Reds followed by a singleton and then another two-runner. It's all they get and it's all they need.

Whereupon Baylor announces that Blair is replacing Ruffin in the Rox pitching rotation.

In the Post, it is pointed out that Jay Gainer, who just got his first at-bat a couple of minutes ago, already has more homers than Dale Murphy, Daryl Boston and Alex Cole. Combined.
In favor of stuffing it: Mark Kiszla suggests that the best thing fans can do to squeeze some glory out of this doomed season is to vote often enough to get Galarraga on the All-Star team. "As long as almost 60,000 fans show up for every game

at Mile High Stadium, they might as well make themselves useful," Kiszla says, encouraging spirited stuffage of the All-Star ballot box.

Laurel Walters stuffed. She punched out a box of 2,250 cards a game for five games. Total: 11,000 votes.

In front of the tube in Central City: Jack Hidahl watches a double steal and makes an observation: "Players don't do double steals. Managers do double steals."

And after yet another after-the-homer fireworks display in Cincinnati, Jeff Aiken says, "If the Rockies did that every time somebody hit a home run at Mile High, they'd go broke."

Although this isn't one of those superstation games the Rockies have blacked out in the Denver area, Hidahl points out that it doesn't matter up here. Central City is outside the blackout zone. "Central gets all the Cubs and Braves games—even when they play the Rockies at home."

Gosh. All this, and slot machines, too.

Today's milestone: Cleveland's Ron Hassey caught Len Parker's perfect game vs. the Blue Jays (1981)

The Rockies have now lost five in a row. Their 11-25 record puts them in last place, 11 games out of first and 3.5 games behind sixth-place L.A.

Sunday, May 16: Cincinnati 14, Colorado 2
The first game the Rox lost by twelve.

> **12:15 at Riverfront Stadium**
> **The starting pitchers:** Nied (3-4) vs. Roper (0-0)
> **The W-L pitchers:** Roper (1-0) and Nied (3-5)
> **The attendance:** 35,434
> **The Post headline:** Road kill: Rockies leveled 14-2
> **The News headline:** The beatings go on for Rockies

On the field: This is John Roper's ML debut. After three innings, he's got himself a 12-0 lead. After six, he's out of there. After nine, he's got his first ML win and an attitude—so he tells the world that he's faced tougher lineups in Triple-A. Specifically Buffalo "and maybe the Nashville Sounds."

That's the Cincy pitching story.

Here's the Rocks': The Reds steal four bases before Nied gets anybody out. The kid lasts two innings, giving up five walks before he takes his.

Bryn Smith comes in and allows eight runs in 1/3 inning. At one point, he throws 51 pitches to get one out. Chris Sabo has a 12-pitch at-bat against Smith that ends when Sabo finally gets a single.

The Rockies have now been swept four times. Meanwhile, the Marlins have yet to suffer this shameful disgrace.

Faintly fallacious fractions.

The Rockies have won one of their last twelve games. So says the morning paper.

Throughout the season there is an unending supply of "of their last" stats.

Which never fails to amuse those who realize that you can usually add to one or both of the numbers and still be right.

Indeed, it is true that the Rockies have won one of their last 12 games.

Also true: They've won two of their last 13. And three of their last 14.

Same goes for individual stats.

When they say Eric Young has been successful in four of his last five stolen base attempts, it also means that he's been successful in four of his last *six* stolen base tries.

The Rockies have now lost six in a row (a franchise first). Their 11-26 record puts them in last place, 3.5 games behind the tied-for-fifth Dodgers and Padres. The Marlins are 16-21.

Monday, May 17: San Diego 4, Colorado 0
The first game against—and the first loss to—the Padres.

8:05 at Jack Murphy Stadium
The starting pitchers: Henry (2-3) and Benes (5-3)
The W-L pitchers: Benes (6-3) and Henry (2-4)
The attendance: 15,251
The Post headline: Rockies' bats spend day at beach
The News headline: Rockies take hope from latest loss

On the field: A San Diego radio station sprays artificial snow in the bleachers to welcome the Rockies to town. The chilling display does little to draw in the fans and this turns out to be the first game the Rockies have played before so few onlookers.

Which may be just as well—there are fewer witnesses to the embarrassment *du jour*.

The Padres' Andy Benes throws a sharp three-hitter at the Rockies. For a while, the Rockies' Butch Henry is tough, too. He has a one-hitter through five innings.

Then came the sixth. This is the inning in which the Pods score all of the game's runs. They employ a double, four singles, a wild pitch and a sacrifice fly. (During this episode, Henry allows five straight hits.)

And so the Rockies' futility streak reaches seven games. It's a season high, a franchise high—and an emotional low.

What's wrong with this pitcher? That's what Baylor wants to know—about *all* his hurlers. So more moves are made today. Knudson goes down to the Springs, Holmes and Painter are recalled from same. Outfielder Gerald Young (.053) has shown little, so he, too, is shown the door. [Ultimately, G. Young will wind up with Cincinnati's Triple-A team in Indianapolis.]

In South Denver: A maroon Volvo sits in the rain. It bears the Colorado license plate BAZBAL.

The Rockies have now lost seven in a row and have a record of 11-27, the worst in baseball. They're 13.5 games behind the division-leading Giants. Florida is 16-22. The Mets are 12-24.

Tuesday, May 18: Colorado 2, San Diego 1 (11 innings)
The game that broke the 7-game losing streak.

8:05 at Jack Murphy Stadium
The starting pitchers: Blair (1-0) vs. Eiland (0-2)
The W-L pitchers: Wayne (1-2) and Rodriguez (1-2)
The attendance: 15,347
The Post headline: Rockies win is extraordinary
The News headline: Rockies win as Blair steps into
      breach

On the field: Tight games are a novelty to the battered Rockies, but this thriller turns out just fine. Blair starts for the Rocks and delivers a remarkable performance. He gives up but one run in nine innings. Normally, that'd be good enough for a win, but the Rockies put only one run of their own on the board so the game rolls on into bonus innings.

Finally, in the eleventh, Charlie Hayes sacrifices in Castilla and Darren Holmes comes in to shut down the Padres in the bottom of the stanza.

This is Holmes' second strong performance since his return from the littles.

While having a beer just before going to see Forever Plaid: "I don't know what to do when the Rockies are on the road." Response: "They don't seem to know, either."

Today's milestone: Eric Young's birthday (1967)

The Rockies now have a 12-27 record, still the worst in baseball. It puts the Rocks 3.5 games behind the Padres for sixth place. The Marlins are 16-23 and the Mets are 12-25.

Wednesday, May 19: San Diego 7, Colorado 3
The first time a Rocky hit two homers in a game.

> **8:05 at Jack Murphy Stadium**
> **The starting pitchers:** Painter (0-0) vs. Harris (3-5)
> **The W-L pitchers:** Harris (4-5) and Painter (0-1)
> **The attendance:** 12,773
> **The Post headline:** Padres brush Painter's dream
> **The News headline:** 7-3 loss spoils Painter debut with
> Rockies

On the field: Lance Painter, a draftee from the Padres' farm system, appears in his first ML game, and has a great quote: "What a guy to start your major league career with...Tony Gwynn. Why can't he bat second?"

Painter's debut is ruined by the San Diegans when the Rockies' defective defense lets the Padres have two runs in the first and then, in the fifth, allows the home team to turn five hits into another three runs.

The Rocks score all their runs via the long ball, all lead-off shots. Boston becomes the first Colorado to knock two in one game. Jerald Clark gets one against his former teammates.

The Padres' winning pitcher, Greg Harris, has now won three in a row.

Off the face: Bruce Ruffin's mustache.

Off the team: Pitcher Mark Knudson. The Northglenn native and former Denver Zephyr turns down the option of returning to the minors.

Instead, after a wild eleven-day career with the Rockies, he retires.

Knudson appeared in four games for the Rox, pitched 5 2/3 innings, had no decisions and wound up with an ERA of 22.24.

His last ML victory was on opening day in 1991 when he pitched the Brewers over Nolan Ryan and the Rangers.

In the seats of Jack Murphy Stadium, there are few customers. As every self-satisfied Rockies fan knows, the Padres have pared their payroll down.

Way down.

All the way down to the size of Colorado's. As a result of the departure of their most talented—and expensive—players, crowds have shrunk in Jack Murphy.

But there's another angle to the story, says fan Tom Reynolds. The Padres have the smallest region to draw from of any big league club. "To the west, there's water. To the east, there's desert. To the north, there're the Dodgers and Angels. And to the south, there's Mexico.

"It's really a very tiny area, geographically and populationally," Reynolds says. "It's not at all like the situation for all the other teams that have sizable regional fan bases."

Then there's the team with an entire time zone.

The Rockies now have a 12-28 record. The Mets have won 13 and lost 25—and they've also lost their manager.

Jeff Torborg was just fired and replaced by Dallas Green. (The Mets' record, it is noted, is one game better than the embarrassing 1962 version was at this stage of the season.)

The game that saw an 11th inning go-ahead homer go to waste.

2:05 at Jack Murphy Stadium
The starting pitchers: Reynoso (2-2) vs. Taylor (0-3)
The W-L pitchers: Harris (3-0) and Holmes (0-3)
The attendance: 22,098
The Post headline: Rockies' 5-4 loss all too familiar
The News headline: Rockies' road demolition continues

On the field: It was one of those games manic-depressives love. In the top of the eleventh inning, Dante Bichette homers the Rockies to a 4-3 lead, but then in the bottom of the inning, with just three outs standing between the Rockies and victory, Darren Holmes takes the mound.

Next thing you know, Fred McGriff blasts a two-run homer—off Dante Bichette's glove—and the Padres get the win.

Bright spot: The second HR of Danny Sheaffer's big league career. The first came on his second ML at-bat in 1987.

After starting all 40 games before today at third, Charlie Hayes rests in favor of Jim Tatum. But Hayes doesn't miss the game entirely. He pinch hits. Actually, he pinch strikes out.

In the hope of improving their struggling pitching staff, the Rocks acquire Mark Grant from Houston. And Fredrickson is demoted to Colorado Springs for issuing way too many walks.

Stuck on the Rockies.

Dick Veit's crew of house painters (Bonnie Brae Painting) listens to today's game. But it's not necessarily because they want to. For years, they've listened to KOA's lineup of talk show folks—Tom Martino, Andrea Van Steenhouse, etc.—while they worked. Now, after all this time, they *have* to listen to the Rockies. Because their radio is so splattered with paint, it's stuck on 850 on your AM dial.

The Rockies have now lost two in a row, have a 12-29 record and are in last place. The Marlins are 17-23. The Mets are 13-25. The season is now 1/4 completed, so people are projecting the Rocks to 47-115 by the end of the season, more or less.

Friday, May 21: Los Angeles 8, Colorado 0

Dale Murphy's first start for the Rockies in left field.

8:35 at Dodger Stadium
The starting pitchers: Nied (3-5) vs. Hershiser (4-4)
The W-L pitchers: Hershiser (5-4) and Nied (3-6)
The attendance: 51,818
The Post headline: Dodgers hand Nied more woes
The News headline: Dodgers batter Nied, Rockies

On the field: Orel Hershiser hadn't pitched a shutout in four seasons until today. He five-hit, no-walked the Rockies while David Nied gave up four walks, eight hits and six runs in five innings. Nied is now 0-5 in his last six starting assignments.

New Rocky Mark Grant permitted the Dodgers to score twice in his two-inning debut with Colorado.

The Rockies have now lost three in a row, have a 12-30 record and are in last place, 16.5 games behind the Giants.

New York's record is now 13-26.

Saturday, May 22: Los Angeles 4, Colorado 3

The game Butch Henry thought he had won.

8:05 at Dodger Stadium
The starting pitchers: Henry (2-4) vs. Astacio (2-3)
The W-L pitchers: McDowell (2-0) and Henry (2-5)
The attendance: 50,537
The Post headline: Rockies dodge victory
The News headline: Another victory vanishes

On the field: Going into the bottom of the sixth, the Rockies have a 3-2 lead. Butch Henry appears to have things pretty much in control until that fateful sixth when Piazza singles in Davis to tie it and Reed singles in Wallach to go ahead—with a bit of help from double-clutching Nelson Liriano's late throw—and the Rockies fail to return the favor.

The alarmists point out that the Rockies have lost 16 of their last 18 games. (Which means their last 19, of course.)

The Rockies have now lost four in a row and have a 12-31 record.

This puts them in last place, 16.5 games out of first and 7 games behind the sixth-place Padres.

Florida's record is 18-24. The Mets are 14-26.

Sunday, May 23: Los Angeles 4, Colorado 0
The game that left the Rox playing .273 ball.

2:05 at Dodger Stadium
The starting pitchers: Blair (1-0) vs. Martinez (2-3)
The W-L pitchers: (3-3) and Blair (1-1)
The attendance: 48,343
The Post headline: California dreamin' Rockies
    nightmare
The News headline: Latest loss puts Rockies 20 games
    under .500

On the field: The hapless Rockies wind up their three-game series with the Dodgers with the knowledge that they managed to score but three runs in the 27 innings they played.

In today's contest, the purples get just three hits.

Only the second game of the season—when the Mets' Saberhagen held the Rox to two—was a more pitiful outing.

So far.

Rockies' starter Blair shuts down the Dodgers for six innings, then lets them assemble three runs out of some singles and stolen bases in the seventh. All they needed.

In today's Post, a giant headline spells out a large part of the Rockies' problem and, at the same time, misspells it: "Rockies just can't wait for Galaragga's return."

In front of a TV set in a bar back in Denver, a customer comes in and sees that the game isn't on.

The bartender explains: "It's all over."

From the bar: "Yep. Four to zip."

Another habitue adds a positive note: "Single digits, though."

In Elizabeth, Carl Kay claims he's the first to fly an official team flag over his house. According to Kreck in the Post, he probably is. Kay works for the company that makes the flags and he glommed onto the first of the first shipment and quickly ran it up his flagpole.

In the mountains west of Denver, a cowboy has an opinion.

"I don't think Colorado's team should have farm teams." Sandy Hoffman says. "We should have *ranch* teams."

The Rockies have now lost five in a row and have a 12-32 record, the worst in ML baseball.

May 24 is an off day, but it was the day that Allison Knudson, wife of Mark, the first Rocky to retire, becomes the first former Rockies pitcher's wife to give birth to triplets.

It was also the day the Cincinnati Reds replaced their manager, Tony Perez. The new skipper is the Mets' old one, Davey Johnson.

Tuesday, May 25: Colorado 7, Houston 5
The first visit to the Astrodome (and the Rox' first victory over Houston).

6:05 at the Astrodome
The starting pitchers: Painter (0-1) vs. Hamisch (4-2)
The W-L pitchers: Wayne (2-2) and Hernandez (2-1)
The attendance: 18,812
The Post headline: Rockies win 7-5, believe it or not
The News headline: Rockies mesh rally, relief for sweet win

On the field: The first meeting between these teams, the Rocks' first visit to The Dome, and their first victory over the Astros. Another first: Nelson Liriano's first home run in the bigs since April 20, 1990.

The Rockies snap their five-game losing streak with the help of Daryl Boston's fourth homer in the last six games. And with some timely hitting from Jim Tatum. His two-run, pinch hit double in the eighth breaks the tie.

A highlight for most Rockies fans was the fact that the bullpen delivered four innings of strong relief pitching. Baylor uses six relievers in all, and none gives up a run.

Oddly, Gary Wayne gets the W although he didn't retire a batter. When he came in, there were two outs. After two pitches, the third out was made when Steve Finley was caught stealing.

In the next inning, while Wayne is still the pitcher of record, the Rockies pulled ahead for good and Wayne gets a very strange W. So strange, in fact, that it's only happened thrice in major leagues in the past ten years.

The Rockies now have a 13-32 record, which puts them in last place, 17.5 games out of first and 6.5 out of sixth. The Marlins are 19-25 and the Mets are 14-29.

Wednesday, May 26: Colorado 3, Houston 2
The first time a Rocky struck out the side.

> **6:05 at the Astrodome**
> **The starting pitchers:** Reynoso (2-2) vs. Portugal (4-2)
> **The W-L pitchers:** Smith (2-3) and Jones (1-4)
> **The attendance:** 22,267
> **The Post headline:** For Bichette, it was astronomical
> **The News headline:** Rockies start believing they can win

On the field: Reynoso strikes out the side. That is a highlight. So is his 5+ innings of quality hurling. A pair of timely Bichette singles drive in all of the Rockies runs.

The Rox are one win away from their first series sweep. And from winning three in a row for the first time.

On a plane headed for Colorado Springs is Jay Gainer. His 12 days up with the big club were noteworthy in that he got that homer in his first at-bat and that he goes back to the Sky Sox without having set foot in Mile High. He joined the Rockies at the beginning of their road trip and left them near its end.

The Rockies have now won two in a row (which ties their all-time longest winning streak) and have a record of 14-32. Still in last place, five games out of next-to-last.

The Rockies' first loss to Houston.

6:05 at the Astrodome
The starting pitchers: Nied (3-6) vs. Drabek (4-5)
The W-L pitchers: Drabek (5-5) and Nied (3-7)
The attendance: 22,372
The Post headline: Rockies can't fill in the blanks
The News headline: Astros prolong Nied's days of misery

Somewhere in Houston: Gebhard and Baylor meet with Dale Murphy, the result of which is the seven-time All-Star announces his retirement.

It is a sad moment, but nobody is very surprised.

This is met with mixed feelings by the fans back in Denver.

One one hand, everybody wanted him to get HRs 399 and 400 for the Rockies.

On the other, his bat just wasn't delivering the punch everybody wanted, expected, and hoped for.

He was 6-for-42 with seven RBI and just one extra base hit (a double) and one run scored as a Rocky.

On the field: Everybody said this is a must-win game for 24-year-old David Nied, who started out fast and has pretty much lost confidence in himself.

But a couple of bad innings leave him with a five-and-dime night: Five runs on ten hits in five innings.

Which makes Nied's *next* outing the must-win game.

The Astros avoid the sweep on Doug Drabek's seven-hitter—and the Rockies avoid the three-game winning streak.

The Rockies now have a record of 14-33 and continue to reside in last place.

(Upon hearing on KYBG that the Rockies' two-game winning streak is over, fan Frank Graffeo observed that perhaps, when you've won just two games in a row, it isn't a winning streak. "It's more a winning stripe.")

Friday, May 28: Philadelphia 15, Colorado 9

The Rockies' first meeting with
—and first defeat by—the Phillies.

7:05 at Mile High Stadium
The National Anthem: Denver City Limits
The first ball: Robert Vessa, Sr. (7-11)
The starting pitchers: Henry (2-5) vs. Rivera (2-2)
The W-L pitchers: Rivera (3-2) and Henry (2-6)
The attendance: 58,312
The Post headline: Creamed by Philadelphia
The News headline: Philadelphia wins comedy of errors vs. Rockies 15-9

On the field: The Phillies start fast, hitting up Butch Henry for four runs on three hits in the first inning alone. And they never quit, piling up 20 hits before the evening is over.

The Rocks almost make a game of it when they score two in the seventh and another two in the eighth to make the score a semi-respectable 11-8. But the Phillies put the game out of reach with four in the top of the ninth off Jeff Parrett.

Galarraga's back in the lineup after being out since May 9 with an hamstring injury. He gets two hits.

Chris Jones makes his first start for the Rox and singles in his first AB.

In the stands: Fans enjoy following Chris Jones' batting average as it goes from 1.000 to .500 to .333 to .250.

But they're grumbling over the fact that the Rox had *seemed* to be over the give-the-other-guys-ten-or-more-runs syndrome. It had been ten games since they allowed their opponents to go double digits on them. But now this.

In Dick Kreck's column, Jim Mullen's comments in Entertainment Weekly magazine are quoted: "The worst team in baseball is drawing the most fans. Now every owner wants one."

In hopes of hosting the All-Star game in Denver in 1996, the Rockies have sent an official bid to the commissioner, Jerry McMorris announced today.

The Avalanche.

A fan has an idea that borders on greatness.

Dick Veit: "You know how everybody says we shouldn't be doing the wave because it is a football thing? How about we do something that's completely *ours*.

"What if we do a wave-like thing from the *top* of the the stands down. We'd call it The Avalanche. It would be perfect for Colorado's team! Aren't we the only team in all of sports with snow on its logo?"

Yes. But how would people know it was headed their way?

"Hmm. We'll have to work on that."

Today's milestone: Don Baylor's minor surgery (1993)

The Rockies now have lost two in a row and have a record of 14-34. This puts them in last place 5.5 games behind the Padres. Florida's record is 21-26. The Mets are 15-30.

Saturday, May 29: Philadelphia 6, Colorado 0
The first major league shutout at Mile High.

1:05 at Mile High Stadium
The National Anthem: Amy Carlon
The first ball: Tom Flanagan
The starting pitchers: Blair (1-1) vs. Mulholland (5-4)
The W-L pitchers: Mulholland (6-4) and Blair (1-2)
The attendance: 56,263
The Post headline: Rockies lose, then shake up pitching
   staff
The News headline: Rockies' offense runs dry

On the field: Unfortunately, the Rockies aren't the shutouters. Rather, they are the shutoutees.

Terry Mulholland hurls the zeroes at them, distributing six hits over the course of his complete game victory. At no time does a Rock get past second.

And the Rockies hit only two fair balls past the infield.

Amazingly, Philadelphia's outfielders record no putouts for the day.

It is noted that it wasn't until the 23rd ML game played in Mile High that the shutout came to pass.

In the stands: "You can't go from last to first unless you're last."

"You mean you have to be last first?"

"That's right."

In the News: Bob Kravitz writes an entire column "without one mention of the local professional baseball team."

And brags about it.

New Yorker and New Yorkers know the feeling. Today, New Yorker magazine appeared on newsstands with a cartoon depicting the Mets' dugout. Most of the players are just sitting there with glum expressions on their faces.

One speaks: "Maybe we weren't meant to express ourselves in this particular medium."

We know the feeling. Matter of fact, so far this season, the Mets have expressed themselves in only two more games than the Rocks have.

Today's milestone: Charlie Hayes' birthday (1965)

The Rockies have now lost three in a row, have a 14-35 record and are in last place, 17.5 games out of first and 6.5 out of sixth. Florida is 21-27.

Sunday, May 30: Philadelphia 18, Colorado 1
The worst defeat.

1:05 at Mile High Stadium
The National Anthem: Willis Reed
The first ball: Nichole Birdsong (5th grade) and Carl Nance (6th grade)
The starting pitchers: Painter (0-1) vs. Greene (6-0)
The W-L pitchers: Greene (7-0) and Painter (0-2)
The attendance: 56,710
The Post headline: Black (and Blue) Sunday
The News headline: Phillies humble Rockies

On the field: The visit from the representatives of the City of Brotherly Love hasn't been very brotherly.

Or lovely.

How do you top a 15-9 drubbing (Friday) and a 6-0 thrashing (Saturday)?

With an 18-1 clobbering, of course. The season's most massive differential.

Phillies' starter Tommy Greene's NL-leading ERA gets even lower and so do the Rockies.

After retiring 12 of the first 13 Phils he faced, Painter suddenly loses it. The Phils explode for five runs in the fifth and another five in the eighth—each explosion powered by three home runs. Even Greene homers today.

While the Phils feast on Rockies' pitching for 19 hits, the Rocks nibble on Greene for just six. Fortunately for shutout avoidance, one of those is a Galarraga blast in the seventh.

Amid all this madness, Castellano makes his ML debut.

In the stands: The P.A. reminds men to please remove their caps for the National Anthem. Nobody can remember getting reminded before.

And folks yuk it up over the Chris Bermanesque nickname given to the Rockies' right fielder by a Post sportswriter. According to Jim Armstrong, he's Dante Bichette Hit-the-fan.

Two traditions: One is the number Young and Cole do on the batting box when they first come to bat. The other is the fans' making sure they don't forget.

On this warm Sunday afternoon, someone starts singing "Send in the Clouds."

Fantalk: "Kruk is one guy who can go to a biker bar without a tattoo."

"Hell, Kruk doesn't even need a *bike*."

After reflecting on the Phillies' easy manhandling of the Rockies: "Maybe Baylor was wrong to have that no-beard rule. Look what facial fur has done for the Phillies!"

More: "Oh, my God! The Rockies are wearing their Sunday uniforms! They're bad luck!"

"What Rockies uniforms aren't?"

"Good point. Maybe they should play naked."

A reasonable question: "Who's pitching?"

"Painter."

"Is this the guy who cut his ear off?"

The Phillies' cover boy Darren Daulton is seen talking to the Hooters poster girl. Which elicits this: "I want the pick of the litter."

When Girardi is brought in to pinch hit for Painter: "Oh, boy! We've got two catchers in the game and no pitcher."

Spotted: A CR cap in *Zephyrs'* colors. A promo for a Littleton restaurant, Cafe Rio.

A prediction made in the second inning by John M.: "In the bottom of the ninth, EY's gonna put this game into EIs." (As it turns out, EY doesn't come to bat in the ninth.)

A comment about Incaviglia: "He's the ballplayer most likely to be willing to sell a vowel."

And the South Stands, in clear defiance of The Rules, rejects Daulton's fifth-inning home run. Yes, it is tossed back onto the field. Which puts Bichette in no small peril.

No small peril—*miniscule.*

After the game, Baylor says this about Denver's fans: "They're just dying for some heroes and when we can give them some, this will be a fun place to play."

On the radio: KOA, which has a feature called The Play of the Game, selects, as *the* play of the game the *last* play of the game. The one that ended the suffering for Rockies players and fans, alike.

At a wedding at St. Vincent's early that evening: Rockies exec Roger Kinney sighs and says, "Well, at least they missed the extra points."

The Rockies have now lost four in a row, have a 14-36 record, and are in last place. Florida is 21-28.

Monday, May 31: Colorado 6, Pittsburgh 2
The Rockies' first meeting with —and first victory over—the Pirates.

7:05 at Mile High Stadium
The National Anthem: Rep. David Skaggs (D-Colo.)
The first ball: Daniel Valot (Total Petroleum)
The starting pitchers: Reynoso (2-2) vs. Wakefield (3-4)
The W-L pitchers: Reynoso (3-2) and Wakefield (3-5)
The attendance: 47,665
The Post headline: Rockies halt skid 6-2
The News headline: Reynoso rescues Rockies

On the field: Like a good car salesman, Reynoso makes a sale on the last day of the month. In fact, Reynoso is now the only Rocky with a positive win-loss record. He isn't overpowering, but he manages to get out of jams, so Baylor lets him go all the way.

Although no Rocky pitcher has yet to record a shutout, neither of the two runs Reynoso allows are earned, so this game can be called The First Shutout Ever—In Spirit.

Meanwhile, the purple pinstripers put up some numbers that, to everyone's relief, actually stand up.

With two outs in the third, a Sheaffer double plus a Bichette triple plus a Galarraga single equals two runs.

Then, in the fifth, the Rox bat around and add three more.

Later, with two on, Van Slyke scared the popcorn out of everybody in the park with a screamer that was just barely foul, but Reynoso came back and got him to hit into a double play.

In the stands: Trivia fans are trying to remember that on the Rockies' first Memorial Day, they won their first game from the Pirates.

The Pirates' leftfielder, Al Martin, has locals talking: "I'm pretty sure he's an appliance dealer in Denver in the off season."

Oh yeah? "Sure. He's a lefty. And he's a Martin."

During the seventh-inning stretch, Charlie Jones showers the fans below the press box from which he broadcasts with boxes of Cracker Jack.

A fan on mascots: "I'm not bullish on the bear."

And on the pitiful state of the team's team of hurlers: "You'd think that with Coors behind the team we'd have lots of pitchers."

In the eighth inning, a wave develops. The first reaction: "Call security!" The second: "Let's start one going the other direction and maybe they'll wave themselves into the next county."

When it appears we're going to actually win it, Miles Cortez cries out: "It's a miracle!"

On the way out of the park, the PA system serenades the happy fans with "The Battle Hymn of the Republic," aka "Glory, Glory, Colorado."

In Supercuts salons: You can now get—at no additional cost—"The Rockies Cut." You walk out with the outline of the Rocky Mountains etched into the side or back of your hair.

As Supercuts spokesman Gary Gapp says, "Colorado baseball has gone to our heads."

The Rockies now have a record of 15-36, the worst in baseball. This puts them in last place, 18 games out of first and 5.5 out of sixth. The next worst record, 17-31, belongs to the Mets.

The Rockies' first May: 6 wins, 21 losses. The Rockies won only twice at home in May, both victories for Armando Reynoso.

Tuesday, June 1: Pittsburgh 8, Colorado 6
The last game Bryn Smith pitched.

7:05 at Mile High Stadium
The National Anthem: Pastor Doug Ream (trumpet)
The first ball: Dale Murphy
The starting pitchers: Smith (2-3) vs. Walk (6-3)
The W-L pitchers: Walk (7-3) and Smith (2-4)
The attendance: 45,752
The Post headline: Rockies have no answer for late call
The News headline: Rockies frustrated again

Before the game: A ceremony was held to give Dale Murphy a chance to say goodbye to his Denver fans and for them to return the favor. Following a lengthy standing ovation, Dale pointed out that he's been a very small part of baseball history here, but the enthusiastic reception he's received from Denver's fans will be cherished.

The best part was when the thanks the guys on the team "for letting me act like a kid for a few months."

His poignant remarks were somewhat impaired by a hawker in the stands. "RED ROPES!"

On the field: Bryn Smith is 37, but he's a gamer. So he struggles gamely against the Bucs, holding them to three runs through four innings. Then comes the fifth, during which Orlando Merced gets three of his day's allotment of five RBI with one swing of the bat.

In their losing effort, the Rox put up two runs in each of three innings tonight. Key hits are a two-run double by Cole and a towering, 421-foot Galarraga homer.

Pedro Castellano makes his first ML start and gets his first hit, a double.

Charlie Hayes pinch hits—and thereby keeps his streak alive. Hayes is the only player who has appeared in all 52 games.

In the stands: It is noted that during the pregame salute to Dale Murphy, the scoreboard put up his number, 33. Except that it's 3.

Scorekeepers pull out tufts of hair in the first inning when Galarraga grabs a Clark grounder and turns it into a Van Slyke rundown between third and home. The scoring: 3-2-5-4-1-4.

Speaking of tufts of hair, it is generally agreed that Baylor's making Bryn Smith shave off his beard was probably a major factor in the decline in Smitty's pitching prowess.

A reason is put forth to return home run balls: "We want to help the team save money to buy a pitcher."

A passing vendor: "Become attractive to the opposite sex! Drink Coca-Cola!"

Somebody else remarks that "Tonight's game is not on TV. And it's not live, either, apparently."

After a great catch: "He caught it on the fly!"

"It must've hurt."

A strange conversation that somehow makes sense anyway:

"When did Darren Holmes come in?"

"In the seventh."

"No, I want to know when—what time?"

"You want Mountain Daylight or Greenwich time?"

"Cooperstown."

Today's milestone: John Burke selected in the first round of the ML draft (1992)

The Rockies now have a record of 15-37, which puts them in last place, 6.5 games behind the Padres and 18.5 games behind the NL West-leading Giants. Every other team has 20 or more wins except for the 17-32 Mets. Florida is 22-29.

Tuesday, June 2: Pittsburgh 5, Colorado 3

The day the Rockies' first winning pitcher was released.

7:05 at Mile High Stadium
The National Anthem: Cellular One Choir (26 voices)
The first ball: Jerry Morris (Jeep Eagle)
The starting pitchers: Ruffin (1-2) vs. Wagner (1-2)
The W-L pitchers: Petkovsek (1-0) and Parrett (0-2)
The attendance: 50,122
The Post headline: Rockies can't steal win from Pirates
The News headline: Rockies let another one slip away

Before the game: There is a moment of silence for Hall of Famer Johnny Mize. Mize died earlier today at the age of 80. Mize was known as The Big Cat for the same reasons as Galarraga. He played first base with great smoothness in spite of his size. And he could hit a ton.

On the way out: Bryn Smith. After his hot opening day in Mile High, things went bigtime cool for much-loved brother Smith.

Today, the former Denver Bear is released with a 2-4 record and an ERA of 8.49. He takes with him some fabulous memories: Starting and winning the first ML game played in the Mile High City. Being the first Rocky pitcher to win a game anywhere. Pitching before the largest crowd ever to watch a ML game. Hell, he even shaved his beard for the Rockies.

On the field: The Rockies try to make something happen in the first, but it all pretty much fizzles out when two Rocks are caught stealing. The Pirates' Jeff King (a Colorado Springs native) hits a two-run homer in the fourth. Bichette's solo shot in the sixth is adjudged to be a 452-footer. [This will be his longest of the year and the team's second longest of the season.]

The Pirates throw five pitchers at the Rockies, and it works. The Rox manage just four hits total. Meanwhile, the Bucs touch a trio of Rockies' hurlers for a dozen hits, including the two in the top of the ninth that the Pirates use to turn the 3-3 tie into a win for the Pittsburghers.

Pitcher Keith Shepherd makes his Rockies debut and the kid impresses.

Gold Glover Van Slyke's error is his first in 92 games. As they say. (Which means it's his second in 93 games.) But to make up for it, he goes 4-for-5 at the plate.

Galarraga begins the day at .400, ends it at .397.

In the stands: Vendor: "Frozen yogurt!"

Fan (a little too loud): "Yuck."

Vendor: "What's the matter, afraid of a little culture?"

In the bottom of the second inning, we find the pitcher and the ump examining the mound in the rain. Organist Shockney suggests a Plan of Action: "Mr. Sandman."

Fantalk: "If baseball is a religion, how come it hasn't gone New Age—with hugging the person on each side of you during the seventh inning stretch?"

And when the fans yell out, "CHARGE!" some respond with "CAN'T!" Because there are no ATMs in the ballpark.

The Rockies now have a two-game losing streak and a 15-38 record. This puts them in last place, 19.5 games out of first—and 6.5 games behind the sixth-place Padres.

The only other team that hasn't yet gotten its win column into the twenties is the Mets, who languish in their own personal cellar with an 18-32 record.

Thursday, June 3: Colorado Springs 4, Colorado 2

The game that hurt the most—but didn't count.

3:35 at Sky Sox Stadium
The National Anthem: Pikes Peak Achord
The first ball: Katie Pritchard
The News headline: Rockies and Nied go down on farm
The Post headline: Nied exits early with ailing elbow

On the field: The Rockies' top farm club is wearing those cheap, adjustable souvenir caps, a rinky-dink no-class cost-saver gaucherie in the eyes of many Rockies fans. Hell, even Dikeou's Zephyrs wore sized caps.

But in spite of their lower minor league headwear, the Sky Sox have no trouble manhandling the major leaguers.

Nied doesn't look good, giving up a couple of hits in the

first, a homer to Sean Ross in the second, and a triple in the third before exiting the game with an elbow injury, the seriousness of which will not be known until magnetic resonance testing.

Fredrickson replaces Nied and promptly gives up a home run to Roberto Mejia.

John Burke finishes up for the Rox and looks good during his two-inning stint.

The Springs' pitchers, Thompson, Metzinger, Moore and Allen, hold the big league club to six hits. And average a strikeout per inning. And give up zero runs until Clarke's clout in the closing stanza

In the stands: Before the game, Jack Kisling had a question: "The Rockies are an expansion team now. What I want to know is, if they lose to Colorado Springs, will they be a contraction team?"

Upon learning that the game was going to be a 7-inning encounter, Diane K. had some questions, too: "Do they have a fifth inning stretch—and when do they stop selling beer?"

To amuse themselves, a busload of fans from Denver (who had stopped for a few at Murphy's on their way down) decides to cheer for no reason. And they do, which causes the other fans to wonder what the hell.

"This," one of the conspirators admits, "is why we have to do away with baseball."

Then they notice the Sky Sox's premier attraction—the hot tub down the right field line which the Sky Sox rent out at $75 per game. After a squinty-eyed appraisal of the contents of the tub, one fan makes this observation: "I'd only pay five bucks to go nekkid with them."

Fans also notice the sign which proclaims that this is "THE WORLD'S HIGHEST PRO BALLPARK, ELEVATION 6531 FT." Remembering that Baylor had Denver's elevation displayed on the wall of Mile High Stadium to reduce the opposition to weak-kneed pushovers, there is comment about Don Baylor's petard. Yes, his own petard.

On the way out of the park, a grumbler opined that "the farm team ought to fly to Philly tonight."

In the restrooms: While using the facilities at Sky Sox Stadium, one can listen to the radio account of the game. The idea of piping KOA into the restrooms of the big league ballpark has been suggested to the Rockies, but—like the fans in Mile High's restrooms—they're not listening.

Another invidious comparison with the big league team: They sell a cheap scorecard here. It's just 50¢. And it includes up-to-date stats on both teams, including broken-out stats on pinch hitting plus bases stolen *and caught stealing*.

The Rockies charge three bucks for their hefty program-cum-scorecard and it provides none of that info.

On the way back to Denver: David Hartley discusses his quest to see a game at every ML ballpark: "My wife works for the Denver Zoo, so whenever a trip to a city with a big league team comes up, we both go. Typically, we go to a game on Friday night, then visit the local zoo on Saturday. I'm collecting ballparks and she's collecting zoos."

Somebody with one of those baseball-fact-a-day calendars pulls out today's fact. It's about a monster home run—estimated at 520 feet—that Harmon Killebrew hit in Metropolitan Stadium. The seat the ball struck when it landed was painted orange to mark the spot.

Which brings up a sore spot among longtime Denver baseball fans: The spot where Joey Meyer's enormous belt landed. It, too, had been marked so people could look up there and marvel. But it, like the bell Haraway used to ring, apparently was deemed to be Minor League and was done away with.

"Of course it was minor league," sputters Don L. "all of our baseball history was minor league until this year."

If the head fits...

A new Official Publication has been officially published. It's called If I Were A Rockie (sic) and it is a baseball story for children. What you're supposed to do is get a photo of the kid and tape it on the inside back cover. The book is die-cut so that you see the kid's face on every spread—as a member of the Colorado Rockies. Naturally, the kid is ultimately called into the critical game and hits the winning homer.

Interestingly, the manager of the Rockies in this book is a white guy. And the newspaper that reports the winning home run is called the Morning Gazette. Guess the author, Joseph C. D'Andrea, is a furriner.

Friday, June 4: Colorado 2, Philadelphia 1
The first victory over the Phillies.

5:35 at Veterans Stadium
The starting pitchers: Blair (1-2) vs. Mulholland (6-4)
The W-L pitchers: Blair (2-2) and Mulholland (6-5)
The attendance: 43,333
The Post headline: Blair holds tight rein on Phillies
The News headline: Rockies prove a point to Phillies

On the field: It's the team with the best record in the major leagues going against the team with the worst.

Nevertheless, the game is zip-zip after eight.

The Rockies' Blair is tough. He comes within two outs of pitching the first shutout in the history of the franchise.

The Phillies' Terry Mulholland is even more Mulholland-esque than usual. He strikes out a career-high 14.

In the Rockies' portion of the ninth, the scoring begins. Galarraga doubles in Jones. Then, Hayes doubles in The Cat to make it 2-0.

We go to the bottom of the ninth. Jordan, pinch hitting for Mulholland, and Morandini each double. That's one run for the Phillies.

Turns out to be the only one when Gary Wayne comes in and gets the last two outs.

Girardi injures himself while swinging in the ninth. Sheaffer has to take over his AB with a 1-2 count. (He takes strike three.) The seriousness of Girardi's affliction won't be known until later.

For his heroics in stifling Kruk and Daulton, Wayne collects his first save of the season. [As it turns out, it his only.]

In University Hospital, an MRI exam disclosed a tear in a ligament in David Nied's right elbow. The docs say he'll be out for a month at least.

The Rockies now have a 16-38 record. They are in last place, six games behind the sixth-place Padres.

The Mets' record is better: 18-33. The Marlins' record is better yet: 23-30.

Saturday, June 5: Philadelphia 6, Colorado 2

The game the Rockies raised the ERA of the National League's ERA leader.

5:05 at Veterans Stadium
The starting pitchers: Reynoso (3-2) vs. Greene (7-0)
The W-L pitchers: Greene (8-0) and Reynoso (3-3)
The attendance: 43,837
The Post headline: Rockies can't hit Greene, fall 6-2
The News headline: Phils' Greene shuts down Rockies
     again

On the field: In the beginning, it looks like Tommy Greene is going to giftwrap this one for the Rox.

His wild pitch lets the Rockies take a 1-0 lead in the first. But it's just a tease from the National League ERA leader (1.87).

The two runs run Greene's ERA up a tick and it provides a moral victory of the smallest kind.

But it's the only one today.

Because, in the second, the Phils put up three on a couple of Reynoso walks and doubles. They'll need no more.

Galarraga gets three of the Rockies' seven hits off Greene. He's now at .408.

A cruel statistician points out that Chris Jones has seven hits in 18 at-bats. Which is one more than Dale Murphy had in 42 at-bats.

In Helena, Montana: Like many Montanans, Jerry Metcalf is a fan of the Seattle Mariners. But now that the Rockies have come to the Mountain Time Zone, he has adopted them, too.

"The Mariners are my American League team and the Rockies are my National League team," he says. "I'm waiting for them to meet in the World Series before I decide which team is really my favorite."

Wait, wait, wait.

The Rockies now have a 16-39 record. This puts them in last place, 19 games out of first and six behind the Padres who are in sixth place. Florida is 24-30. The Mets are 18-34.

The first game Chris Jones homered twice in.

11:35 at Veterans Stadium
The starting pitchers: Ashby (0-3) vs. Schilling (6-1)
The W-L pitchers: Schilling (7-1) and Ashby (0-4)
The attendance: 55,714
The Post headline: Phils have Sunday feast
The News headline: It's another black Sunday

On the field: Andy Ashby is quickly bloodied (13 hits and nine runs) and when he leaves the game in the fourth, the Phillies have a comfy 9-2 edge.

The Rockies get three runs back in the fifth and another two in the seventh (both innings include two-run homers by Chris Jones), but the effort falls short

The Cat's average is now up to .417. The one steady factor in a rocky Rocky world.

The Rockies have now lost two in a row and have a 16-40 record. (The chilling thing is that the Mets had the same record at this point in their inaugural 40-120 season.)

June 7 is an open date and the day the National League announces the Player of the Week: Andres Galarraga. Although Andres had gotten the honor thrice as an Expo in '88, it is the first time a Rocky has been awarded this accolade. Well, when you bat .600 for a week, people tend to notice.

Tuesday, June 8: Colorado 4, Pittsburgh 1
The first visit to Three Rivers Stadium.

5:35 at Three Rivers Stadium
The starting pitchers: Ruffin (1-2) vs. Wagner (1-2)
The W-L pitchers: Ruffin (2-2) and Wagner (1-3)
The attendance: 16,722
The Post headline: Rockies wait out the rain for victory
The News headline: Rockies pitchers snuff Bucs

On the field: Ruffin and Shepherd combine for a four-hitter, making this the first Rockies game to embody such stinginess. Indeed, the Pirates managed to score once in the first inning, but that was all they'd get all evening.

Meanwhile, Andres the G. is up to an amazing .421 batting average, after hammering out three- and four-baggers to help propel this rain-interrupted game into the Rox' W column.

The Rockies now have a 17-40 record (.298), are 19 games behind the Giants, and remain in last place, 6.5 games behind San Diego. The Rockies are the only team playing below-.300 ball. Even the 19-36 Mets—whose luckless pitcher Anthony Young lost his 20th straight decision tonight—are playing .345.

Wednesday, June 9: Pittsburgh 4, Colorado 1

The first loss at Three Rivers Stadium.

5:35 at Three Rivers Stadium
The starting pitchers: Blair (2-2) vs. Neagle (1-1)
The W-L pitchers: Neagle (2-1) and Blair (2-3)
The attendance: 30,628
The Post headline: Rockies' sweep dreams come to halt
The News headline: Rockies leave Blair hanging once
more

On the field: Martin's two-run home run in the third breaks a 1-1 tie and the Pittsburghers never look back.

Or need to.

The Rockies' only run comes in the first and after that, they run themselves out of anything that vaguely resembles a scoring opportunity.

Blair has an estimable outing for the first six innings. But, during his nearly three dozen innings of moundwork for the Rox, he's been supported by exactly *four* runs.

The Blair/Holmes combo provides zero walks to the Pirates. Only the second game of the season that has seen the opposition bereft of freebie bases.

After "maybe 15 attempts," Danny Sheaffer steals his the first base of his career.

Smiles for the Dittohead.

In **Sports Illustrated,** there's a piece by Littleton's Rick Reilly about how Coloradans are turning out in enormous numbers "to cheer their puny Rockies." Choice tidbit: "Baylor could put nine toaster ovens on the field and attendance might not be different. Come to think of it, neither might the results." Reilly says Rockies fans treat their team "like freed hostages." He also says that fans aren't sure yet about what to do at a baseball game, claims some yell "Balk!" every time an opposition pitcher tries a pickoff, and points out that people bring gloves even when they're sitting under overhangs.

Quel embarrassment! He says we chant "Dee-fense!" and (gasp!) do the Wave.

Ah, but he says that "One *enjoys* the Rockies. One *endures* the Broncos."

Sounds good, whatever it means.

Also of note: Reilly eschews the -ie as he writes about "Rocky games" and "Rocky fans" and "Rocky merchandise" and "Rocky history."

The Rockies now have a record of 17-41 and are in last place, 20 games behind first and six behind sixth. The Marlins are 26-31 and Mets are 19-37.

June 10 is an open date, but in 1991 it was the date that Fay Vincent announced that Denver and Miami were the two applicants chosen by the expansion committee to join the National League.

Friday, June 11: Colorado 5, Houston 4
The first win for Parrett.
But he hates it.

7:05 at Mile High Stadium
The National Anthem: Billy Joe Royal
The first ball: Mike Wilson (7-11)
The starting pitchers: Reynoso (3-2) vs. Portugal (4-2)
The W-L pitchers: Parrett (1-2) and Hernandez (2-2)
The attendance: 57,136
The News headline: Rockies survive close call—at last
The Post headline: Rockies bail out Parrett in 8th, 5-4

On the field: The game see-saws back and forth and goes into the eighth with the Colorados ahead 4-3.

Winning pitcher Parrett is not real happy about what happened then. "Winning pitcher? Winning *vulture* is more like it." So said because instead of protecting Reynoso's one-run lead, he lets the Astros tie it up on a homer by Servais. Then. when the Rockies get the lead back, Parrett gets the W.

And Holmes makes it stand up in the ninth.

In the stands: It is noted that Ron Hassey always sprints out to his coaches' box. "If that's a superstition, it ain't working."

After scanning the Astros' roster to make sure there isn't anybody on the team named Jack, a plot is hatched. "To drive the Astros crazy, let's call 'em all Jack. Like when one of 'em whiffs, we'll yell out, 'Nice swing, Jack!'"

Two fans watch a couple of young men sauntering by looking real cool. "No matter what they say, I wouldn't want to go back and be that age again."

"Well, then, I've got good news for you."

The Astros' starter, Mark Portugal, causes a clot of fans to struggle to remember some other players whose last names are countries. Ray J. suggests there was once a Steve Nigeria a long time ago, but nobody's buying it.

On the Astros' white shoes: "It's O.K., it's after Memorial Day."

And: "Here, when somebody says the pitcher is 24, you don't know if it's his age, his number or his ERA."

A sign in the Rockpile when the score was tied in the eighth: "Bring in Elway."

A foul goes into the stands, eliciting: "Give it to your dad!"

And there is discussion of the item in Dear Abby that discusses the correct way to face when you're struggling to pass people who already seated in a theater or church. (One assumes this includes ballparks.) "It may be easier for the late arrivals to turn their backs to those who are already seated," writes a reader, "but I would much prefer having a stranger's navel within a foot of my forehead that having his bottom within an inch of my nose."

As mentioned, there is discussion.

The Rockies now have a record of 18-41. This puts them in last place, 20 games out of first and 6.5 behind the Padres.

Saturday, June 12: Colorado 14, Houston 11

The game the Rockies came back from a 7-0 deficit to win.

7:05 at Mile High Stadium
The National Anthem: Don Smith, St. Andrew's United
    Methodist Church Bell Choir
The first ball: Eric Dunham (Yale Elementary)
The starting pitchers: Ashby (0-4) vs. Drabek (5-6)
The W-L pitchers: Shepherd (1-0) and Jones (3-5)
The attendance: 60,864
The News headline: Rockies' rally rocks Astros
The Post headline: Galarraga revives Rockies, 14-11

On the field: Talk about come from behind. The Rockies allow the Astros to run off to a 7-0 lead, but still battle back to win. Against a strong team with a Cy Young pitcher on the mound.

A crucial participant in the comeback is a Sr. Galarraga. In the fourth, he swats a two-run homer. Then, in the eighth, he singles in a run to break the tie and ignite a five-run explosion.

Besides Cat, today's heroics are provided by Messrs. Hayes (four hits), Bichette (another four) and J. Owens (three). J. gets the first big league RBI of his career.

The total number of Rockies hits is 20, a franchise record.

In the stands: Fantalk: "Do they have a five-run rule like they do in Little League?"

And: "They're playing the Beatles' song, 'Help.'"

"No, that isn't the Beatles song. That's the Rockies song."

John Mason: "Excuse me, I am going to do my first Major League yell." Whereupon he bellows the following: "DRABEK, GET YOURSELF A DECENT TAILOR, YOU BUM!"

Within 20 minutes, D. Drabek had given up four runs.

At a wedding reception, guests are wondering to themselves why, of all days, Ancel Martinez and Gina Lombardi picked today to get married. After all, the schedule had been out long before Ancel and Gina booked their bash. And you'd think Ancel would know better. He is, after all, in the employ of KOA. And the interview he did with Armando Reynoso yesterday—Ancel translated—was fascinating.

The reception, held in a 5th floor loft of The Ice House,

provided a great view of the ballpark. More than a few attendees looked longingly out at Mile High, shining brightly in the dusk. And wondered why nobody had brought a radio.

Then Father Tony Judge, who had presided at the ceremony earlier, decided it was time to leave. Quickly, a plan was put together. When he got to his car down in Union Station's parking lot, he would listen to the game on KOA until he got the score, then he'd signal it up to the reception. Each pump of the right arm would signal a run on the good guys' side of the ledger. The left arm would indicate Astros runs.

Nine...to...*nine*.

Why, of all days...

The Rockies now have a two-game winning "streak" and a 19-41 record which is good enough for last place, 20 games out of first and 5.5 games behind the Padres. The Marlins are 29-31. That's awfully close to .500.

Sunday, June 13: Rockies 9, Houston 1
The first sweep *for* the Rockies.
And a lot of other firsts.

> **1:05 at Mile High Stadium**
> **The National Anthem:** LaTanya Hall
> **The first ball:** Jose Santiago
> **The starting pitchers:** Ruffin (2-2) vs. Swindell (5-5)
> **The W-L pitchers:** Ruffin (3-2) and Swindell (5-6)
> **The attendance:** 60,349
> **The News headline:** Rockies sweep away blues
> **The Post headline:** Hot Rockies bats sweep Astros

On the field: The Rox launch themselves on a two-out two-run Galarraga homer in the first, then coast along with a slim lead until the eighth when they score a sixpack of runs on three walks, a balk, a wild pitch and five singles.

This is the Rockies' first six-run inning. When Hayes scores on a balk, he is the first Rockies player ever to do so.

And Bichette has seven straight hits, a personal *and* franchise high.

Meanwhile, Ruffin has a nice outing, striking out the first five Houston batters he faces (a Rockies first) and winding up with eight Ks (ties the team record).

It is a sweep for the Rockies, their first ever.

In the stands: The Rockies fans, after just 30 home games, now hold the all-time attendance record for expansion fans. The breaker of the Blue Jays' 1977 record is said to be Robert Ladd of Broomfield. (How appropriate, fans notice, for a Broomfielder to be honored on this, the day of the Rockies' first sweep.)

As previously noted, Ancel and Gina just got married. (See yesterday's report on their baseball-deprived reception.) But they're not on their honeymoon yet. First, they had to treat their out-of-town friends to a Rockies game. A block of 50 seats was put to good use. Excellent use, as it turned out.

Marveling over Ruffin's blowing away of the first five Astros he faces: "How do you spell Ruffin? *With five Ks.*"

Is ARA an enemy of the planet? From the looks of the beer cups—plastic type 6—they're not recyclable.

The shame. In the top of the seventh, there are five circuits of The Wave.

A money-making plan: "I'm going to bring a Magic Marker to the games and offer to draw CRs on the foreheads of people wearing their ball caps backward for a buck."

A cruel query: "Did Will Clark break his arm yesterday?" Didn't hear anything about it. "Damn. That would have gotten Andres into the All-Star Game."

And: "Is Galarraga an American?"

"Anybody who hits .413 is an American."

"I'd go so far as to say that anybody who bats .413 ought to be President."

When the East and West Stands combine to do their classic "GO!" (pause) "ROCKIES!" chant, Jane D. asks: "Don't you think they should be yelling 'Stay! Rockies!' or is that premature?"

There's discussion of the way organist Shockney stops playing the instant a batter steps into the batters' box: "Does he stop playing when the batter sets his foot down in the batters' box—or when he *breaks the plane* of the batters' box?"

When Art Howe is tossed out of the game, a fan suggests that it wasn't anything he said to the umpire that was offensive. "It was Seed Breath." From eating too many sunflower seeds.

When John M. shows up in the fourth, he is asked "Are you early for tomorrow's game?"

Out: Nelson Liriano. He's been sent back down to Colorado Springs.

The Rockies have now, for the first time ever, won three in a row. They have a record of 20-41 and are in the cellar. The Marlins are 30-31 and aren't. But with the Mets in possession of a 19-41 record, the Rockies are no longer carrying around the worst record in ML baseball. (It's a burden they've borne for the last 37 days.) As somebody says, "You can stop comparing the Rockies to the '62 New York Mets. Now you can compare them to the '93 Mets."

Monday, June 14: Los Angeles 9, Colorado 4
The Dodgers' first visit to Denver.

7:05 at Mile High Stadium
The National Anthem: Xavian Raile, 12
The first ball: Zach Gray
The starting pitchers: Blair (2-3) vs. Astacio (4-4)
The W-L pitchers: Astacio (5-4) and Blair (2-4)
The attendance: 51,475
The News headline: Baylor exit highlights loss to LA
The Post headline: Dodgers frustrate Rockies 9-4

On the field: Former Denver Bear Tim Wallach knocks in three of the Dodgers' nine runs and the Rockies' winning streak ends—and their losing streak to the Dodgers extends to four.

But Galarraga's hitting tear continues. He goes 4-for-4 including a solo homer in the 7th. His BA is now up to .425. And he's become the first Rock to homer in three consecutive games.

The Rockies are down, 6-2, when Baylor argues a called ball which leads to his ejection.

This is the first time Baylor's been tossed as a manager.

The three unearned runs the Dodgers garner in the eighth (with the aid of two Rockies miscues) put the game away.

In the stands: "Tommy Lasorda eats bologna right off the loaf. Not even slices."

It is noted that DiamondVision is screening a new style of player portraits. The backgrounds of them all appear to be a raging snowstorm in progress. Interesting. But strange.

The Rockies now have won 20 and lost 42 and have slipped back below the 20-41 Mets in the battle for the worst record in baseball.

Tuesday, June 15: Los Angeles 12, Colorado 4
The first game with two bench-clearing brawls.

7:05 at Mile High Stadium
The National Anthem: Tagana DeCluette, 14, and the Voices of Faith (surely the longest rendition of the season)
The first ball: Bob Beelenberg (Metro Brokers)
The starting pitchers: Henry (2-6) vs. Martinez (4-4)
The W-L pitchers: McDowell (3-0) and Shepherd (1-1)
The attendance: 55,772
The News headline: Galarraga, Rockies go down fighting
The Post headline: Rockies go down swinging in brawl

On the field: It's not the show the Rockies' management wanted their team to put on for baseball's owners. The Horsehide Honchos are in town for a summit meeting re expanding the playoffs.

The fights take place in the seventh and eighth innings. Their genesis is the classic escalating they-hit-us-so-we'll-hit-'em-back scenario. It's triggered by Shepherd's smite of Cory Snyder followed by Shepherd's taunt to come-and-get-me! Naturally, it's a bench-clearer.

The next outburst of ill temper is provoked by Galarraga's slide into Jody Reed at second with spikes high. Very high. Fight-startin' high.

Indeed, Reed is spiked and Round Two begins.

The organ is right there with "Who's Sorry Now?" And, later, with the Beatles' "We Can Work It Out."

After order is restored, Baylor finds himself tossed from his second game in two days.

Other ejectees: Charlie Hayes, Ramon Martinez, and Shepherd.

Until it is severed, the Rocks' Shepherd had a streak of 13 consecutive scoreless innings going.

(Speaking of fights: When Shepherd was a boxer—and he was—he was known as The Apache Kid.)

Mike Piazza is the Dodgers' hitting (the other kind) hero: He hits a pair of homers and drives in five runs.

Galarraga continues to be the Rockies' hitting phenomenon: He goes four-for-five and raises his ML-leading average to .435. [*This will turn out to be his highest of the season.*] When he grounds out in the ninth, it ends his streak of nine straight hits, a team record and but one shy of the NL record.

After the dust clears, the Rockies realize that they had a 3-2 lead and a fighting chance going into the seventh but wound up losing big-time—12-4.

The Rox are now 0-5 against the Dodgers.

In the stands: The P.A. announcer: "If you have any problems, contact your usher." Bill K.: "I told her I marital problems, but she was no help."

In the minors: Today was the day a ban on chewing or smoking tobacco during games or in the clubhouse in the minor leagues went into effect.

The Rockies have now lost two in a row, have a 20-43 record, and are in last place, six games out of sixth. At 30-33, Florida is in fourth place in the Eastern Division.

Wednesday, June 16: Colorado 7, Los Angeles 6
The Rockies' first victory over the Dodgers.

> **7:05 at Mile High Stadium**
> **The National Anthem:** Suzy Nelson
> **The first ball:** Christopher Lloyd impersonator
> **The starting pitchers:** Reynoso (3-3) vs. Gross (5-4)
> **The W-L pitchers:** Reynoso (4-3) and Gross (5-5)
> **The attendance:** 51,765
> **The News headline:** Reynoso survives Dodgers,
> weather
> **The Post headline:** Rockies end L.A.'s spell

On the field: After five straight losses to L.A., the Rockies finally get to put one in the win column. Reynoso goes eight innings, holding Los Angeles to two runs, but when the relief corps comes in—after a 67-minute rain delay—it looks like something horrible is going to happen. Again. Indeed, the Dodgers score four runs in the top of the ninth, three on Jody Snyder's three-run homer.

You could almost hear the entire time zone breathe a sigh of relief when the Rocks escape with the victory. Empty-base homers for Hayes and Boston. Charlie's shot flies 437 feet. [Ultimately, this is his longest homer of the year and the team's third longest.]

Mark Grant gets the save. [This will be his only save of the year.] Daryl Boston knocks the Rockies' first homer into the South Stands.

Andres Galarraga goes 1-for-3, so his average plummets to .433. A number crunchy kind of guy has it figured out: Andres G. can fail in his next 83 trips to the plate without dropping below .300.

Daryl Strawberry delights the fans by striking out thrice.

In the stands: The lame "actor" who throws out the first ball is promoting some new movie. Which some fans think is a crass commercialization of one of baseball's cherished traditions. To make it worse, the promotional ninny takes the mike and speaks to the crowd about today's game "between the California Rockies and the Los Angeles Dodgers."

The boos drown out the groans.

There's much talk about the Dodgers now being primary rivals, after last night's fights and all. "Forget the fish," Darrell T. says, "the Hollywoods are closer. And more fun to beat. Besides, they're in our division."

Between pitches, the stands are voting for Galarraga for the All-Star game. Voters using ballpoint pens to punch ballots soon learn that six ballots is the maximum that can be gang-punched at one time.

The scoreboard tells us that Boston has 0 SBs. But is that 0 out of 0 attempts—or 0 out of 10 attempts? *The Purple People Watchers want to know.* And want the scoreboard to tell them.

The heavens rumble, then open up. Umbrellas pop open as the Rockies suffer the first mid-game rain delay at home. It's a 67-minute job in the sixth inning.

"Look!" a happy fan says, "my beer is full again!"

And it gets so cold that Diane K. says, "Right now, I'm in favor of global warming."

You can't go home again.

Not everyone is waterproof, apparently.

Because some consider leaving during the rain delay, maybe go out to their cars or even head home.

And if the game is resumed, they say they'll just come back to the ballyard.

Oh no you don't.

One of the Rockies' many rules won't let you.

The scoreboard has warned:

PATRONS LEAVING THIS STADIUM CANNOT BE READMITTED.

Evidently, the only place that recognizes Rockies ticket stubs is Shotgun Willie's.

"Dammit, if I want to come back to see the end of the game, I'll *buy* another ticket!"

Oh no you won't. By then, all the ticket windows are all closed. Yep, when you're out of *this* ballpark, you're out of luck.

A sign spotted (and photographed) by a Rockies' fan at the Texas Rangers' ballyard:

"If you are going to re-enter stadium have your ticket stub initialed by gate attendant."

So civilized.

And in Texas, even.

Today's odd fact: Only three teams don't have the names of their players on the backs of their home uniforms—the Rox and the two Sox.

Today's milestone: The anniversary of the first Rockies win ever when the Bend Rockies beat Boise, 6-4, on Will Scalzitti's grand slam on the eighth (1992)

The Rockies now have a record of 21-43 and are in last place, five games behind the sixth-place Padres. The Mets are the only team in the majors to have won fewer games. They're 20-43. The Marlins are 30-34.

Thursday, June 17 is an open date for the Rockies and it's a good thing. It means that they won't fall any further behind the Marlins, who now are now ahead of the Rox by 9.5 games.

Friday, June 18: San Diego 11, Colorado 1

The game that almost got rained out but, unfortunately, wasn't.

7:05 at Mile High Stadium
The National Anthem: The 17th Ave. All Stars
The first balls: Jeremy Hartshorn and Jeff Flint
The starting pitchers: Ruffin (3-2) vs. Harris (6-7)
The W-L pitchers: Harris (7-7) and Ruffin (3-3)
The attendance: 52,159
The News headline: Rockies take a step backward
The Post headline: Not a prayer: Padres romp 11-1

On 38th Avenue: The message on the signboard in front of Lehrer's Flowers read "GO ROCKIES REIGN OVER THE PADRES." And reign it did. All day long.

On the field: Water. Lots of it. KOA said that the game might start as late as nine or ten p.m. Suddenly, the rain stops, the tarp comes off, and the ball game—an artistic disaster for the home team—gets played after all.

Greg Harris goes all the way for the Padres, tossing a no-walk masterpiece, and has solid backing from his batsmen.

The Rox' starter, Ruffin, doesn't make it through the first inning when he lets the Padres score four. They score another three in the second off Fredrickson and ride a fat lead all the way to the final stanza. That's when Hayes smacks a lead-off homer to avert the shutout. It is pretty much the only good thing a Rock did all evening.

In the stands: John M. takes advantage of the sparseness of the crowd and stretches out. "You know, this is more like it!"

Diane K. is glad to see John. "Know why I'm happy you showed up? I forgot my cigarettes."

"Oh," says John, "you haven't heard then. It's Day 18."

A fan brings today's page from his baseball-fact-a-day calendar. Says that on this date in 1969, the Padres lost, 19-0. "So," he points to the scoreboard, "that's a 30-run swing."

A fan imagines a Rockies fan sticking up a 7-11: "Give me all the money in the cash register—and a No. 5 pin."

Ken Kirkland: "We appreciated the fact that the beer vendor we had in our section the other night knew that there is no 'r' in the word, 'beer.'"

This isn't Wrigley Field. Or is it?

There's an anti-throwing-the-ball-back movement. And a T-shirt that says, "Ain't No Ivy Here. Keep The Ball."

And yet, in the Padres' end of the fourth, Bell homers. And, in spite of the P.A. warning that "Any fan throwing objects onto the field, including home run balls, will be subject to ejection and criminal prosecution," a Rockies fan promptly throws it back. The thrower is then thrown out.

We'd like to see that tried at Wrigley.

Since many fans wonder why the hell our fans can't do what their fans do if we want to, the Fans' Ombudsman puts the question the Bob Gebhard.

His response:

"When the season began, we looked on the throwing back of opposing home run balls onto the field as an amusing expression of contempt and an imitation of fans' behavior at Wrigley Field. In short order, we found that fans who had caught opposing home run balls were being harassed to the point of threats of bodily harm for failure to throw such balls back onto the field...in light of the fact that such a ball can pose a threat to an unwary outfielder, we determined that we could best eliminate the difficult situation by including these balls in our general stadium prohibition concerning items being thrown on the field. I don't know what other clubs do about this problem. I'm not aware that this practice is common anywhere other than Wrigley Field."

To which a fan wonders why it's no problem in Wrigley.

And why nobody thinks twice about the balls that the players from both teams throw up into the stands throughout games.

Are they threats to unwary *fans*?

Today's milestone: Andres Galarraga's birthday (1961)

The Rockies now have a record of 21-44 and reside in last place, 22 games behind the first-place Giants. San Diego is in sixth place, 5.5 games ahead of the Rockies. Florida is 31-35.

Saturday, June 19: Colorado 17, San Diego 3

The game that set the Rockies' record for runs scored.

7:05 at Mile High Stadium
The National Anthem: NorWest Bank Choir (all eight
of them)
The first ball: Nick Hawkinson (Upper Deck)
The starting pitchers: Blair (2-4) vs. Taylor (0-4)
The W-L pitchers: Blair (3-4) and Taylor (0-5)
The attendance: 55,603
The News headline: Rockies pummel Padres
The Post headline: Blair, Rockies give Padres hit fit, 17-3

On his front porch, when the paper bearing news of tonight's
game arrives, Dick V. opens his paper. "I saw the score, 17-3,
and thought 'Oh, no, not again!'"

On the field: The Rockies score eight times in the third inning,
two more than their previous single-inning high. The Rockies'
17-run total beats the franchise's previous high by three.

Four RBIs for Alex Cole and pitcher Willie Blair are both
personal single-game bests.

Yes, Blair. All the Rocks—including the pitcher—get hits
tonight. And Charlie Hayes gets his third homer in as many
games. Naturally, The Cat gets three more hits and is now
batting .434.

More on Blair: He'd gone hitless for the season until the
third inning when he bunted himself on—and a run in. Then, in
the seventh, he stepped to the plate with the bases loaded. And
unloaded a base-clearing double. Three more RBI.

In the stands: The organist makes some real strides. Today, he
gives Andres Galarraga a theme song. The Big Cat strides to
the plate to the tune of "Pink Panther."

But some fans favor making "What's New, Pussycat?"
the theme song of the Rockies' first real hero. Mainly because
after the the song's title phrase is played, everybody in the
stands could/would/should yell, "Oh-oh-oh-oh-oh." Try it. You
may hate it.

Thank you, Dizzy Dean.

Years ago, when Diz was a baseball broadcaster, he kept score of the games as he called them.

One day, somebody peered over Dean's shoulder and saw a notation on the scorecard that wasn't in anybody's scorekeeping lexicon. It said, "WWO." What does it mean, Dean?

"It means it was a Wasn't Watching Out."

In a ballpark full of distractions, this has proven to be a handy bit of shorthand. Tonight, Jack Hidahl adds another. It's somewhat more specific.

His scorecard includes RHGO.

It means it was a Redhead Haltertop, Goosebumps Out.

Speaking of scorecards, a fan points out that scorecards have places, from left to right, for players' numbers, then their names, then their positions.

"But the P.A. guy gives us that information in another order. He'll say 'batting second, catcher, number seven, Joe Girardi.'

Sure would be handy if he gave us the info in scorecard order."

And Sandy L. says she saw a cartoon that said that "research has shown that wearing a baseball cap backward lowers one's IQ by as much as 50 points."

The Rockies now have a 22-44 record and reside in last place in the NL West, 22 games behind the leaders, 5.5 games behind the next-to-last. The Marlins are 31-36.

Sunday, June 20: Colorado 3, San Diego 1
A win for Fathers' Day—and a new two million attendance record.

1:05 at Mile High Stadium
The National Anthem: Pump Boys & Dinettes (Arvada Center)
The first ball: Allen Brandt (Colo. Lottery)
The starting pitchers: Henry (2-6) vs. Whitehurst (2-3)
The W-L pitchers: Reed (2-2) vs. Mason (0-5)
The attendance: 63,661
The News headline: Rockies finding ways to win
The Post headline: Castilla's slam grand nonetheless

On the field: This is the Rockies' sixth victory in nine games. (Also the sixth victory in ten games.)

Vinny Castilla, hitting and fielding solidly, emerges as a new Rocky hero. It's his lead-off homer in the seventh that breaks the 1-1 tie in a tense, well-played game some describe as the best they've seen this season.

Baylor uses five pitchers strategically and all were effective.

Although he permits the Padres no runs in 5 2/3 innings, starter Butch Henry doesn't get the W.

In the record book: The Rox hit the one-million attendance mark on Mother's Day, so it was only right that they break two million on Father's Day. Accomplished in a mere 36 dates, it is the quickest any franchise has ever reached the two-million milestone. Until today, Toronto had the record with 41. They set it in '92.

The Rockies designated Ralph McCray as No. 2,000,000. He's a father (of twins) from Aurora. Works for U S West.

Many are amused that the person said to be the one-millionth was a mother and the two-millionth turned out to be a dad. Sometimes, it appears, coincidences are made, not born.

Yet another coincidence: The Rockies' opponents on Fathers' Day is...the Padres.

To celebrate, have a pop.

In the parking lot: A Chevy Nova with Colorado plates— DBLPLA.

In the stands: It is Colorado Lottery/King Soopers Barbecue Apron Day. Some number of fans received aprons. Most didn't.

And it was HOT. How hot was it? It was so hot that the people in the South Stands crowded into the shade of the scoreboard. As it moved, they moved.

It was noted that Bonnie Brae AARP was one of the groups in attendance. And suggested that their official cheer is "Eh?" As in, "Give me an 'Eh?'" The group: "Eh?"

And there's a new record in the stands tonight. *Seven* votes for Galarraga with one poke of the ballpoint pen.

A fan: "My progressive lens glasses are not suited for Section 424. I've got to change one or the other."

A sign: "Life's short. Play Zimmer."

That the scoreboard is now running the Coors Cutter Homerun Ball Race should be noted. Or maybe not. A fan shakes his head. "Can you believe 50,000 people will watch something so dumb?"

Charlie Hayes gets caught in a base running blunder, then, in the inning that follows, makes a nice throw to nail a runner. Which brought this comment from a female fan: "Isn't is amazing that when a guy makes a bonehead base running mistake for the last out, he often makes the next good play on defense."

She is bought a beer.

The Rockies now have a two-game win "streak" and a 23-44 record. They are in last place, 3.5 games behind the Padres and 22 games behind the leaders, the Giants. The Floridans are 31-37, the New Yorkers 20-47.

Monday, June 21: Colorado 5, Cincinnati 4 (10 innings)
The first home game that went into extra innings.

7:05 at Mile High Stadium
The National Anthem: Jim Salestrom
The first ball: Jamie Brazzel, Easter Seals National
    Poster Child
The starting pitchers: Armando Reynoso (4-3) vs.
    Jose Rijo (6-2)
The W-L pitchers: Reed (3-2) and Reardon (1-1)
The attendance: 51,835 (largest in ML today)
The News headline: Rockies settling old scores
The Post headline: Bichette sticks it to Reds in 10th

On the field: Going in, the Rockies were even in extra-inning games, 2-2, but all the oversized ones had come on the road. Here is a first for Mile High Stadium. The timing is right, too. After all, this is the longest day of the year, perfect for having the longest game (in innings) of the season (so far).

Reynoso semi-struggles along for 8 2/3 innings, giving up four. The Rockies match that with four consecutive singles in the fourth, followed by a Castilla triple.

Finally, the tenth inning—and the game—comes to an

abrupt and rewarding end for the home fans when Dante bashes a double, sort of, over the Reds' shallow-playing centerfielder with two out and two on.

Bichette *would* have had a double if he'd bothered to touch second base on his game-winning poke. But when he saw the winning run cross the plate, he didn't bother.

In the stands: Perhaps emboldened by the Reds' dominance of the Rockies during their visit to Cincinnati last month, quite a few red C caps are in evidence tonight.

Witnessing his first Rockies game in person tonight is Jim Cullinane. He was the Denver Bears' radio voice for 19 years, from '75 to '84.

Cullinane knows Don Baylor and says "He's so intense. He's on fire all the time. I don't think he's laid back in his sleep."

We knew them when. (Well, maybe we didn't.)

On the way into the park, fans get copies of ROOKIE LEAGUE courtesy of Fleer and discover that it comes with a pack of fifteen baseball cards.

A typical set of cards includes some guy named Charlie Hayes who plays third for the New York Yankees and the Los Angeles Dodgers' second baseman, Eric Young.

One doesn't know whether to be happy with these rare treasures or honked off by their lack of Rockiesness.

The Rockies now have a three-game winning streak, a record of 24-44, and a home in the cellar of the NL West, three games behind the sixth-place Padres. The Marlins are 31-38.

Tuesday, June 22: Cincinnati 16, Colorado 13
The most total runs scored in a game.

7:05 at Mile High Stadium
The National Anthem: Wende Harston
The first ball: Michael Amidei
The starting pitchers: Ruffin (3-3) vs. Smiley (3-9)
The W-L pitchers: Wickander (1-0) and Grant (0-1)
The attendance: 58,597
The News headline: Rockies lose slugfest 16-13
The Post headline: Reds' machine gears up again

At noon on the Mall: The Rockies and KOA put on a rally for Andres Galarraga in front of Prudential Plaza.

The alleged purpose: To honor The Big Cat, who now has an astronomical batting average of .431.

The real purpose: To hand out fistfuls of All Star Ballots to try to move The Big Cat up from fourth or fifth place in the voting for NL first baseman.

People are voting like crazy. Because, as they say, they want Galarraga to be on the All-Star team.

Much of Denver seems not to understand that every team has at least one player in the All Star Game and Andres is a shoo-in to be the Rockies' representative.

Galarraga knows, of course, and he is gracious in his remarks made to the throng along the mall. He not only says he was "really hoppy," he also admits he is "very hoppy."

Not so with the ESPN cameraman who is smacked by a mall shuttle bus. Embarrassed, perhaps, but not injured.

On the field: Mark Grant's first decision is an L, and it comes in the scoringest game so far this year.

Yes, it's the year's highest-scoring game in the National League's highest-scoring park.

[As it turns out, the 29 runs scored today will be the most scored in the majors this season. It won't be matched until the post season, in Game 4 of the World Series, when the Blue Jays and Phillies beat up on each other to the tune of 15-14, a win for the Phils.]

Kevin Mitchell is in the lineup for the Reds tonight. It's his first appearance at Mile High. He gets two doubles, a triple, and a home run.

The Rox have two four-run innings and, in the third, they score five. Chris Jones gets two home runs in one game for the second time this month.

Charlie Hayes, frequently mentioned but rarely in the same paragraph as hustling, steals three bases today, a club record. Indeed, he records the Rockies' first theft of home.

All of which says much about his *potential* for hustling. Or perhaps it says much about Baylor's persuasiveness.

Galarraga continues his torridity. He's three for five, including a home run.

In the stands: There is much frivolity over Jack Guthrie's suggestion in this morning's News that a different ball be used in Denver to compensate for the thin air. "Whiffle comes to mind," says Tony P.

The parking lot with the wildly fluctuating rates went down to $8 for tonight's game. It's often up to $10 and even $15.

Zima has made the scene in the Beers of the World stand on the concourse. How's it doing? The guy manning the booth says it has displaced Rockies beer as their best seller.

Speaking of overpriced, it is noted that Pizza Hut's little pizzas have gone down from $7.50 to $5.50. What's the story here? A passing pizza peddler is asked. "We went down two inches and two dollars at the beginning of this homestand."

With the proliferation of runs in tonight's contest, a scorekeeping fan says he's glad he brought two pencils.

Somebody points out that the East Stands yell GO! and the West Stand yell ROCKIES! but the fans seated in the middle, between home and third, have no role in the powerful chant.

"Yes, we do," John N. replies. "We're the *pause*."

According to the P.A. announcer, a promotion awarded some lucky fan "a free pair of glasses from Lenscrafters." Which led to a cry: "Give 'em to the ump!"

And a heated argument about coolers breaks out. "I think Rockies fans should use blue Coleman insulated jugs to bring their beverage of choice to the games, not red ones," Don K. says. "Blue is closer to purple."

"A better idea would be to bring one of each. Blue and red *make* purple."

In the tradition of Fenway Park, people are hawking peanuts outside the park. Indeed, the value is better. Two dollars instead of three. But the peanuts seem to be strangely tiny. Dwarf peanuts, really.

The explanation: "I think they were grown near Rocky Flats."

A savvy fan: "The best deal of all is to get your peanuts at King Soopers for $1.29 a pound. Compare that to three bucks for eight ounces or whatever it is!"

A Galarraga fan: "If we got everybody to vote for Andres every time either team makes an out for one entire game, he'd be the starting firstbaseman for sure."

Steve Basch: "This game has been delayed by runs."

And: "They're going to have to mow the grass before this game is over."

And: "If they go past midnight, can you bring your pitchers back in again? It's a new day."

Hal Moore left late, at 9:21, but it was just the fifth.

The Rockies now have a record of 24-45. This puts them in last place, three games out of next-to-last. The Marlins: 32-38.

Wednesday, June 23: Colorado 15, Cincinnati 5
The last game in the first winning homestand.

3:05 at Mile High Stadium
The National Anthem: Keith Carradine
The first ball: Wade Phillips
The starting pitchers: Parrett (1-2) vs. Pugh (3-8)
The W-L pitchers: Parrett (2-2) and Pugh (3-9)
The attendance: 60,282
The News headline: Rockies hit road with romp
The Post headline: Mile High finally where heart is

On the field: Clobber. Drub. Rout.

The Rockies stick their first winning homestand (8-4!) into the old memory book. And note that The Big Cat got a hit in all 12 games.

Tonight, the Rocks let the Reds sneak ahead 2-0 and then Sheaffer strokes a three-run homer. (Before the game is over, Danny and Vinny Castilla will have become the first Rocks to knock in five runs in one game.)

Castilla goes 4-for-5, including a pair of home runs.

An anemic single gives Galarraga his 1,000th hit, but that's all for today. This drops him down to .427.

In the stands: The Colorado Symphony closes down its offices, puts the operation in the hands of a handful of volunteers, and spends the afternoon in a big block of seats up in section 404.

All the Symphony folk are cheering for Vinny Castilla because the CSO's Sandy Lasky is getting a new dog on Friday. Its name: Vincent Van Go!

Fueled by the media, folks are thinking that Galarraga's fabulous numbers plus the enormous ballot-punching crowds that come to Mile High may well make The Big Cat a starter in the All-Star game.

Mark Zessin, the Andy Frain honcho in charge of distributing All-Star ballots in the ballpark: "Sixty thousand people show up and everybody wants 500 ballots."

Piper Stevens: "I've been listening to Hal and Charlie on KHOW. They're pretty knowledgeable. I'd like to hear them broadcast a game."

Once again, one of the Rockies' Rules is the subject of grumbles. It's that No Flash Photography decree. "Can't you just hear Bichette?" a fan asks. "I lost it in the photography!"

Why the No Flash rule? The Fans' Ombudsman asked Bob Gebhard.

"We banned flash photography so as not to create a danger or distraction to a hitter facing a pitched ball or to a fielder attempting to field a batted or thrown ball. I don't know what other ball clubs have decided to do concerning this issue in their own parks."

Nothing, probably. Except maybe to snicker a bit at the Rockies' policy.

Tonight, a new bell has been brought to the park to mark the Rocks' runs with dings. A bigger, better bell. Most of all, a louder bell. After the seventh inning, it gets a real workout: *Seven* dings.

In the Reds' ninth, Barry Larkin bats a ball into the stands. In flagrant disregard of the Rockies' Rule No. 47B, the ball is thrown back, rejected by the fan who caught it.

Across the stadium, a guy jumps up and yells "Eject that bastard!" Just kidding.

Returning from the concession stands, a guy struggles to get back to his seat. He's juggling two beers that're filled to the brim—until he splashes some on Pat Milstein's sandaled feet. Which results in this request from a nearby fan. "Can I lick your toes?"

There seems to be a heady theme to tonight's game. Some fans recast the lyrics to "Take Me Out To The Ballgame." The new line: "For it's one, two, three beers, you're out..."

Somebody points out that the IBM Tale of the Tape only reports the distance of the Rockies' home runs in Mile High Stadium. "They only measure homer homers."

A philosophical note is heard from a fan who is AWOL from his job: "Work, shmurk. Ditch it and go to a ballgame. Work'll be there tomorrow, but the ballgame won't."

In the fifth inning, with The Color Purple ahead, 6-3, no outs and a man on first, Dante comes to bat and a fan sighs, "I can't wait for spring training."

In the newsstands: Baseball Weekly's cover story is about John Olerud and Andres Galarraga, the two guys who have a shot at batting .400 this year.

A cartoon suggests how Cat can finish the season over that lofty threshold. Among them: "Be allowed to bat against own team's pitching staff once a week." And "Make pact with the devil (in exchange, Satan gets chic purple Rockies cap)."

Hmm. Last Rockies cap we saw was black, except for the CR and the button on top.

In ignorance, KUSA-Channel 9 anchor Ward Lucas is quoted thusly: "I knew that a pro team meant a lot to Denver, but..."

But we've had a professional baseball team in this neck of the rocks for many decades, Ward.

In a suburb of Washington, D.C.: An angry knife-wielding wife cuts off her husband's penis, adding credence to the theory that people living in cities without major league baseball have an elevated level of marital strife.

The Rockies now have a 25-45 record and are 22 games behind the first-place Giants. The Marlins are 32-39 and are 18 games behind their divisional leaders, the Phillies.

Thursday, June 24: San Francisco 17, Colorado 2
The Rockies' first visit to Candlestick Park—and first humiliation there.

2:05 at Candlestick Park
The starting pitchers: Blair (3-4) vs. Burkett (10-2)
The W-L pitchers: Burkett (11-2) and Blair (3-5)
The attendance: 39,827
The News headline: Giants bring Rockies back down
The Post headline: Rockies mugged in broad daylight

On the field: The first trip to the 'Stick brings the Rocks back down to earth.

In 96° weather, the hottest game of the year for Colorado, San Francisco is the team that's really hot. They get 20 hits and, for all practical purposes, the game is over after two.

Robby Thompson belts a pair out, Will Clark and Mark Carreron each tag one, and Barry Bonds hits the third grand slam of his career to welcome the Rockies to the ballpark everyone loves to hate.

For only the eighth time this season, Galarraga goes oh-fer. This snaps his 12-game hitting streak.

In Channel 9's conference room: Joe Franzgrote, KUSA's President: "The Rockies will in all likelihood sell more tickets this season than any other sports team in the history of this planet."

On ESPN: There's a piece about Galarraga's sensational hitting in which it is pointed out that he's batting way over .400 in spite of the fact that his speed (or lack thereof) makes infield hits mighty rare and—this hurts—"he never gets to face Rockies pitching."

The Rockies are now 25-46. They're in last place, 23 games behind the Giants and 3.4 behind the sixth-place Padres. Florida's record is 32-39. (The Marlins just picked up last year's NL batting champ, Gary Sheffield, in yet another odoriferous Padres "trade.")

Friday, June 25: San Francisco 7, Colorado 2
The game in which Jayhawk hit the first home run of his ML career.

> **8:35 at Candlestick Park**
> **The starting pitchers:** Henry (2-6) vs. Hickerson (0-1)
> **The W-L pitchers:** Hickerson (1-1) and Henry (2-7)
> **The attendance:** 30,722
> **The News headline:** Rockies pitchers take another beating
> **The Post headline:** Rockies get bell rung again

On the field: The Giants run up a 6-0 lead before the Rockies manage to cross the plate for the first time. Butch Henry gives up all seven runs the Giants score. A trio of relievers relieve him, and none gives up a run, but it's too late.

Jayhawk Owens collects his first big league homer, a solo blast, in the fifth.

In two games at the home of the NL West leaders, the Rox have been outscored 24-4.

The Rockies have now lost two in a row and are in last place with a 25-47 record. Only the 21-50 Mets have a worse record.

Saturday, June 26: Colorado 5, San Francisco 1
The Rockies' first win at Candlestick.

2:05 at Candlestick Park
The starting pitchers: Reynoso (4-3) vs. Wilson (5-3)
The W-L pitchers: Reynoso (5-3) and Wilson (5-4)
The attendance: 39,327
The News headline: Reynoso rides to rescue again
The Post headline: Reynoso a Giant killer

On the field: Armando Reynoso is tough.

Today, he allows just seven hits and struggles only in the late innings. But he survives to add another complete game (his fourth) to his résumé.

Freddie Benavides enjoys the first four-hit day of his career, and Galarraga contributes two of each, hits and RBI. The Cat is at .420.

San Francisco's run comes on a round-tripper by Royce Clayton. Which brings to ten the number of homers that Reynoso has given up this season—all solo shots.

In his home near L.A., Roy Campanella died. Heart. Age 71. Campy was the man who gave Don Zimmer his nickname, "Popeye."

The Rockies now have a 26-47 record, and are in last place, 23 games behind the Giants and 3.5 games behind the sixth-place Padres. Florida is 33-40. The Mets are 21-51.

Sunday, June 27: San Francisco 5, Colorado 0

The first time the Rockies are shut out at Candlestick.

2:05 at Candlestick Park
The starting pitchers: Leskanic (0-0) vs. Swift (9-4)
The W-L pitchers: Swift (10-4) and Leskanic (0-1)
The attendance: 45,408
The News headline: Swift makes quick work of Rockies
The Post headline: Rockies dealt Swift loss

On the field: Curt Leskanic makes his ML debut and begins shakily. He hits the first man he faces, then walks the next on four straight pitches. And little goes particularly right for Leskanic or his teammates the rest of the afternoon.

Bill Swift pitches very quickly and the game is completed in a minute short of two hours.

With the help of Colorado's baserunning boners, Swift faces the minimum 18 Rockies through the first six innings.

He even manages to induce Galarraga to strike out thrice en route to a rare day without a hit.

The Rockies now have a record of 26-48. This earns them sole possession of last place in the NL West, 2.5 games behind the Padres. Curiously, the Rox have identical 13-24 records against the National League's East and West divisions.

Monday, June 28: Don Baylor's 44th birthday. His gift: A day off. Curiously, it was on this date in 1987 that Baylor, batting DH for the California Angels, was struck by a pitch for the 244th time in his career. The record.

Tuesday, June 29: Atlanta 6, Colorado 4

Baylor's first victory over an umpire.

5:40 at Atlanta-Fulton County Stadium
The starting pitchers: Ruffin (3-3) vs. Smoltz (6-7)
The W-L pitchers: Smoltz (7-7) and Ruffin (3-4)
The attendance: 48,974
The News headline: Rockies strike out against Braves 6-4
The Post headline: Blauser snuffs 7th-inning rally

On the field: Ump Kerwin Danley calls a balk on Ruffin when he throws to Andres who is ten feet off the bag. Seems that in the AL and the minors, it *is* a balk when the infielder isn't in a reasonable position to apply a tag. But this is the NL and Baylor is wise to the fine points of the game, so he argues—and wins.

Other than that, a three-run outburst by the Rocks in the sixth, and a minor threat in the seventh, Colorado fans watching on TV have little to cheer them.

John Smoltz mows down the Rockies with ease. They whiff a dozen times and the Braves run their dominance of the new kids to 5-0. (Atlanta is the only team the Rockies haven't managed to beat at least once.)

Galarraga is one-for-four and drops to .411. Cat still hasn't oh-fered in two games in a row.

In Dick Kreck's column, the idea of installing a mountain skyline fence at Coors Field is once again raised. And praised.

The outfield wall would be bumpy and would match the mountainscape looking west from Denver. Pikes Peak would be at the left field foul pole, Longs Peak at the right. "It's a home run right over Mount Evans!"

It would be our ivy, our Green Monster, our special thing that makes Coors Field special.

The Rockies are now 26-49 on the season, have lost two in a row, are in last place, 24.5 games behind (2 behind the Padres). At 22-52, the Mets are worse.

Wednesday, June 30: Atlanta 3, Colorado 2
The second time the Rox went into the ninth tied with the Braves —and lost.

5:40 at Atlanta-Fulton County Stadium
The starting pitchers: Blair (3-5) vs. Avery (9-2)
The W-L pitchers: Wohlers (2-0) and Shepherd (1-2)
The attendance: 48,791
The News headline: Rockies fumble their way to another loss
The Post headline: Gant lifts Braves over Rockies 3-2

On the field: It was horrible, really. Two errors in the third (both by -gasp!- Galarraga) led to Atlanta's first run.

Each team gets a run in the fourth. Atlanta gets its via a homer by Gant. Colorado gets its the old-fashioned way—it earns it.

In the seventh, Bichette homers the Rockies into a 2-2 tie. And that's the score when the game goes into the bottom of the ninth.

Then it happens. A double and two sacrifices and another L is added to the Rockies' record.

Really quite disheartening for Willie Blair and Keith Shepherd, both of whom pitch strong games.

The Rockies now have a three-game losing streak and a record of 26-50. This puts them in last place, two games behind the sixth-place Padres and 24.5 games behind the division-leading Giants. The Marlins are 34-42, the Mets 23-52.

The Rockies' first June: Won 12, lost 15.

Thursday, July 1: Atlanta 4, Colorado 0

The first shutout by the Braves.

5:40 at Atlanta-Fulton County Stadium
The starting pitchers: Reynoso (5-3) vs. Glavine (9-3)
The W-L pitchers: Glavine (10-3) and Reynoso (5-4)
The attendance: 45,252
The News headline: Braves shackle Rockies
The Post headline: Braves' Glavine blanks Rockies to
    end 1-6 trip

On the field: It's Thursday, so the Rockies take a dive. They've won just one Thursday game all season. Tonight's Braves win makes it a 7-0 series for Turner's team.

The Braves' Tom Glavine flings just 92 pitches on the way to a four-hit shutout.

Galarraga, who's been struggling at the plate of late, gets one of the four and keeps his head above .400.

Meanwhile, Atlanta manufactures a run in the first inning out of a couple of singles. They make it 3-0 on Bream's home run in the fourth. Then Reynoso is replaced by newly acquired reliever Scott Service, who debuts by quickly allowing the Braves to score runs #3 and #4 on an Olson homer in the sixth.

The Rockies have now lost four in a row, have a record of 26-51, and are in last place, 25 games out of first and 2.5 games out of sixth. The Marlins are 35-42. The Mets are 23-53.

Friday, July 2: Chicago 11, Colorado 8
The game with seven Rox pitchers. To no avail.

> **7:05 at Mile High Stadium**
> **The National Anthem:** Blues Traveler
> **The first ball:** Rebecca Miller (Coca-Cola)
> **The starting pitchers:** Henry (2-7) vs. Hibbard (7-4)
> **The W-L pitchers:** Bautista (3-2) and Shepherd (1-3)
> **The attendance:** 62,037
> **The News headline:** Pitching betrays Rockies again
> **The Post headline:** Sosa and Cubs batter Rockies 11-8

On the field: Twenty-one hits by the Cubs, six by Sosa.

Indeed, the procession of Rockies' pitchers is wretched. Tonight, the worst performances of the seven moundsmen is turned in by starter Henry (eight hits and five runs in 2 1/3) and Service (six hits and three runs in 1 2/3).

The Unmagnificent Seven let the Cubs score in every inning but the fourth and ninth.

Galarraga shows up, though. Cat delivers two doubles and leaves the park with a .403 average.

Not that it did much good, but the Rockies' batters hit nine doubles tonight, a franchise record.

In the stands: Bill Koerber has proclaimed himself as the judge of goodness of performances of the National Anthem. His criterion, apparently, is *Not Messing With It.*

The Rockies have now lost five in a row, have a 26-52 record, and are in last place in the NL West. Florida is 36-42 and is next-to-last in the NL East. The Mets are 12.5 games further back!

124

The Colorado Rockies' first come-from-behind-in-the-9th win.

7:05 at Mile High Stadium
The National Anthem: Vikki Rae Jordan
The first ball: Don Gallegos (King Soopers)
The starting pitchers: Leskanic (0-1) vs. Castillo (2-5)
The W-L pitchers: Reed (4-2) and Myers (1-2)
The attendance: 63,826
The News headline: Rockies light it up in 9th
The Post headline: Rockies' fireworks burn Cubs

On the verge: Andres Galarraga goes 1-for-4, which drops his average to .401. But it is announced today that he has been named June's National League Player of the Month.

The trivia-packed mind of Barrie Sullivan points out that the last National Leaguer to bat .401 for a season was Bill Terry. 63 years ago.

On the field: The bottom line is that the Rockies score three runs in the bottom of the ninth inning to overtake the Chicago Cubs and win the game, 5-4.

As is traditional, Leskanic struggles in the first and gives up a couple of runs. (Then he settles down and allows just one hit over the next five innings.)

Bichette put the Rox' first run up with a solo homer in the opening inning.

When the final inning arrives the score is Cubs 4, Rockies 2. And on the mound for the Cubs is Randy Myers—who has recorded a save in 25 of his last 26 opportunities.

Whereupon: With one out, Tatum draws a walk, Castilla, Hayes and Sheaffer all single, Young walks to load the bases and up steps Chris Jones. Who singles in the winning run to the delight of all.

Yes, all. Because no one has left the park. Because there are post-game fireworks in the offing.

In the stands: Some hoped for an extra-inning game. A verrry long extra-inning game. To push the post-game fireworks to the *actual* Fourth of July.

It is noted that there is a wind. To make the Chicagoans

feel at home.

It works for Ryne. In the minds of many—including Ryno—he gets his 2,000th career hit in the first. But on the scorecards of some, the ball that got past Eric Young shouldn't have, and it was an error, and the Sandman does not get #2,000 this night in this city.

Naturally, someone starts a rumor that Ryne Sandberg is somehow related to Carl. After all, they're both Chicago boys.

Speculation: "If David Cone married Edith Head..."

And: "If Jim Tatum had kids, they'd be Tatum Tots."

A Cub fan visiting from Chicago asks: "Why don't they show the game on those TVs by the concession stands?"

Gee. What a concept.

In the bottom of the eighth, for the first time ever, the *West* Stands begins the GO! (pause) ROCKIES! chant with the ROCKIES! part. It is, indeed, a great day.

On the air: Jeff Kingery tells his KOA audience that this is "the best game of the season."

In a hotel room in Montreal: Don Drysdale died. Age 56. Heart.

The Rockies now have a 27-52 record and reside in the cellar of the NL West, three games beneath San Diego. Florida is 36-43. The Mets are 24-54.

Sunday, July 4: Colorado 3, Chicago 1
The game that should've been the Rockies' first shutout.

7:05 at Mile High Stadium
The National Anthem: Chris & Maggie
The first ball: Nick Wright
The starting pitchers: Parrett (2-2) vs. Morgan (5-8)
The W-L pitchers: Parrett (3-2) and Morgan (5-9)
The attendance: 59,259
The News headline: Intense Parrett bears down on Cubs
The Post headline: Parrett sets up Cubs for 3-1 fall

On the field: Independence Day would've been a good day to get that first shutout.

Indeed, the Rocks' pitching staff notches its first 0 ERA game of the season, but no shutout.

Former reliever Jeff Parrett starts and is tough for 6 2/3 innings, giving up just three hits and one unearned run. (Via a dropped third strike by Sheaffer.)

Just about everybody contributes to the Rox' offense.

Galarraga goes two-for-four, ends the day with a .402 BA.

In the stands: When Galarraga snags a passing soft drink cup and sticks it in his pocket, there is concern. "That could throw off his delicate balance."

Giddy with the moment, a fan breaks out into song: "Here a Frain, there a Frain, everywhere a Frain Frain."

Followed by the refrain.

In the ladies' rest room: Janine Turner (Northern Exposure's Maggie) is spotted touching up her makeup. Not surprising, since the newspapers have determined that she and Cubby firstbaseman Mark Grace are itemized.

Today's Milestone: Vinny Castilla's birthday (1967)

The Rockies have now won two in a row, have a record of 28-52, and are in last place, two games behind the Padres. The Marlins are 36-44.

Monday, July 5: Chicago 10, Colorado 1
The game that marked the first season's halfway point.

> **7:05 at Mile High Stadium**
> **The National Anthem:** Douglas County High School (a dozen or so)
> **The first ball:** Allen Pridemore, 8
> **The starting pitchers:** Blair (3-5) vs. Harkey (5-2)
> **The W-L pitchers:** Harkey (6-2) and Blair (3-6)
> **The attendance:** 55,185
> **The News headline:** Home-run bug bites Blair, Rockies
> **The Post headline:** Cubs hammer Rockies 10-1

On the field: It's the Cubbies' final visit to The Frenzied Confines for 1993. They begin making sure they'll have nice memories of Mile High in the fourth when they bat around on Blair and take a 4-0 lead. The partisan crowd has zip to cheer until the seventh, when the Rocks open with three hits. Alas, they are able to manage but one score from it, the minimum required for shutout avoidance.

This is the 19th game in which the Rockies' pitching staff has been victimized for double-digit run production.

Ryne Sandberg smacks his 2,000th hit. According to reports, the Rockies' classy general manager Bob Gebhard sent Ryno a bottle of champagne to mark the occasion—but Cubs management did nothing.

In the stands: The Nuggets' sign is observed by about a third of those in attendance. That's the one out there in the Nuggies' parking lot, the annoying one which tells time and temp and gives a countdown to the Nuggets' season—and pointedly flashes the logos of products that compete with the brands that paid very large dollars to be sponsors of the Rockies. No doubt, the Rockies would like to see it EJECTED and maybe even ARRESTED.

But it provides much-needed diversion on a day like today. Yup, it's still one minute later in Nuggetville.

When John Mason blows out his flip-flops: "Going barefoot in the men's room here is something I don't think I want to experience."

Highlight of day in the stands: In the fourth, a guy in section 117 caught a foul ball off the bat of Cubs' centerfielder Wilson—in his cap!

Accountant Randy Hay busily tracks Galarraga, noting that, at 8:14, after grounding out 6-3, the Cat has slipped to .3992094, but when he doubles at 9:01, he's back up to .4015748. To round it off.

When the Rocks are down, 9-1, the musical selection is "I Believe in Magic." But nobody does.

Fantalk: "Oh well, I guess there'll be one game like this in a season.

And: "We may have to resort to the ultimate thing you can do when a game gets really ugly. We may have to yell 'UP IN FRONT!'"

The stuffing of the ballot box for Galarraga is over.

No longer do ushers push fistfuls of ballots at you as you enter. "I kind of miss not voting," says a fan.

Someone develops a new stupid yell that's supposed to distract the Cubs' Steve Buechele. Here's how it goes. "Give me a Bue!" "Bue!" "Give me a Chele!" "Chele!" "Forget the Chele and what've you got?" "Bue!"

Eleven-year-old Caitlin Kreck has a question for her dad:

"What if a guy hit a home run and then died of a heart attack and couldn't run around the bases?" Good question. Dad is stumped. He calls on the Fans' Ombudsman to investigate same.

The F.O. gets this answer from umpire Eric Gregg: "We'd get a new runner and the run scores," Gregg straightfaces, "and we'd just have to get rid of the dead body."

After the game, fans use the fact that the season is half over to project the final numbers.

"Let's see... We've won 28, so we'll double that to get the final number of wins—56. And we'll double Galarraga's batting average, too. We project him to wind up the season with a batting average of .800."

Nobody wants to do it, but somebody has to. So the Rockies' season's losses, 53, are also doubled. Hmm. That appears to exceed the much-to-be-avoided one-hundred.

Getting real serious about these matters, the fans double the Marlins' record and get 72-90. Not bad. Even considering the payroll.

The numbers on the 'board bring sad news, then good.

After failing to hit his first two times at-bat, The Big Cat's BA plummets below .400 to .399. He later gets a hit and goes home at exactly .400.

Today's milestone: The Major League owners officially awarded a National League franchise to Denver and the Colorado Baseball Partnership announced the team will be known as the Colorado Rockies and revealed the team logo (version one, with the baseball flying toward the mountains) (1991)

The Rockies now have a 28-53 record and are in last place, three games behind San Diego.

Tuesday, July 6: Colorado 8, Florida 3

The game that started off as a total disaster and went uphill from there.

7:05 at Mile High Stadium
The National Anthem: Joyce Campana (Central City
    Opera)
The first ball: Todd Macey, 7
The starting pitchers: Reynoso (5-4) vs. Hough (4-8)
The W-L pitchers: Reynoso (6-4) and Hough (4-9)
The attendance: 47,528
The News headline: Rally-minded Rockies blow by
    Marlins
The Post headline: Rockies elude Marlins

Through the turnstiles clicks the 2.5 millionth fan of the
inaugural season today.

On the field: Reynoso gives up a home run on the second pitch
of the game, but winds up upping his record at home to 4-0, with
the help of two-run homers by Andres and Dante. One each.

Galarraga's blast, a 473-footer, will wind up as the
longest anyone hits in Mile High all season. It is, however, his
only hit in three at-bats and after the game, he's batting a sliver
under .400 for the first time since June 4.

Reed provides a frightening adventure-in-an-inning when
he is summoned to protect the Rox' 4-3 lead with a man on in
the eighth. First thing he does is walk a guy and hit another to
load the bases. Then, three pitches later, he is out of the jam.
Got a pop up and a line out.

In the stands: When Henry Cotto smacks the second pitch of
the game over the wall, someone says, "Oh, well, it's only a
game." The time is noted: 7:08, the earliest that statement's
ever been made. At a night game.

Some fans buy extra provisions (primarily beer) tonight
in preparation for a particularly lengthy game. Seems they've
heard that the pitches of Marlins' knuckleballer Charlie Hough
take a long time to get to the plate.

Some fans—it's unclear which team they are for—begin a
cheer which goes like this: "Hough! Hough! Hough!"

130

Which brings this response from a well-meaning fan: "Do you guys need the Heimlich maneuver?"

Somebody points out that Hough was drafted by L.A. back in 1966. And somebody else notes that "I was still alive and well then."

"It's just 86° at game time," says Regis G. "The Marlins probably think it's a little chilly."

Bob the Beerman: "Would you like some peanuts to wash down that beer?"

And observers of such phenomena claim that this is the first day that iced tea is offered in the stands. ($2.)

Fantalk: "I read they're giving patches to the Rockies players who want to quit using tobacco."

"Wish they'd give 'em patches for their *pants*."

And: "Wonder where umpires come from?"

"As children, they were told to CLEAN YOUR PLATE!"

And: "What's the name of that baseball clown guy?"

"Al Schacht? Max Patkin? Dante Bichette?"

Fans had put forth substantial effort to make Galarraga a starter on the All-Star team. Now word has it that many of the ballots—perhaps tens of thousands of them—are going to be trashed by the vote counters because it is obvious that they were gang-punched.

This news sets not well with the faithful, some of whom are said to have punched ballots at the rate of a thou per ball game. With the encouragement of the Rockies.

And it raises questions. Did Rockies management—very big on rules—know the rules of All-Star balloting and counting? If no, why not? If yes, why didn't they pass that info on to the fans so they could've kept their ballots from being invalidated?

Bill Koerber makes this tasteful observation: "Andres Galarraga is the only guy in baseball whose last name sounds like the noise you make with mouthwash."

And Bill Hook notes that the opposing team should be called the Florida Marlin. Singular. Because fish are typically spoken of in the singular no matter how many there are. As in "I caught three trout, five bass, and two swordfish." All agree with the wisdom of this observation.

But then, with a name like Hook, he should know of what he speaks.

[The thrower of tonight's First Ball, Todd Macey, is the son of Neil Macey, a key figure in the battle to bring MLB to Denver. Macey the elder acquires a sequence of pictures of the younger's one-shot on the Mile High mound, has them blown up and framed and puts them on display in the reception area of his office in the DTC.]

The Rockies are now 29-53, and are in the cellar of the NL West by two games. The only other team in the majors that has yet to win its 30th game is the Mets. The Hapless Nine is 25-56.

Wednesday, July 7: Colorado 6, Florida 5
The game the Rockies won after falling five runs behind.

> **7:05 at Mile High Stadium**
> **The National Anthem:** The Plaids
> **The first ball:** Doug Watson (Wendy's)
> **The starting pitchers:** Shepherd (1-3) vs. Hammond (10-4)
> **The W-L pitchers:** Reed (5-2) and Harvey (1-2)
> **The attendance:** 50,707
> **The News headline:** Jones' heroics rescue Rockies again
> **The Post headline:** Ruffin a hit; Rockies roll

On the field: It's the first start in Shepherd's major league career. Auspicious it ain't. When he leaves in the third, the herder has given up two two-run homers and put his team into a five-run deficit.

With Hammond on the mound, a winner of eight decisions in a row, the Marlins appear to be in the fishbird seat.

Then the Rockies turn the ball over to Bruce Ruffin, and, later, to Steve Reed, and the Marlins get no more runs this day.

But the Rockies do. A Sheaffer homer in the third makes it 5-1. A Galarraga triple in the fourth leads to another score. And Ruffin takes bat in hand to open the fifth. Ruffin, who hasn't gotten a hit in over three years. Naturally, he strokes a double and scores when Jones does the same. In the seventh, Benavides knocks in two. And then, in the ninth, Young gets on, steals second, goes to third on a ground out, and, with two out, scores on Jones' single.

The five-run deficit is gone like day-old cotton candy. And the Marlins' losing streak is extended to five.

In the stands: In Section 107, Row 13, six guys play a game that Justin Franks and his pals invented while at Arizona State.

Here's how it works: The first guy gets the first batter, the second gets the second, and on and on, using all batters from both teams (including pitchers) rotating through the six players.

When your batter gets a single, all the other guys pay you a buck. Two bucks for a double and so on up to four bucks for a homer. (There is one additional rule: When your guy is a base runner and gets thrown out attempting to steal, you give the money back.)

Todd Vollmer was the big winner, winding up fifty or sixty dollars ahead. The big loser, Rob, winds up minus $25.

Today's other losers of note include Andres Galarraga, who wasn't voted onto the All-Star team after all. After all those votes. In fact, he finished fourth among firstbasemen behind John Kruk, Fred McGriff, and Will Clark.

The Rockies have now won two straight, have won 30 games (and lost 53) and are in last place, two games behind the Padres.

Thursday, July 8: Colorado 3, Florida 2

The first game won by Leskanic
—and the first sweep of the Marlins.

3:05 at Mile High Stadium
The National Anthem: Amy Carlon
The first ball: Dode Hammack (Continental Airlines)
The starting pitchers: Leskanic (0-1) vs. Rapp (0-0)
The W-L pitchers: Leskanic (1-1) and Rapp (0-1)
The attendance: 56,807
The News headline: Rockies sweep Marlins
The Post headline: Doors opened for Leskanic

On the field: In its long history, Mile High Stadium has never seen a genuine, nine-inning no-hitter, and the last one-hit game was thrown by Ryne Duren back in the fifties.

That's what they say.

(Others say Duren hurled a no-hitter, but it was in a seven-inning game.)

In today's contest, Leskanic is super-effective, shutting down the Marlins (or Blowfish, as a certain commentator calls them on KOA) on just one hit in 6 2/3 innings.

The Marlin's first hit comes in the third when their pitcher, Pat Rapp, lucks himself a bloop single in the third, *the first hit in his ML career.*

Shutout hopes vanish when Darren Holmes gives up a pair of hits, the second of which was a homer.

[As it will turn out, this will be Leskanic's only W of the season.]

In the stands: Brooms are in evidence. Whisk. Fireplace. Plastic. And, of course, full-size, but with sawed-off handles to comply with the NO STICKS rule. With the sweep o' the Floridans, they are soon employed to good effect.

"How," a fan wonders, "can they have a NO STICKS rule and still sell pennants?"

Evidently, this is a riddle wrapped in an enigma inside an infield fly rule. A ballpark conundrum that nobody will ever comprehend.

After staring at his scorecard, a fan discovers that four of the Marlins—Cris Carpenter, Alex Aries, Bret Barberie and Walt Weiss—have first and last names beginning with the same letter. And *none* of the Rockies do. The closest is Steve Reed.

Cookie Rojas is coaching third for the Marlins, which causes fans to think of all the other baseball luminaries whose first names are pastries. But they could only come up with one—Pie Traynor. It was decided that Bake McBride doesn't count. And Candy Maldonado is a confection. And Carmelo Martinez is misspelled.

The Rockies' fans have already put up attendance numbers that are larger than all but four teams achieved last season. More amazingly, they've surpassed the single-season attendance records of 12 franchises. And it is just July. Early July.

The organist makes a good point when he challenges a questionable call by the ump with "It Ain't Necessarily So."

Bobby D. has come up with a new inner-city pronouncement to yell at the men in blue: "Dis the umpire!"

From heaven (or someplace that's quite near it), comes the announcement. Galarraga is Bobby Cox' choice as the Rockies' representative on the All-Star team. Yes, every team gets to have one. Charlie Hayes is of the belief that the 1993 model ought to have two from the Rocks and can and does put forth a strong argument in favor of his selection as a reserve. After all, Hayes sits with numbers of .310, 12, and 52.

Maybe if, every once in a while, he ran like hell...

The Rockies have now won three in a row and have a record of 31-53, good enough for last place, a game out of next-to-last.

Friday, July 9: Colorado 5, St. Louis 4

The first win for Marcus Moore. And the first time the Rox won four straight.

6:35 at Busch Stadium
The starting pitchers: Parrett (3-2) vs. Arocha (6-3)
The W-L pitchers: Moore (1-0) and Smith (2-2)
The attendance: 41,466
The News headline: Rockies pull out another
The Post headline: Rockies HRs trump Cards 5-4

On the field: At 8:50 MDT, Marcus Moore flings his first ML pitch. He tosses only five of them in relief to retire the side in the 8th inning, but his timing is great because, in the top of the 9th, his teammates come back to take the lead on a pair of homers off Lee Smith (!) by Danny Sheaffer and Chris Jones and wind up winning their fourth in a row—a first.

To say St. Louis was stunned by this turn of events would be correct.

Jones has been responsible for more heroics in the last week than you can shake a bat at: Last Saturday, his ninth-inning hit won it for the Rox. Last Wednesday, ditto. And now tonight.

And the three pitchers victimized by the young Rock? Bryan Harvey, Randy Myers, and Lee Smith.

Galarraga has gone hitless for consecutive games for the first time of the season, and has dropped to .390.

The Rockies have now won four in a row (for the first time in their history) and have a record of 32-53. They remain in the cellar, 25 games out of first, but are just three percentage points behind the Padres.

Saturday, July 10: St. Louis 9, Colorado 3
The game that Brian Jordan won all by himself.

6:05 at Busch Stadium
The starting pitchers: Henry (2-7) vs. Osborne (7-3)
The W-L pitchers: Osborne (8-3) and Henry (2-8)
The attendance: 53,146 (largest in Busch Stadium history)
The News headline: Henry hits rock bottom
The Post headline: Cardinals punch Henry's ticket

On the field: Jordan goes 4-for-4, knocks in three and scores two himself. That's enough.

That's enough to put an end to the Rockies' longest win streak—four—of the season.

That's enough for Don Baylor, too. After Butch Henry's lackluster performance, he is sent down to the Springs.

On the warpath: Randy Rutherford, owner of the Champion Brewing Co., is circulating a petition to *force* the Rockies to put players' names on their backs.

His friends hope that petitioning isn't against one of The Rules, like flash photography in the stands.

The Rockies are now 32-54 on the season, which puts them in last place in the NL West, but only barely. The Rox are three percentage points behind the 33-55 Padres.

Sunday, July 11: Colorado 4, St. Louis 1
The game that pulled the Rocks out of last place.

12:15 at Busch Stadium
The starting pitchers: Reynoso (6-4) vs. Tewskbury (9-6)
The W-L pitchers: Reynoso (7-4) and Tewksbury (9-7)

The attendance: 44,105
The News headline: Hot Rockies finally make break from cellar
The Post headline: Rockies climb out of cellar

On the field: Baylor juggles his starters to give Reynoso this extra start before the All Star break and is almost rewarded with the Rockies' first-ever shutout.

Almost.

Still, the Rox' take the series from the Cardinals, a team that had just swept the plenty powerful Braves in their previous series. Reynoso tosses seven strong innings, and gives up just five hits and one unearned run. A passed ball by Sheaffer sets up the Cards' solitary score.

Reed is super tough in his two-inning stint as the closer and gets the first ML save of his career.

The Rockies' batting heroics are provided primarily by Clark, who is 3-for-4 with a two-run homer.

Today's milestone: Andy Ashby's birthday (1967)

At the All-Star break, the Rockies have a record of 33-54, which pulls them out of last place just in time to be subjected to the national spotlight.

They are now in sixth place of the NL West, 25 games behind the Giants and a game ahead of the Padres. Atlanta is in second place of the division, nine games out of first.

Gathered around a TV set at a party in Denver's Belcaro neighborhood: A fan worries that the Rockies' All-Star rep, Galarraga, won't get into the game.

"I guess," he says, "they probably won't put him in as a pinch runner." Probably not.

On Tuesday, July 13, at 9:13 p.m. MDT: The first representative of the Colorado Rockies in the history of the All-Star Game comes to the plate. It is the eighth inning and his team trails 9-3, which turns out to be the final score. Because, with two men in scoring position, Andres Galarraga pops out to the shortstop in shallow left field. It's his only plate appearance.

Of course, as Woody says, Galarraga's out didn't count against his batting average.

The Denver Restaurant Relief Fund
(A Mid-Season Plea by John Hickenlooper)

In the battle to bring Major League Baseball to Denver, no group worked harder, no group sacrificed more, no group longed lustier than metropolitan restaurant owners.

But we have been betrayed.

Call it the school of hard knocks. I refer to hard knocks of the extra base variety. The barrage of extra-base hits and endless big innings has elongated Rockies games tremendously.

When a game starts at 7:05 and continues almost to 11:00, only the hardiest fans even consider a postgame meal. Indeed, the siren's song of slumber beckons ever so sweetly.

Rockies pitchers have achieved earned run averages that could be mistaken for Olympic diving scores. Not coincidentally, downtown restaurants are averaging an 18% drop in revenues when the Rockies are at home.

What do we need? A Relief Fund. Yes, area restaurants must once again band together. This time to raise monies to bolster the bullpen.

Certainly, Jerry McMorris and the other scions controlling the Rockies will be asked to pay their share. They probably should match the Relief Fund dollar for new dollar.

But it'll be up to the restaurants to take the initiative. A voluntary 1/10 of 1% sales tax, benefit concerts, recycling campaigns—whatever it takes.

At any given Rockies game, 60,000 fun-loving, normally food-oriented citizens of this fair city are being sucked out of the city's restaurant economy.

The time to act is now. The future of fine dining as we know it is at stake.

Thursday, July 15: Chicago 1, Colorado 0

The first game for Roberto Mejia.

6:05 at Wrigley Field
The starting pitchers: Blair (3-6) vs. Morgan (6-9)
The W-L pitchers: Morgan (7-9) and Blair (3-7)
The attendance: 38,765
The News Headline: Mejia debut begins with loss to Cubs
The Post Headline: Rockies draw a blank against Cubs

In the News: Bob Kravitz states that Alex Cole "has the baseball instincts of a wild yak."

On the field: The Cubs' starter goes all the way. The Rockies enjoy a (rare) nicely pitched game, too. Willie Blair pitches seven strong innings and allows just one run (and that of the unearned variety), and yet he loses the game, 1-0. Each team gets just five hits.

Roberto Mejia, the much-heralded future superstar for the Rockies, gets none of them in his ML debut. In first AB, he flies out—at 6:11 MDT. In fact, the barely-21-year-old makes a critical error that leads to the only run of the game. And he strikes out to end an inning with a man on third.

Charlie Hayes gets three of the five Rockies hits, but was thrown out stealing. As was Cole.

The Rockies are now 33-55 (.375) on the season, and have dropped back into last place a few percentage points behind the Padres and 26 games behind the leaders, San Francisco.

Friday, July 16: Chicago 8, Colorado 2
The first ML hit for Roberto Mejia.

1:20 at Wrigley Field
The starting pitchers: Leskanic (1-1) vs. Guzman (7-7)
The W-L pitchers: Guzman (8-7) and Leskanic (1-2)
The attendance: 39,281
The News Headline: Leskanic's false start a bust again
The Post Headline: Rockies leave their bats at home
  again

In the world of strange trades, the Rockies have traded Butch Henry to the Expos for Kent Bottenfield, the pitcher who was bombed in the home opener and occupies an unenviable place in history as the first hurler to lose to the Rocks.

(Perhaps this explains his hobby. In his spare time, Bottenfield writes contemporary Christian music.)

Two more pitchers are gone. Shepherd has been demoted to the SSox. And, instead of accepting assignment to the Sky Sox, injured Rudy Seañez declared himself a free agent and joined the San Diego organization.

On the field: Guzman permits the Rockies only three hits in the first eight innings and just six total. They manage two one-run innings. Nothing more.

Meanwhile, the Cubs tee off on Leskanic. Already famous for hitting the first guy he faced in his ML debut and walking the next, Leskanic adds to the legend by walking the first two Cubs this afternoon. Moments later, Sammy Sosa's homer gives the Cubs a three-run first inning. Later, another homer, this time by Derrick May, powers another three-run stanza.

Guzman strikes out 11 Rockies and gets 26 of the 27 requisite outs before he leaves.

Meanwhile, the Rockies parade four pitchers, all of whom are tagged for hits.

Roberto Mejia's first big league hit is a double in the ninth which leads to the Rocks' ninth-inning score.

On the Field of Dreams: All is well. Word has it from Iowa that the floods that have done so much damage in the midwest haven't reached the modern-day baseball icon.

The Rockies have now lost two in a row, are 33-56 on the season, and reside in the cellar, 27 games out of first. The Fish have been reeling of late, leaving the Marlins with a 37-52 record. They're now 19 out of first, ten ahead of the last-place Mets.

Saturday, July 17: Chicago 5, Colorado 1
The game in which Alex Cole came the closest to hitting a home run.

> **2:05 at Wrigley Field**
> **The starting pitchers:** Reynoso (7-4) and Harkey (6-3)
> **The W-L pitchers:** Harkey (7-3) and Reynoso (7-5)
> **The attendance:** 39,522
> **The News Headline:** Harkey, Cubs keep stone-cold
>   Rockies in post-break funk
> **The Post Headline:** Rockies don't bat an eye at Cubs

On the field: Held to five hits today, the Rockies continue to be plagued by rampant punchlessness. It takes the Cubs' Mark Harkey just four pitches to mow down the Rox in the fifth.

Through eight, he permits just three hits.

Reynoso gets off to a dandy start, too. Indeed, he pitches four innings of perfection. Then, in the fifth, he lets the Cubbies pick up two runs, and that is all they need.

The Rox escape the shutout when they touch closer Myers for a run in the ninth on a Mejia double followed by a Galarraga single.

Bichette falls below .300 for the first time in a month and a half.

Cole knocks a ball off the ivy-covered outfield wall. It almost ends the longest homerless streak—1,141 at-bats—of any active big league player. Cole is quoted as saying "Almost only counts in horseshoes and hand grenades."

And dancing, Alex.

The Rockies have now lost three in a row, have a 33-57 record, and are in last place in the NL West, two games behind San Diego. The Marlins are 38-52. The Mets are 28-62.

Sunday, July 18: Chicago 12, Colorado 2
The first rain-shortened game in Rockies history.

12:20 at Wrigley Field
The starting pitchers: Parrett (3-2) vs. Hibbard (7-6)
The W-L pitchers: Hibbard (8-6) and Parrett (3-3)
The attendance: 39,022
The News Headline: Baylor sounds alarm
The Post Headline: Rockies are total washout at Wrigley

On the field: Mother Nature is a Rockies fan. Must be. She mercifully ends this one after seven innings.

It began ugly with a capital ug. The Cubs explode for eight runs in the first inning and the game goes downhill—and downpour—the rest of the way.

As Official Gamedom approached, Baylor & Co. try all the stalling techniques known to man hoping to get this game washed away. Double switching. Galarraga consulting with the pitcher (?). Shoelace tying. Even taking strikes. But to no avail.

And so the Rockies suffer their second four-game sweep

of the season. And they can't believe they couldn't go deep once in four games in The Confines.

Meanwhile, the Cubs celebrate having won their first season series from the Rockies, eight games to four. And enjoy seeing their rookie outfielder Kevin Roberson get his first ML hit and, later, his first ML HR.

Galarraga, meanwhile, is skyrocketing downward. His BA has dropped 49 points in the last 21 games. And Mejia's four ML hits consist of one bunt single and three doubles.

The Rockies have now lost four in a row, have a record of 33-58, and are in last place, two games behind San Diego. The Marlins and Mets records are 38-53 and 29-62.

Monday, July 19: Florida 3, Colorado 1
Bottenfield's first start as a Rocky.

5:35 at Joe Robbie Stadium
The starting pitchers: Bottenfield (2-5) vs. Bowen (4-9)
The W-L pitchers: Bowen (5-9) and Bottenfield (2-6)
The attendance: 34,703
The News Headline: Punchless Rockies fall to Marlins 3-1
The Post Headline: Rockies' bats remain ice cold in the Florida heat

On the field: Before the game, Baylor calls a team meeting. He juggles his lineup, too. Anything to snap the four-game draught since the All-Star break. But soon it is a five-game draught.

Kent Bottenfield drives in the Rockies' only run, but ruins his initial outing by giving up a trio of runs on four hits in six innings.

Of course, the Rocks could've given him a little more offensive support. They got men to third with one out on several occasions, but failed to score.

All of this notwithstanding, Baylor is reported to say he wouldn't trade his team for the Marlins' squad. Even with Weiss, Sheffield and Harvey thereupon.

The Rockies have now lost five in a row, have a 33-59 record (.359) and are in last place, two games out of sixth. Only the Mets have a worse record, 30-62.

Tuesday, July 20: Colorado 6, Florida 3
The Rockies' first game played without batting practice.

5:35 at Joe Robbie Stadium
The starting pitchers: Blair (3-7) vs. Hammond (10-5)
The W-L pitchers: Blair (4-7) and Hammond (10-6)
The attendance: 31,852
The News Headline: Rockies reel in Marlins
The Post Headline: Rockies answer wake-up call

On the field, which is wet: The rain stops in time to play the game, but not soon enough to permit batting practice. No matter. The Rox score six runs, matching their total for the five previous games since the All-Star break, all of which were deposited in the L column.

The Rockies' bats catch fire the same night the press box area of Atlanta-Fulton County Stadium does.

Highlights include the biggest blast in Joe Robbie's ML history—a 455' shot by Andres Galarraga. And The Big Cat's Big Stretch to make the dramatic double play with the bases loaded that ends the sixth and keeps the Rockies in the lead, 3-2.

Then, in the top of the seventh, Dante Bichette puts the game away with a three-run blast.

The win gives the Rox a 7-4 record against the Florida Fish & Game Dept. (as Woody Paige calls them), which means The Purple has guaranteed itself a win in the season's battle vs. The Teal.

In the New Yorker: A cartoon shows a disgruntled TV watcher whose wife makes this observation: "I see we're not wearing our Mets cap." It hasn't come to that in Denver. Yet.

In King Soopers: Kellogg's Frosted Flakes with Tony the Tiger wearing a Rockies uniform. According to the box, Frosted Flakes are fat free. So they won't be confused with certain members of the team.

The Rockies now have a record of 34-59, good enough for a spot in the NL West's cellar, 28 games behind the leaders (S.F.) and two games behind the sixth-place Padres.

Wednesday, July 21: Florida 6, Colorado 4

The last game of the season against those other expansionists.

5:35 at Joe Robbie Stadium
The starting pitchers: Leskanic (1-2) vs. Rapp (0-2)
The W-L pitchers: Rapp (1-2) and Leskanic (1-3)
The attendance: 32,129
The News Headline: Rockies fall to Marlins again and limp home
The Post Headline: Rockies don't feel like award-winners

On the field: The Rox lose the last game between the expansion teams this year, but win the season series anyway, 7-5.

Florida's rockie pitcher Pat Rapp helps himself with two RBI en route to notching his first ML victory.

Letting the opposing pitcher single on an 0-2 count is one mistake by Rox hurler Leskanic that ultimately undoes him. Another is failing to put down a sacrifice bunt with a man on and no outs in the third.

And it isn't helpful when Ruffin comes in to relieve Leskanic and promptly gives up a two-run HR to Gary Sheffield.

A ninth-inning rally fueled by doubles by Hayes and Clark pulls the Rox to within two, but it stalls when Young strikes out with a man on. The Rockies now crawl home after winning just one on their seven-game road trip.

In an article about Brooklyn's in the Post, Kreck says that Wayne Stivers is displaying some of his collection of baseball memorabilia in the sports bar. Including, according to the article, "Bunting from the 1955 World Series."

A phony, like so many so-called baseball collectibles.

Everybody knows that Jim Bunting was with Detroit in '55 and the Tigers were *not* in the series that year.

Today's milestone: Lance Painter's birthday (1967)

The Rockies now have a 34-60 record (.362) and continue to reside in the NL West basement, two games behind the Padres and 29 behind the leaders, San Francisco.

144

The first game in Denver with a mascot in attendance.

7:05 at Mile High Stadium
The National Anthem: Charles Wesley Choir (about 70 voices)
The first ball: Dan Issel
The starting pitchers: Reynoso (7-5) vs. Tewksbury (10-7)
The W-L pitchers: Holmes (1-3) and Burris (0-1)
The attendance: 56,013
The News Headline: Rockies' surge stuns Cardinals
The Post Headline: Rockies pull ace on Cards

In the Post: Credit Jim Armstrong for coming up with a primo nickname for Mile High Stadium. He calls it "the frenzied confines." Which accurately describes the scene as the Rockies win the fourteenth of their last 20 home games.

On the way in: A peddler of $1 outlaw scorecards cries out: "Get your Homestand Flyer—it's something to read while the Cardinals change pitchers!"

Prophetic. The Cards make four pitching changes en route to today's loss.

On the field: In the first inning, the Rockies take a 2-0 lead on consecutive home runs by Bichette and Galarraga. Would've been 3-0 if leadoff batter Cole hadn't been thrown out after stealing second—and then oversliding it.

Galarraga continues to hit, going three for four to pump his average up to .382.

And Reynoso continues to pick people off first base in the first inning (he's done it thrice now) and holds the Cards to two runs through five innings before he's touched for three in the sixth. The Rocks enter their half of the eighth trailing, 6-3, but emerge with a tie built out of singles—and two runs walked in on eight straight balls thrown by reliever Omar Olivares.

Now comes the ninth inning. After the DiamondVision shows a piece of "Animal House" where John Belushi exhorts the tough to get going (a new touch and one everybody seems to get a big kick out of), the Rockies respond.

Mejia opens with a bunt single. When Bichette follows with a double, Mejia is thrown out trying to score. But Bichette makes it to third on the throw and scores on Clark's sac fly.

In the stands: The Cardinal's mascot, Fredbird, hoo-hahs his way through the stands to mixed reactions. Joe Judge, visiting from St. Louis, knows who's inside the Fredbird suit. It's Tony Simokaitis, a front office operative for the Cardinals.

Joe to Fredbird: "Hi, Tony!"

Fredbird: "Hi, Mr. Judge! How are you? These fans out here are nutty!"

This from a guy dressed up like a bird.

A new sign greets those who would use the space behind the box seats as an aisle: PLEASE DO NOT USE AS AN AISLEWAY. All admire the coinage of the new word and hope it will soon be included in the dictionarybook.

The Nuggets' annoying sign over by Big Mac flashes a timely announcement: YOU'VE SEEN THE 'HORSE' PITCH – CALL 893-6700 TO SEE WHAT HE DOES BEST.

A plane flies over with another electric sign: HAPPY BIRTHDAY MARSHA.

Not counting planes overhead or the Big Mac atrocity over there, a fan counts sixteen inside-the-park advertising signs that can be seen from your seat in Mile High Stadium. (Sixteen more than you can see from your seat in Wrigley Field.)

So many signs. So many that a fan says, "It's starting to look like the Blue Bonnet around here."

At the top of the sixth inning, the groundskeepers not only smooth out the basepaths, they install fresh bases. And they do it very speedily, too. Watching this, a fan calls out: "Just call Base Monkey. Ten minutes and you're on your way!"

It is 80° at game time, so most of the starters eschew the undershirt. A fan points out that the only exception is Galarraga. "Because, in Venezuela, it's winter."

All this talk about attendance records brings this observation: "We will also set an all-time record for the most fans that have seen their team lose games in a single season."

This is the first game wherein five of the Rockies' starters speak Spanish. And the first with Freddie Benavides starting at third. And the first with an all-Latino infield.

So how do you score a double play that goes from

The Rockpile. That's where you'll find the cheapest seats in the Major Leagues. The regulars in the front row will cheer for anything. The arrival of the center-fielder at center field will do it. The dweller of the Rockpile pictured below employs a great deal of wishful thinking as he implores the batter *way over there* to hit a homer into his hat way out here.

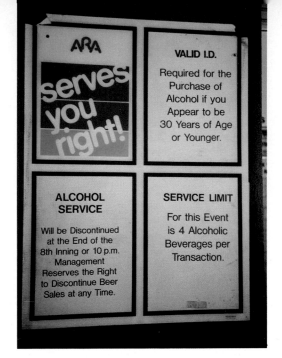

ARA. The concessionaires that control the beer taps at Mile High have different rules in Arlington Stadium (photo above) than they do in Mile High. Check the deal ARA gives Texas Rangers fans, then compare it with the sign posted behind Joyce and Joan, big sellers of Coors Light all season long in Mile High Stadium.

Marketing. A giant Cracker Jack box appeared on the scene, all the better to separate fans from $3.75. *($3.75 for Cracker Jack?)*

Bob the Beer Man (Donchez) became an instant celebrity when he loudly made the most of his vendor number, the lowest of them all.

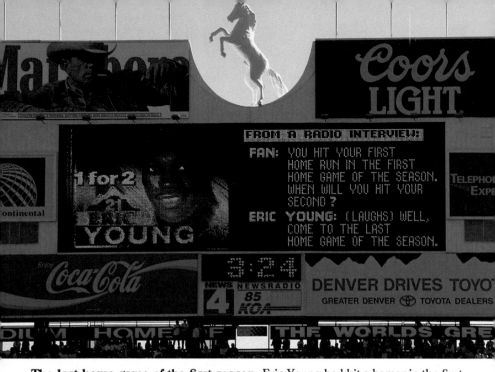

FROM A RADIO INTERVIEW

FAN: YOU HIT YOUR FIRST
HOME RUN IN THE FIRST
HOME GAME OF THE SEASON.
WHEN WILL YOU HIT YOUR
SECOND ?

ERIC YOUNG: (LAUGHS) WELL,
COME TO THE LAST
HOME GAME OF THE SEASON.

The last home game of the first season. Eric Young had hit a homer in the first home game, but no more—until the last one.

Goodbyes all around. After the game, the Colorado Rockies walked the perimeter of the playing field, saluting the best fans in the history of sports. The salute was, of course, reciprocated.

Reynoso to Mejia to Galarraga? "Uno–cuatro–tres."

And when a Cardinal bounces a ball through the left side of the infield, a fan grumbles: "With three shortstops out there, you'd think that one of 'em could've gotten that."

The Rockies now have a 35-60 record (.368) and are one game behind the sixth-place Padres. The Giants have a commanding ten-game lead in the NL West. Atlanta is second, ten games back.

Friday, July 23: St. Louis 13, Colorado 11
The game in which Mejia hit his first ML home run.

7:05 at Mile High Stadium
The National Anthem: Randy Mayfield
The first ball: Ryan Slattery, 7
The starting pitchers: Parrett (3-3) vs. Watson (1-0)
The W-L pitchers: Watson (2-0) and Reed (5-3)
The attendance: 58,513
The News Headline: Cards deal Rockies odd loss
The Post Headline: Cards fly by Rockies

On the field: The evening is hot (84°) and so are the teams. 'Twas a hitfest, with each team averaging nearly two an inning.

The Cards open with three runs in the top of the first and the Rockies come back with three of their own in the bottom, a highlight of which is a double steal which allows Bichette to notch the year's' second steal of home for a Rock

Mejia's homer—his career first—helps the Rox take a nice 6-3 lead in fifth, but it doesn't last long.

In the next inning, the Cards put four doubles together with an assortment of walks, singles and Rockies errors to score *eight* times.

Andres gets four hits and both Benavides and Young got three, but it's small consolation. The Rox wanted the W.

In Bob Gebhard's mind: A plan is cooking to acquire pitcher Greg Harris from the Padres. Harris tossed a three hitter at the Rox on June 18.

In the stands: It's Coca-Cola Lapel Pin #8 Night.

It is also, apparently, scam-in-the-stands night. Here's how it goes: When Roberto Mejia hits his first ML homer, Stieg Corell, wearing his old baseball mitt out there in the left field stands, *catches* his first ML homer. So far, so swell. But some fast-talking lowlife tries to scam 'em both out of the historic orb.

This guy says he'll take the ball to Mejia and get, in return, a jersey and a signed ball and off he goes. Turns out this guy is not a Rockies rep, so he's chased down by some guys who are and the ball is returned to Corell.

After the game, Corell and his three young sons are taken to the clubhouse to meet Mejia, whereupon the prized spheroid is turned over to the guy who smacked it over the fence in the first place. A grateful Roberto Mejia makes sure that Corell & Co. get baseballs all around, signed and dated.

The Cards' mascot, Fredbird, is surprised to meet a little kid—about five years old—wearing a tiny fredbird costume.

A father and son watch the game wearing Cardinals caps and CR caps. Yes, each is wearing two caps. Dad explains: "He's rootin' for both teams, just like his dad."

The scoreboard tells us that among tonight's groups in attendance is the "RUSH LIMBAUGH FAN CLUB – DENVER CHAPTER." In honor of which Baylor uses only right handed pitchers tonight—Bottenfield, Reed, Moore and Holmes.

The organist plays "Sixteen Tons" when Lankford comes to the plate. A good song for a heavy hitter, but *not* for an opposing batter. "Freddy, My Love" is a good choice for Benavides in the eighth inning, however. And Freddie [sic] responds with a double.

After Galarraga is issued a base on balls, an angry fan yells to the opposing pitcher: "Don't you know you're supposed to walk the dog, not walk the cat?"

Brandt M. and John C. were 7-0 on the season until tonight. Their personal win streaks are snapped by the loss.

In the Post, there's an eyewitness account of Charlie Hayes turning down autograph seekers with a sarcastic muttering of "thanks for the votes."

The **Rockies now have** a 35-61 record (.365) and reside in last place, one game out of sixth.

Saturday, July 24: Colorado 9, St. Louis 8
The NL night game attendance mark is broken—and The Cat is hurt.

7:05 at Mile High Stadium
The National Anthem: A quartet from the University of Wyoming Choir
The first ball: Lewis & Floorwax
The starting pitchers: Bottenfield (2-6) vs. Osborne (9-3)
The W-L pitchers: Bottenfield (3-6) and Osborne (9-4)
The attendance: 71,784
The News Headline: A wild win for Rockies
The Post Headline: Rockies win 9-8; Galarraga hurt

On the field: The Cardinals take a 4-0 lead in the second, but the Rockies take it right back when they match the Cards in the bottom of that inning—then add three more on Charlie Hayes' three-run homer in the next.

Bottenfield gets the win even though he gives up six runs in five innings and the ironic aspect is lost on no one: This is the guy the Rox faced in their first home game and thrashed soundly for their first victory. Now he's one of ours.

Bottenfield also can claim to having pitched before Mile High's two largest crowds of the season—tonight and in the home opener when he started for Montreal.

The victory is welcome, but when Mejia and Galarraga get tangled up going after a foul ball in the ninth inning, the crowd bids farewell to the latter. It's a leg injury. And all hope that The Big Cat will be back tomorrow to continue his battle back to .400 (with 2-for-3 tonight, he's now at .392).

In the stands: It's Beer Mug Night. And it's a night that lasts for three hours and 51 minutes, the longest nine-inning game in the NL this season. (Another 27 minutes would've tied the record for the longest nine-inning game in ML history.)

The crowd tops the heretofore unapproached record attendance mark for a night game (67,550 at L.A.—in the

Coliseum—on 4/12/60).

Jane Cady suggests that on nights with mobs like tonight's they should have lanes in the concourse. Turning lanes, through lanes—and high-occupancy express lanes for people who're carrying kids piggy-back.

The scoreboard continues to put up the "OUT OF TOWN SCORES" as it calls them. As if we may have thought that tonight's contest between Atlanta and Pittsburgh is being played in Washington Park.

Gilkey's HR for the Cards is rejected by the East Stands. In blatant violation of The Rules.

After umpire Froemming, am amply-upholstered fellow, takes broom to home plate, Pat M. says, "He missed a spot."

What? "The ump didn't get the plate clean."

You're right. "And it looks like he's cleaned quite a few plates in his time."

A semi-sharp-eyed fan reports that the discounts that the Taco Bell stands used to give on multiple purchases of tacos are no more.

A guy wearing a shirt that says, "HE WHO DIES WITH THE MOST TOYS, STILL DIES" sparks a discussion.

"He must not have season tickets."

The idea being that the time you spend in the ballyard isn't counted against you. Therefore, heavy users of baseball won't perish. Ever. Or perhaps this is closer to the truth: As long as the Rockies have their hooks into you for season tickets they won't *let* you die.

The organist has an interesting musical selection to mark the Cat's departure from the game: "Jesus Christ Superstar." Yes.

In the Rocky: Bob Kravitz contends that we are suffering "a particularly virulent strain of Broncomania having returned as Rockiemania, an affliction for which there is only one cure—four straight World Series blowout losses."

He goes on to ding the sophistication of Rockies fans, something that will bring the Rocky Mountain News lots of nasty responses from The Best Baseball Fans in the History of the Planet.

The Rockies now have a 36-61 record (.371) and are in last place, one game behind the Padres.

Sunday, July 25: St. Louis 5, Colorado 4 (11 innings)

The game that sets the attendance record for a four-game series.

1:05 at Mile High Stadium
The National Anthem: Asleep At The Wheel
The first ball: Steve Grein, 9
The starting pitchers: Blair (4-7) vs. Arocha (7-3)
The W-L pitchers: Olivares (3-2) and Wayne (2-3)
The attendance: 65,211
The News Headline: Rockies lose game, Cat
The Post Headline: Cards cuff Rockies 5-4 in 11th

Through the turnstiles: Today's crowd breaks the Rockies own ML record for a four-game series: 251,521. But only by 74 whiskers. (The previous record, set in early may, was 251,447.)

On the way to the game, listeners to KOA hear Tim Smile, reporting on Broncos' training camp, utter these words:
"The Rockies...uh, *Broncos*..." What does that tell you about the balance of power around here?

On crutches: Andres Galarraga. Doctors have diagnosed him as having a a second-degree sprain of the medial collateral ligament in his right knee. Which means is that he'll be lost from the Rockies' lineup for *at least three weeks.*

On the field: Dante tries to keep Galarraga's bat in the lineup, but breaks it his first time up.

Jayhawk Owens does his part with two homers, and the Rockies take a one-run lead into the ninth. With a sacrifice fly— and a little help from a Marcus Moore wild pitch—the Cards tie it up. When it's the Rockies turn, they squander a fine opportunity when Jayhawk Owens can't get a bunt down with two on and no outs. And the game goes into extra stanzas.

Ultimately, three eleventh-inning singles off Gary Wayne give the victory to the Cardinals.

This, the 98th game of the season, is the first to be played under protest. St. Louis manager Joe Torre feels that there's a technical impropriety involving Baylor's double switch in the 11th inning, but when the Cards win, it becomes moot.

In the stands: John M. blames the whole Owens-can't-lay-down-a-decent-bunt-when-we-need-it incident on aluminum bats. "The bats used in high school and college just don't bunt the same as the wooden kind. Besides, when you've got an aluminum bat in your hand, why would you even *want* to bunt?"

John also proclaims that Coors Field will be filled with rednecks. "No matter where you sit, the sun'll be behind you."

And he is dubious about the Cards' footwear. "I don't know if I could get up 162 days a year and put on red shoes."

How do we know that many, many church groups have chosen today to come out to the Green Cathedral? The scoreboard tells us so. Is also reveals the presence of a group that is, perhaps, in need of a bit of churching. The group's name: THE SAINTS THAT AIN'T.

Bill Swartz shows up wearing a new white CR cap. "Ask me how I got my cap."

How did you get your cap?

"I bought a case of Valvoline."

Speaking of caps, a fan wonders—particularly in this time of sensitivity to gender parity—why women don't doff their caps for the National Anthem.

A vendor is selling iced cappuccinos (aka coffee shakes) thusly: "Iced cappuccinos! Coffee shakes! Which do you want?"

Typical mean-spirited groundless anti-ARA comment: Nobody relishes AraServe relish.

When the Cardinals load the bases, the organist plays "St.Louis Blues." This leads to a lot of head scratching in the stands. An appropriate choice of tune, however, is selected to accompany Bichette to bat in the sixth: "Sledgehammer," by Peter Gabriel.

A fan has a theory. "I think Galarraga was hurt by the noise from the crowd." Huh? "Yes, I believe he collided with Mejia because they couldn't hear each other calling for the ball." So? "So there should be a new Stadium Rule: "People who yell during exciting plays will be subject to immediate ejection and arrest."

Last night's game, which ran 3:51, has fans suggesting that baseball adopt a 30-second clock.

With Eric Young in left field, someone suggests that we ought to "go easy on EY. He's playing out of position."

John M.: "Maybe we'll find that there is no position that he's not playing out of."

Looking at the way Charlie Hayes wears his cap on the back of his head, Barbara N. wonders aloud whether Hayes understands the concept of the bill on a baseball cap.

A little razzing for Brian Jordan, a former footballer spending the afternoon in center field for the Cardinals: "Hey, Jordan! Your fly pattern is open!"

And a major error is discovered in the Rockies' Media Guide. They have Zimmer listed as 195 pounds.

The Rockies now have a record of 36-62 (.367) which puts them in last place of the NL West, a game behind the Padres. In the AL West, Kansas City is but two games behind the Chisox.

Monday, July 26: Atlanta 12, Colorado 7

The first ML inside-the-park homer at Mile High.

7:05 at Mile High Stadium
The National Anthem: Nacho Men
The first ball: John Hildebrand
The starting pitchers: Leskanic (1-3) vs. Maddox (10-8)
The W-L pitchers: Maddox (11-8) and Leskanic (1-4)
The attendance: 62,937
The News Headline: Braves pile on Rockies again, 12-7
The Post Headline: Braves make it eight straight

In the News (and Post): It is reported that the Rockies made the largest trade in their history, a deal with the Padres that brings two quality pitchers to Colorado, Greg Harris and Bruce Hurst, both formerly of San Diego. This means that San Diego replaces Colorado as the team with the lowest payroll in ML baseball.

To get the two hurlers, the Rockies had to give up Brad Ausmus, Doug Bochtler and Andy Ashby.

On the field: The Rockies go 0-and-8 against the Braves for the season and, for that matter, the entirety of their existence. The Braves can continue to boast that they're the only team the Rocks haven't rocked.

The temperature at game time is 86° and both teams take turns being hot. The Braves blast four home runs, one of which is Deion Sanders' inside-the-parker—the first in the Mile

High's short history as a big league venue. (Damn. We wanted Alex Cole to do it.)

Charlie Hayes knocks two out of the park, one a grand slam. Benavides gets a rare homer, his first since last August. (When he was on the Reds' side.)

In the stands: Much is made of tonight's color guard. It's USMC. Yes, Marine Corps. And all of them are women.

Another first is the new sign that runs all the way across the top of the South Stands. "MILE HIGH STADIUM HOME OF THE WORLDS GREATEST BASEBALL FANS."

But not the world's greatest punctuators.

There is mumbling that it's too bad the Rockies hadn't glommed onto Harris and/or Hurst a day or so earlier. Maybe *they* could beat Atlanta.

And there is lots of hoo-hah over learning that Leskanic shaves his pitching arm. The idea, all presume, is to cut down on wind resistance. Tonight, he gives up five runs in as many innings, so that stratagem doesn't seem to be working. Another theory is put forth: Maybe Leskanic has just taken Baylor's no beards rule to an extreme.

Tony T. brings a new discovery to the game—Rockies Gum. Official, licensed and everything. He notes that it is made in Canada, so it must be a celebration of the Canadian Rockies. Another gum bummer: It's pink, not purple.

Brian T. reports that the Dugout Store is selling a bear in a Rockies uniform and wonders "Will that be our mascot?"

And there is an attendee who says: "You know, that Rockies guy—number 23 out there—looks like Lasorda." That number 23, of course, is Zimmer.

The sign on the second level says it for everyone: "GET WELL BIG CAT MISS YOU."

When Bichette comes to bat in the fourth, the organist *began to play the Pink Panther theme.*

Speaking of missing persons, at 9:24, the P.A. announcer calls out for the parents of Mike Mieta. Which makes young Mike the First Lost Kid in Rockies history.

Three minutes later, Hal Moore leaves.

The Rockies have now lost two in a row, have a record of 36-63 (.364) and are in last place by a game.

The game in which Castellano hit his first ML homer.

7:05 at Mile High Stadium
The National Anthem: Sherri Hammons
The first ball: Carrie Nolan (Kempe Children's
   Foundation)
The starting pitchers: Reynoso (7-5) vs. Smoltz (8-8)
The W-L pitchers: Smoltz (9-8) and Reynoso (7-6)
The attendance: 54,550
The News Headline: Rockies fall apart after solid start
The Post Headline: Braves still masters of Rockies

Outside the ballpark: The cops are now permitting fans with
extra tickets to sell them across the street from the box office.
Until now, the Rockies had the cops enforcing a 300' distance for
ticket peddlers. (300' from what? Nobody ever said.)

Before the game: Charlie Hayes is smiling and signing. And
fans are laughing and loving.

On the field: Seems like the Braves always score in double
figures in Mile High Stadium. This time, the Rockies look like
they might just break the Braves' jinx. They nurse a 2-0 lead
nearly to the halfway point before the Rockies' ace Reynoso
falters and a four-run Braves outburst with two outs in the fifth
ends the Rox' dreams of their first-ever shutout.

   Castellano's first big league blast helps the Rocks close it
to 6-5 in the eighth, but the Atlantas put the game away when
they explode for four in the top of the ninth.

   Atlanta's McGriff enjoys a two-homers-and-a-triple day.
One of the homers is an inside-the-park job. Amazing. The
Braves got one last night, too.

   A couple of fans await an addition to the list of Mile High
No Nos: "FANS ARE NOT PERMITTED TO BRING UNCUT
FRUIT INTO THE BALL PARK."

   Like they have at C.U. games.

On crutches: Andres Galarraga. With a sprained right knee.

In the stands: Folks who can spell are amused at the sign that wishes HAPPY BIRTHDAY YOU OLD GEASER.

With the bases loaded with Braves and much excitement in the ballpark, Dean, a paid-for-by-the-Rockies hospitality operative, is heard to yell the following (this is an exact quote): "Let's go Deion! Grand slam, buddy!"

The Rockies have now lost three in a row, and have a 36-64 record. This entitles them to possession of last place in the NL West, 31 games behind the Giants and two behind the sixth-place Padres. The Mets are 34-65. The Marlins are 42-57.

Wednesday, July 28: Atlanta 3, Colorado 2
The 3 million mark is reached.

3:05 at Mile High Stadium
The National Anthem: Kerry Smith
The first ball: Mary Beth Vitale
The starting pitchers: Parrett (3-3) vs. Avery (11-3)
The W-L pitchers: Wohlers (5-0) and Reed (5-4)
The attendance: 60,237
The News Headline: Braves tag loss on Rockies
The Post Headline: Braves and ump frustrate Rockies

On the field: This is the Rockies' last chance to beat Atlanta at home this season and it opens with an injury. After facing just three batters, Jeff Parrett leaves the game with a strain in his right elbow.

From there on, the game is tantalizingly close, a rarity for Braves-Rockies games.

The Rockies get 13 base runners, but are able to convert only two of them into runs.

Atlanta gets its go-ahead run in the top of the eighth when Gant leads off with a home run. It turns out to be the game-winner.

But it is the call that home plate umpire Charlie Williams makes in the Rockies' half of the eighth that really whips Baylor and the entire crowd into a frenzy. Williams calls Cole out when the speedster tries to score the tying run from third on a lazy bouncer by Mejia.

Even the Braves' catcher thinks Cole was safe.

The boos are loud and long and last throughout the rest of the game. [*They will continue when Williams is introduced before the Rockies' next game, the day after tomorrow.*]

In the stands: Criley Orton, 70, was designated as the Rockies' 3,000,000th fan of the season. Orton is a retired electrical engineer who was vacationing his way across the country from his home in Ridgecrest, California to his wife's 53rd high school reunion in Iowa.

The Rockies fans have hit three million in just 53 home games. This is a record that won't be threatened anytime soon. It took its previous owners, the Toronto Blue Jays, 61 games.

Three million. That's more than the Yankees have *ever* drawn in a full season.

Fan were delighted, amazed, and suspicious as hell when the One Millionth Fan turned out to be a mother (it was Mothers' Day) and the Two Millionth Fan happened to be a dad (yes, it was Fathers' Day). Now this. What holiday is it, anyway, the fans wanted to know.

Naturally, they asked the Fans' Ombudsman.

July 28th, the Ombudsman discovered (after a visit to the DPL), is Peru's Independence Day. We must assume, then, that this Orton guy from California, our three millionth fan, is Peruvian.

Because we know he isn't independent. Brought his wife.

From the looks of all the burritos in the stands, the nice ladies outside Mile High who are selling aluminum foil-wrapped burritos out of Playmate coolers are doing well.

One fan, however, wins the prize for bringing his Mexican food to tonight's game from the greatest distance. Just back from Cheyenne Frontier Days, he's packing a Taco Bravo from a Taco John's in Wyoming.

The P.A. Voice suggests that those with problems seek out hospitality folks "in white cowboy hats." The Cowboy says that those things are *not* cowboy hats. Not even close.

Diane K. is saving those plastic Inaugural Season cups that soft drinks come in. "I think a service for 24 would make a nice wedding present."

Massive frustration is caused by the tonight's matchup between the Mets and the Marlins. With the Rockies struggling to finish ahead of both in the standings, nobody at Mile High Stadium wants *either* to win.

Fantalk: "Next time The Fish come to town, I'm going to bring some Cotto Salami to the ballpark."

"How come?"

"In honor of their centerfielder, Henry Cotto."

"In *honor* of?"

"To make fun of, actually."

"That's better."

"Gee, I hope it isn't against The Rules to bring a salami to the ballpark."

"It's O.K. as long as it doesn't flash."

In Vail: Galarraga, getting a second opinion on his sprained knee. The Cat has landed in Eagle County.

In absentia: Jeff Parrett. His elbow injury ends the season for him. Channel 2: "Parrett hurts wing, flies home."

In Shea Stadium, the Mets stage a rare two-run rally in the ninth to beat the Florida Marlins—and to give star-crossed hurler Anthony Young a win. This snaps his ML record of 27 consecutive losses.

On pitching coach Larry Bearnarth's moving day, he takes a tumble while carrying boxes of stuff and breaks his ankle.

"I've got a Colorado Rockies foot," says The Bear. "It's purple and black."

Today's milestone: The Expos' Ron Hassey caught Dennis Martinez' perfect game vs. the Dodgers (1991)

The Rockies have now lost four in a row, have a record of 36-65. They continue to languish in the cellar, two games behind San Diego.

Thursday, July 29 is an open date, and a dandy time to take a close look at the Rockies ad that promotes the upcoming FANNIE PACK NIGHT.

Fannie? What goes on? The term for the posterior is fanny. "Fannie" is as wrong as "Rockie."

Unless, of course, they're giving Fannie Maes to the first 20,000 fans.

In that case, it would be dandie.

Friday, July 30: San Francisco 10, Colorado 4

The game that Don Baylor got thrown out of before the first pitch. And Greg Harris' debut.

7:05 at Mile High Stadium
The National Anthem: Keepin' Time
The first balls: Travis Valentine and James Rijos
    (Coca-Cola)
The starting pitchers: Harris (10-9) vs. Brummett (1-3)
The W-L pitchers: Brummett (2-3) and Harris (10-10)
The attendance: 71,710
The News Headline: Rockies go down quietly
The Post Headline: Bonds tape-measures Rockies

In the morning papers: The Rockies run ads proclaiming that their acquisition of Greg Harris is a gift to the fans, a reward for their support.

ENJOY WATCHING GREG HARRIS TONIGHT, the ads say, YOU EARNED IT.

Just before the game: Manager Don Baylor engages umpire Charlie Williams in a loud, long discussion of the latter's flawed call the night before last when it appeared that Alex Cole had scored the tying run.

Along the way, Williams wads up Baylor's lineup card and gives Baylor much flak and, of course, the heave-ho. Before the game has even gotten under way. So bench coach Ron Hassey runs the club.

On the field: Greg Harris makes his Rockies debut. It is, as they say, inauspicious. Bordering on the *sus*picious. The new acquisition gives up eight hits and five runs in four innings.

Even after dumbbell baserunning and a balk fuel the Giants' lead, a Bichette homer brings the Rox within two runs at the end of the fifth.

Not close enough. Bonds soon pops a two-run shot of his own to give the Giants an 8-4 lead which is never challenged.

During mop-up time, Mo Sanford makes his debut with the Rockies, tossing just eight pitches.

In the stands: It's Coca-Cola Lapel Pin #9 Night.

Roz Ogren: "Harris pitches like he's been with the Rockies for some time."

Bill Koerber: "Two complete cycles of the wave. It's sickening."

When it is announced that Dave Dravecky is in the stands, he stands—and so does everyone else.

After hearing yet another recital of The Rules of The Stadium, Steve K. grumbles that "they have more no-no rules here than at a Catholic school."

It goes like this, usually with two readings a game:

After introducing the umps, Mr. P.A. reads the following:
"Ladies and gentlemen: For the protection of players and fans and in the spirit of good sportsmanship, the Rockies request that you refrain from throwing any objects onto the playing field, including home run balls hit into the stands. Such behavior can cause serious injury and violators *will* be ejected and subject to arrest. The Rockies would like you to keep any balls hit into the stands today; however, it is against National League policy to interfere with balls in play by leaning over the railings or coming out onto the playing field. By doing so, you can seriously damage the chances of either team. *Any fan interference must result in ejection.* Please refrain from any abusive language or behavior that may offend those sitting near you. Problems with profanity or alcohol will *not* be tolerated and are grounds for immediate dismissal. Thank you for your cooperation."
For night games, he adds:
"No flash photography is allowed inside the stadium. Please, no cameras with flash."

That's 147 words of warning by day, 160 by night. Times two. No wonder the fans feel battered by no-nos.

Steve, always looking for the fun side of everything, has an idea: "Let's memorize that litany of laws word-for-word and maybe, by next season, everybody in the park can chant it along with the P.A. guy!"

The Rockies have now lost five straight, have a 36-66 record (.353) and are in last place, three games behind the Padres. Only the Mets, at 35-67, have won fewer games.

Saturday, July 31: San Francisco 4, Colorado 3

The night the Rockies broke their own NL night game attendance record.

7:05 at Mile High Stadium
The National Anthem: Eunice Morris
The first ball: Nancy Murray (Rocky Mountain News)
The starting pitchers: Bottenfield (3-6) vs. Swift (14-5)
The W-L pitchers: Swift (15-5) and Bottenfield (3-7)
The attendance: 72,208 [second largest of season]
The News Headline: Giants put Swift end to Rockies
The Post Headline: Rockies lose pitching duel

On the field: For six innings, Bottenfield is working on The First Shutout Ever. In fact, he is leading on a Bichette homer in the bottom of the sixth. But then the Giants' awesome bats come to life. Matt Williams powers the first pitch of the seventh into the stands.

Bottenfield suffers further when he then permits Giants pitcher Swift to knock in two runs with a double. After the dust clears, the Giants have taken a 4-1 lead. The Rockies make a nice comeback with a 2-run outburst in the eighth.

But not enough.

In the stands: It's Kids' Jersey "Day." And it's the "day" the Rockies break the night game attendance record they wrested from the Dodgers a week ago.

In a bar, a zealot explains What's Going On Here. "Denver is wiping out all the attendance records that were set in Toronto last year, records that everybody said would never be touched."

Sandy Hoffman's response: "How insensitive."

In July, the Rockies had a record of 10-17.

The Rockies have now lost six in a row, have a record of 36-67 (.350), and are three games deep into last place.

Only the Mets with a 35-68 record are playing worse ball in the bigs.

The first sweep by the Giants.

1:05 at Mile High Stadium
The National Anthem: Benny Yarbrough (saxophone)
The first ball: David Washington, 14 and Grover Hall
(Martin Marietta)
The starting pitchers: Reynoso (7-6) vs. Burkett (15-4)
The W-L pitchers: Burkett (16-4) and Reynoso (7-7)
The attendance: 72,431
The News Headline: Rockies hit bottom again
The Post Headline: Swept away with a Giant broom

In today's News: Jack Nolan's letter explains his point of view about being a baseball fan. He says that true fans love the game—and love each game they see as individual works of wonderfulness. He says that true fans don't worry about standings. He says that true fans *know* what baseball is about: "Game Day, the crowd, the moment, the Cat, good plays, bad plays, *great* plays." Nolan hopes that Rockies fans will be like Cubs fans who "live for the beauty of the game and for their heroes, win or lose." And says that Cubs fans "learned a long time ago that there is endless joy in baseball if you have the wisdom not to temper your mania."

Before the game: A moment of silence for Ewing Kauffman, the man who made the Royals a first-class baseball operation.

On the field: Not a good way to celebrate Colorado Day. The error-prone Rockies let John Burkett become the NL's first 16-game winner and let the Giants sweep the series.

Poor Reynoso. The Rockies' starter sprinkles six hits over six innings and gives up just one earned run. But there are five unearned ones, too, so Reynoso winds up taking it on the right side of his W-L record.

The Giants' giant inning was the sixth, wherein they make three hits and two Mejia fielding flubs into four runs.

The Rockies enjoy a four-run eighth due largely to Clark's three-run smash. (Clark enjoys his first four-RBI day as a Rock.) But it ain't quite enough. These days, it never is.

One cheering note: Marcus Moore threw a pitch to Will Clark that was a 99 mph job.

In the stands: It's the night those four college sophomores who are visiting 28 ballparks in 28 days drop by Our Yard.

And it's a big night for Martin Marietta. It is said that the rocketeers bought 4100 seats for the game.

It is also said that Giants' manager, Dusty Baker, is moving to Boulder.

Someone says that, "I just met a second baseman named Mejia" and Pat and Diane break into song.

As a gaunt bearded fan makes his way up the aisle for another beer, somebody says, "Look! Even Jesus is here!"

Then: "Wonder what *his* priority number is."

The scoreboard has some bad news. And some more bad punctuation. According to the big board, the Mets are beating the "CARD'S."

The operator of the guess-the-attendance bit gets cute, offering these choices:

> 72,430
> 72,431
> 72,432
> 72,433

The bottom line attendancewise is that the Rockies draw 216,349 for the three-game series, which breaks the record for same that the Rockies set during their home-opening series against the Expos on Aprils 9, 10 and 11.

In Cooperstown, Reggie Jackson goes into The Hall of Fame.

Wearing a NY cap.

Which proves that although Reggie may have been a better player than the average fan, the average fan is a better fan than Mr. October.

Because many a true baseball fan wouldn't have chosen the Yankees' headgear. After all, Jackson played in 1,311 games for Oakland, *more than twice the number he appeared in for the Yankees.*

It is an important point, and one with which Jackson should be jabbed whenever the opportunity presents.

Today's milestone: Alex Cole stole a Cleveland Indians' team record five bases in a game vs. Kansas City (1990)

The Rockies have now lost seven in a row, are 36-68 on the season, and share with the Mets the distinction for having the worst record in the major leagues. (The Rox had managed to avoid the worst-record label since June 13.)

Naturally, the Rockies are now in last place. They are four games out of next-to-last.

Monday, August 2: Cincinnati 6, Colorado 2
The game that gave the Rockies the worst record in the major leagues.

5:35 at Riverfront Stadium
The starting pitchers: Blair (4-7) vs. Pugh (6-10)
The W-L pitchers: Pugh (7-10) and Blair (4-8)
The attendance: 29,088
The News Headline: Eight in a row and counting
The Post Headline: Rockies sustain 8th straight loss

On the field: Pugh tosses a complete game at the Rockies. He gives up nine hits, all singles. Dante Bichette hits three of them.

But the Rockies don't put any runs on the board until there are two out in the ninth. That's when Vinny Castilla hits a two-run homer.

These bottom-of-the-ninth heroics save the Rockies from shutout shame. Plus they extend the Rox' games-with-homers streak to 13. (A notable mark, but not likely to get much note while the team's compiling a massive losing streak.)

The Reds begin to breathe easy when a couple of singles followed by a triple and a double give them a 3-0 lead in the third. Later, a three-run homer by Joe Oliver leads to even more facile aspiration.

Let it also be noted that, in the third, Castilla stole the first base of his ML career.

And Bichette lost a ball in the lights which then bounced over his head for a "triple."

The Rockies have now lost eight straight games, which is a franchise record and have a 36-69 record, the worst in baseball.

Yes, even worse than the Mets who are 37-68. The Rox are in last place, 34.5 games behind the first-place Giants and 4.5 games behind the sixth-place Padres.

Tuesday, August 3: Cincinnati 5, Colorado 4 (10 innings)

The first game with a woman doing the play-by-play on TV. And Sanford's first start.

5:35 at Riverfront Stadium
The starting pitchers: Sanford (0-0) vs. Luebbers (2-2)
The W-L pitchers: Spradlin (1-0) and Leskanic (1-5)
The attendance: 26,982
The News Headline: Rockies let another one get away
The Post Headline: Bullpen fails Rockies in 5-4 loss

On the field: Baylor mixes it up, starting only three of yesterday's starters, and it almost works. Almost.

And loss number nine is the cruelest of all. When Bichette blasts a two-run home run in the ninth off Rob Dibble, smiles break out throughout The Time Zone With One Team—but a lot of television sets.

Soon, the Rox find themselves just one out away from snapping their skein. But when the Reds use a little of this and a little of that to tie it in the bottom of the ninth, smiles fade.

And turn to frowns in the tenth when the Reds turn a walk, a wild pitch and a sacrifice fly into the winning run.

This is the third time Bichette has slammed a go-ahead homer in a late inning, only to have the bullpen give it back with interest.

You can't eat it, drink it, or put it in the W column, but the fact remains: The Rox have now homered in 14 consecutive games.

On the tube: Charlie Jones has another commitment tonight, so his place in Channel 2's booth is taken by Gayle Gardner—who becomes the first woman ever to do play-by-play on a major league telecast. Or maybe the second. Depends on who you believe.

It is obvious that Gayle is soft on the DH. But she wins Colorado hearts when, in the top of the ninth, with the Rox down by one, she makes this prophetic statement: "My analysis of the game is that Dante Bichette has to hit a two-run homer." *Which he does.*

That's what's new. But there's a lot that's old. On this long, long road trip, fans find themselves watching a lot of televised Rockies games. And they are getting real tired of seeing the same old commercials over and over.

Real tired.

Baylors's spot for the News was OK the first couple dozen times. And the bank executives who are proud to be sponsors of the Rockies were great for a while, too. But three or four times a game, game after game?

The Rockies have now lost nine in a row, have the worst record in the major leagues, 36-70, and are in last place, 4.5 games behind the Padres. The Mets, with 37-69, are second worst.

Wednesday, August 4: Cincinnati 9, Colorado 3
The game that ties this season's ML record for futility.

5:35 at Riverfront Stadium
The starting pitchers: Harris (10-10) vs. Roper (1-1)
The W-L pitchers: Roper (2-1) and Harris (10-11)
The attendance: 22,939
The News Headline: Roper is good as his word
The Post Headline: Rockies Red-faced again

Combat and ball: Tonight's the night the Rangers-White Sox game turns into the Wednesday Night Fights, featuring a bout between the legendary 46-year-old Nolan Ryan and 26-year-old Robin Ventura. The latter charges the former on the mound after the former hits the latter with a pitch. Whereupon Ryan, who has punched out more batters than any other man in history, beats out a tune *fortissimo* on the kid's head until the confrontation is stopped by a bemused mob of men in knickers.

On the field: But we have our own score to settle. Everyone remembers John Roper. When the 21-year-old pitcher beat the Rox in his ML debut on May 16, he made zero friends in The Time Zone when he told a reporter that he'd faced better hitting lineups in Triple-A. That's the kind of thing that really furs your duck. Baylor & Co. are quietly seething.

Roper starts against Colorado tonight.

But he doesn't have to eat his words. What he does is pretty much duplicate his last performance, giving up four hits and a run in six innings.

The Reds score four runs in the fourth inning and again in the fifth (Sabo grand slam off Harris).

Roper takes home career ML victory number two. Both at the expense of the Rox.

Bichette: "He pitches like that, I guess he can say whatever he wants."

Clark: "If we don't start hitting, it could get ugly around here."

The Rockies have now tied the two teams who suffered ten-game losing streaks earlier this season (Detroit and California), have a record of 36-71 (.336) and are in last place, five games behind San Diego. The Mets, at 37-70, most closely approach the Rockies' level of futility.

Thursday, August 5: Cincinnati 11, Colorado 4
The game that breaks this season's ML record for futility.

10:35 at Riverfront Stadium
The starting pitchers: Bottenfield (3-7) and Rijo (9-5)
The W-L pitchers: Rijo (10-5) and Bottenfield (3-8)
The attendance: 33,871
The News Headline: Reds rip Rockies, extend misery
The Post Headline: Road woes roll on to San Diego

On the field: Loss number eleven looks familiar. It features bumbling play by the Rocks leading to a drubbing by the _____ (fill in the blank).

Bottenfield is tagged for four in the first and three in the second and, except for Castellano's solo homer in the sixth and Boston's three-run shot in the eighth—which makes it 16 straight games with a Rocky homer—there was little joy in Rockyville.

Eric Young makes his first ML start in center field.

Danny Sheaffer raises eyebrows with his comment that "it seems pretty obvious to anyone watching the game who really cares and who really doesn't."

Just one year ago: The headline in the Denver Post proclaimed that "Rockies plug owner gap." Subheads: "Phar-Mor claims Monus embezzled $350 million" "Replacements step forward quickly after resignations."

In Colorado Springs, it is Baby Dolls Bikini night at Sky Sox Stadium. It is also Bruce Hurst's debut as a pitcher in the Rockies organization. He pitches well for five innings and gets the W.

The Rockies have now lost eleven in a row (the major leagues' longest losing streak of the season), and have the worst record in the bigs, 36-72. The Mets, at 38-70, are next worst.

Naturally, the Rox are in last place. They're 36.5 games out of first and 5.5 behind sixth-place San Diego.

Friday, August 6: San Diego 6-6, Colorado 3-2

The first doubleheader—and first double loss—leaves the Rox with a 13-game losing streak.

> **6:05 at Jack Murphy Stadium**
> **GAME ONE**
> **The starting pitchers:** Reynoso (7-7) vs. Benes (12-7)
> **The W-L pitchers:** Benes (13-7) and Reynoso (7-8)
> **GAME TWO**
> **The starting pitchers:** Blair (4-8) vs. Sanders (0-0)
> **The W-L pitchers:** Sanders (1-0) and Blair (4-9)
> **The attendance:** 41,085 (Free Beach Towel Day)
> **The News Headline:** Rockies have no defense
> **The Post Headline:** Sweep up: Skid hits 13 games

In Denver, Gerald Phipps, 78, dies. A wealthy construction exec, Phipps accepted stock in the Denver Bears in lieu of payment for construction work on Bears Stadium in 1947. Then, in 1965, he and his brother, Alan, paid $1.5 million for the Broncos to keep them from moving to Atlanta.

Jim Burris, GM of the Denver Bears for many years, says of Phipps: "Whatever we have today is because of him and, earlier, Bob Howsam. They were the giants of our town."

On the field: Losses #12 and #13 come easily when the Galarragaless Rockies give little defensive support to their starters. Today, they make seven errors en route to adding two more to this season's longest ML losing streak.

In the first contest, three of the four runs given up during Reynoso's five-inning tenure are unearned. Then, when the Rockies claw their way back into the game to trail by just one, Pitcher Moore throws a sure out past first and into left field. Then, he's replaced by Ruffin who walks four to make it easy for the Padres to score a pair and the Rockies hopes fade to black.

Daryl Boston's home run in the seventh inning extends the Rox' games-with-at-least-one-homer streak to 17 in a row.

That streak ends in the second game, when none of the Colorado batters go deep.

The big hitting news in the second contest belongs to the Padres. Powered largely by a three-run shot by Bean, the San Diegos explode for five in the bottom of the first and pretty much coast from there.

The thing that makes the Rockies' beer go flat is the fact that catcher Owens missed a tag at home that would've gotten them out of that inning with no damage done.

In the eighth, Tony Gwynn gets his 2,000th hit (off Ruffin).

Jerald Clark and his brother, Phil, play first base for their respective teams.

This is the major league debut for Sanders, the Padres' winning pitcher.

Back home: A fan thinks about a phrase out of a song. "The Rockies may crumble…but our love is here to stay."

But only the lonely (and the terminally optimistic) keep their tubes burning until the last out of the last game comes—at 12:32 a.m.

In the stats, Andres Galarraga officially drops out of the NL batting lead. He no longer meets the at-bat criteria.

In the record books, the longest losing streak for an expansion team doesn't belong to the Mets, whose longest succession of futility was just 17. The all-time winless draught belongs to Montreal, which managed a 0-20 sequence in 1969.

In the pit of the Central City Opera House, bass player Andy Holmes notes that it's Act III, Scene II of *Falstaff.* "It's a full count—three and two."

The Rockies have now lost 13 in a row—and have gone 3-20 since the All-Star break. This gives them a record of 36-74 (.327), and puts them in last place, 38 games behind the Giants (who are 9.5 games ahead of the Braves). The Rockies are 8.5 games out of sixth place. The Marlins and Mets have 46-63 and 38-70 records, respectively.

Saturday, August 7 is an open date. Fortunately.

This is the first day in two weeks that the Rockies haven't lost at least one game.

Many of them go to Las Vegas to take their minds off You Know What. At least in Vegas it is *possible* to win.

Which leads neatly to this: After the opera in Central City, musicians gather in The Teller House for beverage and song. Before singing a novelty version of "Rhinestone Cowboy," conductor Stephen Crout reads a list of "Ten Reasons Not to Gamble in Central City."

Reason #5: "The Rockies can't win—why should you?"

Sunday, August 8: Colorado 5, San Diego 2

The game that snapped the 13-game losing streak.

2:05 at Jack Murphy Stadium
The starting pitchers: Sanford (0-0) vs. Brocail (2-7)
The W-L pitchers: Sanford (1-0) and Brocail (2-8)
The attendance: 15,248
The News Headline: Sanford, Rockies bury the streak
The Post Headline: Rockies hit the brakes on streak

On the field (and in the psyche): Whew.

The monkey is off our back.

And it was starting to look (and feel) a lot like King Kong.

At 4:30 p.m., it was official. The Rox' miserable losing streak—the longest in the majors this year and the fourth longest in expansion history—was over.

Mo Sanford had a win and Darren Holmes had his first save since July 24.

Until today, starter Sanford had a substantial drought of his own going. The last time he'd won a ML game was one year and 364 days ago when, right here in Jack Murphy Stadium, he beat the Reds in his ML debut with the Padres. [Today's win will be Sanford's only W of the season.]

Today, Sanford gives up just five hits in seven innings and has a 3-0 lead in the fourth when Castilla's single takes a fortuitous hop over the head of the Padres' leftfielder and metamorphoses into a triple that scores two runs.

This is the first time the Rockies have led in any ballgame in the month of August.

Another break comes when the Padres' Velasquez is called out at home. TV replays shows he was safe.

Both Hayes (in the second) and Boston (in the fourth) are thrown out at the plate.

But Sheaffer and Castilla each acquire two RBI en route to the victory, the first since July 24.

That was many, *many* whiles ago.

So many that well over half of all Colorado Rockies' fans have gotten their hair cut—or, in the case of women fans, "done"—since the Rockies last won a game.

Matter of fact, according to the fan/accountant, one out of every 25 Colorado Rockies fans celebrated birthdays during the long losing streak.

Or tried to.

Bichette: "This ought to turn us around and start a winning streak. We're hot now."

Down on the farm: All four of the Colorado Rockies' farm teams won today, too, making this the Rox' first organizational sweep in history.

Today's milestone: The Major Leagues and the players signed a new agreement which permits the expansion of the National League by two teams (1985)

The Rockies are now 37-74 for the season, are in last place, 36.5 games out of first and 6.5 games out of sixth.

The Marlins are 47-64, ten games ahead of the Rox. The Mets are 39-72, two games ahead.

Monday, August 9: Colorado 3, Los Angeles 2 (11 innings)

The first Rockies win in Dodger Stadium.

2:05 at Dodger Stadium
The starting pitchers: Harris (10-11) vs. Candiotti (10-12)
The W-L pitchers: Reed (6-4) and Gott (4-6)
The attendance: 31,953
The News Headline: (Game too late for Home Edition)
The Post Headline: Two straight: Rockies win in 11

On the field: Finally, Greg Harris looks like the Greg Harris that Bob Gebhard acquired. The struggling hurler struggles little today, goes eight pretty good innings and leaves with the score tied at two apiece.

Rockies relievers Reed and Holmes blank the Dodgers and the Dodgers blank the Rockies until the top of the 11th, when Castilla's sacrifice fly scores Jerald Clark.

Roberto Mejia suffers a five-strikeout day.

The Rockies have now won two in a row (the last time they won consecutive games was exactly a month ago), boast a 38-74 record (.339) and are in last place, 5.5 games behind the Padres. The Mets have won one more game and lost two fewer.

Tuesday, August 10: Colorado 4, Los Angeles 2

Bottenfield's first complete game— and the first time the Rockies have won three in a row on the road.

8:35 at Dodger Stadium
The starting pitchers: Bottenfield (3-8) vs. Astacio (8-6)
The W-L pitchers: Bottenfield (4-8) and Astacio (8-7)
The attendance: 34,163
The News Headline: Bottenfield keeps Rockies on roll
The Post Headline: Rockies jolt L.A. as streak reaches 3

Hours before the game: A woman who identified herself only as "a hard-core Rockies fan" called KOOL 105.1 and requested Arethra Franklin's song, "Respect" which repeats the line, "Just a little bit of respect," over and over.

Says she wants to dedicate the song to Rockies pitcher Greg Harris because she read that he's been wanting to pitch a great game for the Rockies to gain the respect of Denver fans. Last night, of course, he did it.

On the field: In Denver, the pope arrives. But the miracles are happening in L.A. Yesterday, Roberto Mejia struck out five times against the Dodgers. Today, he goes 4-for-4 against them.

The Rockies jump off to a 3-0 lead in the top of the 1st on Boston's homer with leadoff batter Cole on base.

Bottenfield goes all the way, giving up seven hits for his first complete game in 20 ML starts.

The Dodgers score solo runs in the fifth and sixth.

Not on the field: Galarraga and Hayes. The latter is now serving his three-game suspension for charging the mound back in June. The Rox win anyway.

Today's milestone: Jerald Clark's birthday (1963)

The Rockies have now won three in a row (only the Royals, with 4, have a longer streak) and stand at 39-74.

Still, they have the worst record in ML baseball and are deep in last place in the NL West, 5.5 games behind sixth-place San Diego. The Marlins have 10 more Ws and 10 fewer Ls.

Wednesday, August 11: Colorado 3, Los Angeles 2

The game in which Reynoso got three hits.

8:35 at Dodger Stadium
The starting pitchers: Reynoso (7-8) vs. Martinez (8-6)
The W-L pitchers: Reynoso (8-8) and Martinez (8-7)
The attendance: 38,421
The News Headline: Rockies fend off Dodgers
The Post Headline: Rockies top L.A. for fourth straight

On the field: For the third game in a row, leadoff batter Cole opens with a hit. When he scores, the Rockies have notified Ramon Martinez that, unlike the last time they faced him at Dodger Stadium, there will be no shutout.

Another thing that happened the last time the Rox faced Martinez: Charlie Hayes charged the mound. With Martinez on it. Which led, ultimately, to a three-game suspension for the Rockies third-sacker. That won't be repeated today, either. Because Hayes sits out today's game as part of the above-mentioned suspension.

Not only does Reynoso pitch a good game into the eighth inning, he gets *three* hits. Yes, Reynoso. The guy who entered the game dragging a .044 average. That's 2-for-45.

But his batting stats don't get into the papers. Even though the pitchers in the NL comprise 11% of the ABs (except for PHs), you can't look up their BAs in the DP or the RMN.

Today's milestone: Bryn Smith's birthday (1955)

The Rockies have now won four in a row. This gives them a 40-74 record, good enough for last place, 4.5 games behind the Padres. But good enough to be better than one major league team—New York Mets. They're *39-74*.

Thursday, August 12: Colorado 4, Los Angeles 1
The first time an expansion team has swept a four-game series from an established club. Ever.

> **2:05 at Dodger Stadium**
> **The starting pitchers:** Blair (4-9) vs. Hershiser (8-11)
> **The W-L pitchers:** Blair (5-9) and Hershiser (8-12)
> **The attendance:** 38,549
> **The News Headline:** Blair takes his turn as king of hill
> **The Post Headline:** Give them five: Colorado wins
> another

On the field: Boy, this little rivalry with the Hollywoodies is getting hotter with every game.

Today, it is fueled by a three-run outburst in the top of the first highlighted by a two-on-two-out double by Clark. That is all the Rockies need.

Boston's leaping above-the-wall catch robs Snyder of a HR in the seventh.

Blair's CG win is the first in his 35-starts career.

In Joe Girardi's mind, there has to be some amazement. As he comes off the DL, he find himself with five pitchers new to the club since he last caught—Bottenfield, Harris, Sanford, Moore and Leskanic.

On tonight's NBC's national news: Much is made of the thing that makes the ballpark in Colorado Spring unique: The hot tub out the right field line.

Rockies fans wonder what will be unique about Coors Field. What will be special about it. What people will talk about and want to come to Denver to see.

Wrigley has its ivy. Fenway has The Monster. Dodger Stadium has dugout-level seats for VIPs. Camden has its old railroad buildings. Toronto has outfield walls that are the sides of a hotel with rooms overlooking the field. Rockies fans wonder...

The Rockies have now won five in a row (this matches their longest win streak ever). Their record is 41-74, which puts them in last place, 36 games out of first and 3.5 games out of sixth.

Friday, August 13: Colorado 5, Houston 3
The first game won by a homer with two outs in the 9th.

6:05 in The Astrodome
The starting pitchers: Sanford (1-0) vs. Portugal (11-4)
The W-L pitchers: Wayne (3-3) and Jones (3-9)
The attendance: 37,972
The News Headline: Rockies streak to sixth in a row
The Post Headline: The Rockies' magic number: 6

On the field: Trailing by a run with two outs and two on in the ninth, Charlie Hayes pounds a three-run homer off Doug Jones.

Once again, Holmes comes in to stifle the opposition in the ninth to put another tick into the W column and propel the Rockies into the heady realm of the longest winning streak in their history—*six* games.

Winner Wayne: "This is so much fun!"

Baylor, after the game, celebrates with a beer (Coors Light).

Arrest those dogs!

Today is the day we learn that the Hot Dog Diet (aka the Spokane Heart Diet), which calls for hot dogs and ice cream and promises that you'll lose ten pounds in three days, does *not* have the blessing of the American Heart Association.

The disappointment spreads throughout fandom.

And ARA.

Speaking of hot dogs, somebody wondered how much they cost the concessionaire. The Fans' Ombudsman found out that in other ballparks, the 8-in-1 variety (eight to a pound) cost 12¢ each while the 4-in-1 (jumbo dogs) cost 26¢.

That, of course, is just for the meat. It doesn't include cooking, wrapper, bun, condiments—or enormous profit.

In the superstition department there is much amazement. After all, the Rockies' first Friday-the-13th game ever is won by a dramatic home run. By Number 13.

The Rockies have now won six in a row (best in the majors) and have a 42-74 record. This leaves them in last place 36 games from first and 3.5 games from next-to-last. The Mets are 39-76.

Saturday, August 14: Houston 9, Colorado 0

The game that snapped the six-game streak.

6:05 at The Astrodome
The starting pitchers: Harris (10-11) vs. Harnisch (10-8)
The W-L pitchers: Harnisch (11-8) and Harris (10-12)
      (0-3 with Rockies)
The attendance: 41,523
The News Headline: Rockies' streak snuffed
The Post Headline: Doomsday in Dome for streak

On the field: Going in, everyone was aware that the record for consecutive victories by an expansion team stood at seven, set in 1961 by the Los Angeles Angels.

In an effort to tie the record, Baylor started Greg Harris. And why not? Harris' numbers against the Astros were nifty. Careerwise, Harris was 8-0 against them with a 1.22 ERA.

But it soon became clear that the record would survive the day. While Harris is getting semi-shelled, the Astros' Harnisch hangs up a dozen Ks, retires 16 of the last 18 Rockies, and breezes to a nifty three-hitter.

The dearly departed six-game win streak was comprised of two games won by one run, two by two, and two by three.

Today's Milestones: Bears Stadium is dedicated (1948) and Denver area voters pass a 0.1% sales tax to finance a new stadium (1990)

The Rockies now have a 42-75 record and are in last place, 3.5 games behind the Padres.

Sunday, August 15: Colorado 4, Houston 3
The game that gives the Rockies their first 7-7 road trip.

12:35 at The Astrodome
The starting pitchers: Bottenfield (4-8) vs. Drabek (7-14)
The W-L pitchers: Ruffin (4-4) and Hernandez (3-3)
The attendance: 21,690
The News Headline: Rockies rally again, win one for the road
The Post Headline: Rockies kill road slump

On KOA before the game: "We'll carry the papal mass until 12:05, when we'll cut away for a Rockies game."

On the field: With the Astros putting up a pair of runs in the first and Drabek's slider shutting the Rockies down for five innings, it didn't look good for the Boys in the Purple Pinstripes.

But the Rox pick away. Eric Young, in the lineup for the first time in nine days, singles, steals and scores in the 6th. The Rox add two more in the 8th and go into the 9th tied 3-up.

Thereupon, the Rockies combine a Clark single, a Sheaffer walk, and an Astro error to make the run they needed. Would've gotten more if Castellano, with the bases loaded and one out, hadn't mistakenly thought the squeeze had been called and laid down a bunt. Sheaffer, the runner on third, was out by an estimated 89 feet.

In the News, J.R. Moehringer ends a story about Baltimore and Camden Yards with a sweet statement about Denver: "Denver's baseball team is losing. And Denver is winning."

Today's milestone: Don Zimmer married Soot at home plate in Elmira, New York (1951)

The Rockies are now 43-75 (.364). This has them continuing to languish in last place, 36 games out of first and 2.5 games out of sixth. By comparison, the Mets are 40-77 and the Marlins are 51-67.

Monday, August 16 is an open date, and the Rockies remain open to criticism.

Example: In today's Denver Post, Jim Armstrong points out that the Rockies have been caught stealing more times (71) than the Yankees have *attempted* to steal (58).

And the News lists the Rockies' TRAGIC NUMBER. That's the unmagic number of Giants wins and Rockies losses that will mathematically eliminate Our Boys from the NL West pennant race.

The Tragic Number is nine. With 43 games left to play. Could be close.

Tuesday, August 17: Philadelphia 10, Colorado 7

The game that few saw the end of.

7:05 at Mile High Stadium
The National Anthem: Diana Sanchez (received liver
  transplant a year ago)
The first balls: Ken Caldwell (MCI) and Al Jarreau
The starting pitchers: Reynoso (8-8) vs. Rivera (10-6)
The W-L pitchers: Rivera (11-6) and Reynoso (8-9)
The attendance: 63,193
The News Headline: Rockies' rally comes too late
The Post Headline: It's Mile High misery again

On the way in, some, most, or all fans are given NUPRIN buttons. The Nuprin people expect that for weeks and months to come people will still be wearing them because nobody told them it was OK to take them off. And because they just might win something. The Nuprin people are probably right.

Before the game: A moment of silence for Gerald Phipps to mark the passing on of a man who had much to do with Denver's current sports fortunes.

In the air: The rains came. Several times. Which means that the umbrellas came out. Which is why many fans with eyeballs wished that tonight was Safety Goggles Night at the ballpark.

On the field: If the rain isn't enough to dampen things in Mile High, the wheels come off the Rockies in the 8th when they allow the visitors to double, single, homer, triple, walk, and double again before they get Out One.

Ironically, the Rockies have just released a brand new "official scorecard magazine" and its cover features ARMANDO REYNOSO, THE ROCKIES' PITCHIN' MAGICIAN.

With pitching magic in short supply tonight, many fans slip out early.

In the stands: Fans who believe there should be separation between baseball and foot- are filled with admiration for those who keep the grounds in Mile High. They have obliterated the gridironesque stripes from yesterday's football game.

But what color of paint does the grounds crew use that so perfectly matches the grass? The Fans' Ombudsman is called upon to find out.

Head groundskeeper Tom Lujan supplies the answer: It isn't paint, it's a dye called Green Zip. It's very dark green, so he dilutes it with water to match Mile High's turf.

Considering that the stadium has just endured a football game *and* a papal visit, the place appears to be in great shape for a ballgame.

Sharp-eyed fans look for What's New.

First of all, there's Cracker Jack in its new monster size (it's 10" long) to justify its new monster price (it's $3.75).

Also new: There, on the scoreboard, there's a Continental Airlines' new logo (CAL folks call it Spiderman) where, for many weeks, there'd been a clumsily painted blotch obliterating something. But what? FANS WANT TO KNOW. So the Fans' Ombudsman dropped a letter in the direction of Kevin Carlon, Director of Stadium Ops.

Here's the response: "The advertising panel now occupied by Continental Airlines was formerly occupied by United

Airlines before their contract expired."

Speaking of logos, that old logomeister Greg Akiyama wonders if the Rockies' logo is the only logo for any team with snow in or on it.

Allan S. finds Deep Meaning in a snack: "This frozen yogurt reflects cultural diversity. It's brown and white." Thank you, Allan.

And there is grumbling tonight.

Fans grumble when the organ greets the Phils' Dave Hollins with "Davy Crockett."

"Davy Crockett was a hero," grumbles Rich I., "King of the wild frontier and all that. That's not the kind of song we should greet the opposition with. It should be a song that disses him."

Fans grumble again when it is revealed that this is just Federico Peña's first Rockies game.

Fans who majored in English grumble when the scoreboard reports the outcome of the game between the PADRES and the CARD'S. Earlier, fans had wondered who thought that an apostrophe needed to be jammed into CARDS.

Now they know. It's probably the same guy who put this one on the scoreboard: MARIN'ERS.

For some reason, a clot of fans find themselves making jokes about Cole's Minor Daughter. Few are funny. Actually, none are.

In clear defiance of the NO FLASH PHOTOGRAPHY rule, Mother Nature lit up the top of the 6th with a fine display of lightning.

Fan Diane has returned from the left coast where she witnessed the Rox' brutal treatment of the team that makes its home at Dodger Stadium—where, unlike Mile High, the seats have arms on them.

Will the seats in Coors Field have arms? FANS WANT TO KNOW. Once again, the Fans' Ombudsman goes to work.

The answer is yes. Two each. Though you'll have to share.

Where's the money? A concise conversation between a Rockies fan and a Rockies hospitality operative:

"Is there an ATM here?"

"No."

Kind of surprising, really. Folks would leave more money behind if they could get their hands on it.

Where's the pope?

Much is made of the fact that the pope had just visited Mile High, but it didn't seem to do much good for the Rockies. Looking to the heavens, one wonders if, perhaps, arks are in order.

Naturally, many fans wish the pope and Rockies had been in town at the same time so the papal pitcher could've thrown out the first ball.

And the connection is clear: "Upon these Rockies..."

It just wasn't to be.

Remnants of the pope's visit watch the game from the left field stands. Their sign: TORONTO PILGRIMS THANK DENVER, EH?

One fan is reminded of the classic comment made by St. Louis outfielder Joe "Ducky" Medwick when, during World War II, he was among a group of U.S. soldiers who got an audience with the pope.

"Your Holiness," he said, "I'm Joseph Medwick. I, too, used to be a Cardinal."

Today's milestone: Alex Cole's birthday (1965)

The Rockies now have a 43-76 record, which puts them in last place, 36 games behind San Francisco (which is in first) and 2.5 games behind San Diego (which is in sixth).

With a 51-68 record, Florida leads Colorado by 8 games in the race to the expansion gonfalon.

Wednesday, August 18: Philadelphia 7, Colorado 6
The game Johnny Angel took from us.

7:05 at Mile High Stadium
The National Anthem: Jim Honiotes (Jones Intercable)
The first ball: Congressman Dan Schaefer (*to catcher Dan Sheaffer*)
The starting pitchers: Sanford (1-0) vs. Greene (12-3)
The W-L pitchers: Thigpen (2-0) and Ruffin (4-5)
The attendance: 61,056
The News Headline: Phillies still untamed in Mile High
The Post Headline: Taking another bow

On the field: A Darren Daulton liner breaks the little toe on Ruffin's left foot. And the Phillies are on the verge of breaking the hearts of Rockies fans. A win tomorrow and they'll have won 'em all—a sixpack of games—at Mile High.

Today, Sanford labors through four innings, walking five. Philadelphia's starter, Tommy Greene, has problems, too. Bichette homers in the first and comes within a double—the category in which he leads the NL—of hitting for the cycle.

In fact, sloppy fielding almost hands the game to the Rockies. But the Phillies' pond scum-in-residence, John Kruk, knocks a pair of home runs and the dirtballs prevail.

Speaking of dirt, Phillies' manager Fregosi complains about the condition of the field. Welcome to Mudville, Jim.

In the stands: In the bottom of the third, Tom Legueri buys yogurt for his daughter Aryn, 7. Does it have sprinkles? You bet.

"But," as Jim H. points out, "last night, *everybody* got sprinkles."

After Mo Sanford makes many, many pickoff attempts to first, fans start to chant "NO MO!" And one suggests that "Sanford's going to be a candidate for carpal tunnel surgery—for repetitive motion."

Discussion turns to the story about Charlie Hayes early in the season when he is said to have rebuffed an autograph seeker thusly: "What day is this—Tuesday? I don't give autographs on Tuesday."

A fan's response upon hearing this: "As far as I'm concerned, Hayes should be sitting down there in the dugout next to Baylor."

Then there's Jayhawk Owens. Although he's back in the Springs, a Rockies fan who loves him—or at least loves his nomenclature—gushes: "What a great name! I'm renaming all my children Jayhawk!"

After yet another recounting of the litany of fan no-nos threatening ejection and dismissal from the stadium, someone wants to know "what's the difference between ejection and dismissal?"

It is decided that ejection involves the seat of your pants.

Fans are honked off about the organist's selections to welcome the other team's players to the plate. John Kruk gets "Johnny Angel," which contains the line "How we love you!" Dave Hollins gets "Davy Crockett," who is The King of the Wild

Frontier. He also gets "Monster Mash."

Everybody agrees: We should be poking fun at those guys. Like when the organist finally does come through with the playing of M-I-C-K-E-Y M-O-U-S-E for Mickey Morandini.

But listen. He's playing Billy Joel's "Pressure" when Eric Young comes up with men on in the ninth?

Ungood. The proper use of a ballpark organist is as a weapon.

It should distract their guys, relax ours.

They also agree that the clapping hands graphic on the scoreboard is lame. "We're not the live audience for a TV sitcom," Leslie C. says. "*We'll* decide when."

I am not a Kruk: Bill Hook, the landscape painter, says: "I always get John Kruk mixed up with Jim Palmer." But Bill, you've got the eye of an artist. How can you say such a thing?

"We artists see the inner beauty."

In the News, Tracy Ringolsby reports that "the outlook is bleak for Galarraga attaining the 502 plate appearances he needs to qualify for the National League batting title."

But he points out that oh-fers can be added to his at-bats if necessary to bring it up to 502 and The Cat could still win.

The Rockies have now lost two in a row, have a 43-77 record and are in last place, 3.5 games behind the Padres. Florida is 51-69 and the Mets are 42-78.

Thursday, August 19: Colorado 6, Philadelphia 5
The last chance to beat the Phillies at home in '93—and Freddie B. did it.

3:05 at Mile High Stadium
The National Anthem: USAF Marching Band of the
  Rockies
The first ball: Pat Stokes (Anheuser-Busch)
The starting pitchers: Blair (5-9) vs. Jackson (9-9)
The W-L pitchers: Moore (2-0) and Mason (4-9)
The attendance: 53,443
The News Headline: Rockies rally by Phillies
The Post Headline: Rally breaks new ground

On the field: The Rockies' nine-game losing streak at home is blown away by Freddie Benavides' three-run home run.

Going into the bottom of the eighth, the Phillies have what they believe to be a comfy 5-1 lead.

Then a Clark triple, a Castilla double, a Girardi walk, and a Young single precede Freddie B's heroics. Five runs score, the Rockies take a one-run lead, and Holmes comes in to face the meat of the Phillies' order. No problemo. Down go Kruk, Hollins and Daulton, 1-2-3.

Finally, a victory over Philadelphia. And finally, a victory in Mile High in the month of August, the Rockies' First Ever.

In the stands: Fans are abuzz over the newspaper reports that rookie hurler Curtis Leskanic, 24, was arrested in Littleton early Tuesday morning (aka late Monday night) and charged with DUI. Says he swerved to avoid a deer, says that's why he put his '91 Beretta on its side.

And there is serious consideration given to recommending that Benavides change the spelling of his first name to Freddy. That -ie is just too wimpy for a three-run homer blaster.

Alan Dumas is madder'n hops (and barley). Seems he bought a season ticket. Seems it turned out to be located in the Family Section. Yes, the no-drinking section. "That," Alan grumbles, "should be against the law."

On the way home: Peter Milstein grumbles that "I don't think much of Daryl Boston, but he's been pretty good on the road. And I haven't been very fond of Benavides, either. He's hasn't done much for us—until today. So who do I hate now? Might have to go back to Charlie Hayes."

Today's milestone: Scott Fredrickson's birthday (1967)

The Rockies now have a 44-77 record and languish in the NL West's cellar, 37 games out of first and 1.5 games behind the mighty San Diego Padres.

Friday, August 20 is an open date, but one that finds the Rockies' five Latino players at a private reception with 300 members of Denver's Hispanic community at the Chili Pepper. It was *autógrafos, fotografías,* and *compañerismo* all around.

Bruce Hurst's debut. The Cat's back. And the Rockies sweep their first doubleheader.

3:05 at Mile High Stadium
The National Anthem: Voices of Faith Choir
The first ball: Bill Husted
    GAME ONE
The starting pitchers: Harris (10-12) vs. Hillman (1-6)
The W-L pitchers: Harris (11-12) and Innis (1-3)
    GAME TWO
The starting pitchers: Hurst (0-0) vs. Jones (1-0)
The W-L pitchers: Reed (7-4) and Jones (1-1)
The attendance: 60,613
The News Headline: Galarraga returns, Rockies sweep
The Post Headline: Rockies take two from Mets

Through the turnstiles: Interestingly, today's baseball game outdrew the Broncos exhibition game last night against the Dolphins. The score: 60,613-to-59,383.

On the field: The doubleheader provides an opportunity for the Rockies to display both halves of the H&H acquisition from the Padres on one day. With another H slamming the door in relief.

In the first game, Harris is victorious for the first time as a Rocky. But the big ovation is for Andres Galarraga, back in the lineup after missing as many games as there are beers in a case of Coors. In the first game of the twin bill, The Cat is oh-fer plus a sacrifice fly. Harris gives up just four hits in seven innings, though two were homers. When he leaves, the game is knotted, 3-3. But that just sets the stage for yesterday's hero, Freddie Benavides, to single in the winning run in the bottom of the inning. By the end of the day, Freddie has raised his BA 18 points.

In the second contest, Hurst leaves in the fourth with tightness in his shoulder—and a 6-1 lead consisting largely of four RBI by Jerald Clark, another former Padre. Hurst had been sharp, facing just nine Mets in the first three stanzas. In spite of a couple of scary innings by Leskanic and Moore in which the Mets get five back, the Rox rule (as they say on TV).

In both games, Holmes shuts down the Mets for the last four outs. He's now been successful in his 14th consecutive save opportunity. And he has the first two-save day of his career.

In Westword, Bill Gallo will describe today thusly: "I don't know what your idea of hell is, but Saturday's doubleheader between the last-place Colorado Rockies and the last-place New York Mets—all five hours and 42 minutes of it—might have come pretty close."

Gallo was also critical of the two minute, fifty-one second National Anthem, characterizing it as "a 78 recording played at 33 rpms, only under water." Further, he notes a local sportswriter's quip: "Expansion baseball? That's expansion *singing.*"

In the stands: It's Picture "Night." Everybody gets a team picture—of the Rockies team *du* opening day. Which resembles the team *du jour* only slightly.

In response to the P.A. announcer's daily recitation of The Rules, which include an admonition not to throw things, a fan asks nobody in particular "How about epithets?"

Another warning is displayed on the scoreboard: DON'T PARK IN RESIDENTIAL AREAS AROUND MILE HIGH STADIUM. Which brings up an interesting point: If you had parked thus and went out and moved your car to a parking lot, how would you get back into Mile High? There is that pesky NO RE-ADMITTANCE decree. So if you go out and move your car you might as well go home.

Fans notice that the scoreboard also makes mention of today's DOUBLE HEADER. So spelled, one assumes, because there is a space between the games.

And a new sign now appears behind first and third bases. DO NOT SET OBJECTS ON DUGOUT, it says. An artistic fan wonders: "What about *objets?*"

There is discussion of Bobby Bonilla. "How old is he, anyway?" "Thirty." "Hmm. He's old enough to be called Bob. Almost old enough to be Robert." And talk then turns to Eddie Murray.

Today's crowd pushes the season's attendance past 3.5 million by an even 100.

Speaking of the Rockies' latest hero, a fan confesses that "I always want to call him Benny Fredavides. It's easier to say."

Bill Hook really came equipped for today's game. Soon,

those around him realize that Bill is wearing a different cap for each inning. This goes on through the entire first game. Whereupon it is revealed that Hook is only prepared to go a-hat-an-inning for *one* game.

There's more. Bill also has a meatball sandwich. He is a generous sort, so he turns to Bill K.: "Want a bite?" The reply: "No, I was bitten by a dog once and I didn't like it."

Bill K. has a semi-heartwarming story for those around him. Says he went to the Gart Bros. in Southwest Plaza yesterday to buy a new baseball scorebook. "They didn't have any, so they tried to sell me a lacrosse scorebook." No way. Instead, he went home and designed a baseball scorecard just the way he likes it and had Busy Bee Office Supply on Kipling make him 40 copies.

The organist plays "One" from A Chorus Line to welcome the Mets' shortstop Baez to the batter's box. Because Baez' uniform bears that number, no doubt. But should Our Organist be characterizing their shortstop as "a singular sensation"? Nah. Then how about "One Is The Loneliest Number"? Yeah.

Entering the ballpark, Grace and Doug F. reveal that they have yet to see the Rockies lose in Mile High Stadium. Facing a doubleheader, it sounded like a streak headed for a snapping. But no.

Toward the end of Game Two, provisions are running low. The stadium's supply of nachos and tacos has been exhausted. And a vendor is heard to shout: "I've got one more Coke. *The last of its kind!*"

Speaking of exhausted, in spite of a big crowd and there being many hours for beer-addled minds to wander from the subject at hand, nary a single wave is seen all afternoon. Not even a ripple.

A spectacular catch by Eric Young does, however, elicit salaams from the East Stands.

John M.: "I think the Rockies and Mets are close enough to minor league baseball that their doubleheaders should be seven-inning games."

And Tana W. comforts a Mets fan: "There, there. It'll be all right." That Tana really plays fast and loose with the truth, doesn't she?

Bill Gallo notwithstanding, adding a pair of wins to the old W-L record is recognized to be a highly rewarding use of a day.

Hey, let's play three!

Today's milestone: Danny Sheaffer's birthday (1961)

The Rockies have now won three in a row, are 46-77 on the season and are tied for sixth (and last) place in the NL West with San Diego. The Marlins have won a sixpack of games more than the Rockies. The 42-80 Mets will have to play one game above .500 ball the rest of the way to escape a 100-loss season.

Sunday, August 22: Colorado 4, New York 3
The first sweep of the Mets.
And the escape from the cellar.

1:05 at Mile High Stadium
The National Anthem: Julie Young Christofferson
The first ball: Shannon Dyer, 11 and Daniel Gaverich, 8
The starting pitchers: Bottenfield (4-8) vs. Fernandez (2-3)
The W-L pitchers: Muñoz (1-0) and Fernandez (2-4)
The attendance: 70,064
The News Headline: Rockies leave Mets in their dust
The Post Headline: Rockies drop Mets deeper into abyss

On the field: Today's win gives the Rox a sweep of the three-game series. (Until this visit, the Rocks were 1-4 vs. the Mets.)

Both teams employ the long ball today. Girardi knocks his first Mile High home run in the first to give the Rockies a 1-0 lead. It lasts 'til the sixth when two homers put the Mets ahead.

But not for long. In the bottom of the inning, Galarraga blasts a two-run homer and the Rocks are back on top.

But not for long. The Mets eke out a run in the top of the seventh to tie it up, 3-3.

But not for long. Here comes Freddie Benavides to open the Rockies' end of the seventh. He nails the first pitch for a homer—and has delivered the game-winning hits in three of the last four games.

Encouraging sight: Bottenfield pitching six-plus strong innings. Oddly, all four of his appearances at Mile High have been been in front of crowds of 70,000+. But Muñoz, making his first appearance for the Rox just a couple of hours after coming up from Colorado Springs, gets the W.

In the stands: It's Kids' Backpack Day. And a day that brings much anguish to fan/daddy John Mason.

"All week, my four-year-old daughter has been looking forward to coming to the game and getting her Rockies backpack. Today, she's too sick to come to the game, so I told her that I would go to the game and bring home a backpack for her.

"Boy, was I wrong. I showed a picture of my sick kid and her unused ticket for today's game to the guy handing out the backpacks, but he wouldn't give me one. So I went to another gate and that guy wouldn't, either. So I went to Guest Relations and the same thing happened. She's really going to be disappointed."

Jennifer Moore, executive assistant to Jerry McMorris, soon hears the story. And takes care of John's plight. A Rockies backpack comes in the mail a couple of days later addressed to Casey Mason. Yes, *Casey*. As mentioned, John Mason is a fan.

A fan analyzes the mobility of the Rockies' infield of Galarraga, Mejia, Benavides, and Hayes: "First base can't move; second moves too much, short moves back and forth, and third won't move."

Which inspires Len S.: "Here's a new game. Every time Hayes moves, we have to drink a beer."

John M.: "Sorry, but I'm not ready to go on the wagon."

A fan reports a real estate notice in this morning's Post: Marsha Antonucci has sold 80 Cherry Hills Farm for $1.8 mil.

A fan tells where he's been: "I spent the top of the fifth in the men's room, standing in line. Wishing I could hear KOA."

Another fan comments on the survey the Rockies are conducting on the concourse: "The question I wanted to be asked was 'If they have ARA at Coors Field will you ever go?'"

The most common exchange between fan and vendor undoubtedly goes like this:

"Coke!"

"Got Diet?"

"No."

"O.K., I'll take one anyway."

A survivor of the West Stands which is responsible for the "ROCKIES!" part of the popular "GO!" (pause) "ROCKIES!" chant says the sound is so loud that it hurts.

A fan looks around at yet another mindboggling crowd and comments:

"As usual, more crowd than necessary."

The Rockies have now won four in a row and have a record of 47-77, good enough for sole possession of sixth place, a game ahead of the Padres. The Marlins are in sixth place in their division with a 52-72 record.

Dante Bichette: "We've even got a chance to catch Florida."

Monday, August 23: Colorado 3, Phillies 2 (13 innings)
The longest game.

5:35 at Veterans Stadium
The starting pitchers: Reynoso (8-9) vs. Greene (12-3)
The W-L pitchers: Wayne (4-3) and Mason (4-10)
The attendance: 40,481
The News Headline: Bichette's homer in 13th gives
　　Rockies fifth straight
The Post Headline: Bichette blast levels Phillies

On the field: Finally. Dante hits a last at-bat blast that isn't matched by the opposition. His solo shot in the 13th stanza (an umpire's dozen?) knocks off the NL East-leading Phillies and ends the longest game (4:03) in franchise history.

Benavides strikes out thrice, the first time this season.

Bruce Ruffin (a former Philly) steps back onto the mound in Veterans Stadium for the first time in a couple of years and pitches three perfect innings. This was Bruce's first appearance since last Wednesday when Darren Daulton's shot broke the little toe on his left foot.

Let's run it into the ground dept.:
As mentioned, Ruffin was once a Philly. Or a Phil. But not a Phillie.

These days, of course, Ruffin is a Rocky. Or a Rock. But not a Rockie.

In the Post, Jim Armstrong observes that "Avoiding last place in the National League West isn't the Rockies' only goal. They also want to avoid 100 losses and maybe, just maybe, catch the Marlins in the expansion derby. Yes, it's late August, and even the Rockies are scoreboard-watching."

In other news: The Broncos trade The Vance to the Vikings.

The Rockies have now won 5 in a row, 12 of their last 15, and stand at 48-77, in 6th place, 35.5 games out—a game ahead of the Padres. (Florida is now 52-72 and in 6th place in the East, ten games ahead of the 42-82 Mets.)

Tuesday, August 24: Philadelphia 4, Colorado 2
The first game lost to a pitcher from Aurora.

5:35 at Veterans Stadium
The starting pitchers: Blair (5-9) vs. Jackson (9-9)
The W-L pitchers: Jackson (10-9) and Blair (5-10)
The attendance: 43,419
The News Headline: Jackson halts Rockies' win streak
The Post Headline: Jackson, Phils crash Rockies party

On the field: The Phillies turn three Rockies miscues in the second inning into as many runs—and that is all Aurora Central grad Danny Jackson needs. Looking like the Jackson of a couple of years ago, he one-hits (Galarraga) the Rox through seven innings, gives up a run in the eighth, then turns it over to his relievers who keep the Rockies from coming from behind.

Bichette throws out Incaviglia when the Phllies' outfielder singles, then takes a too-casual turn around first.

Mitch (Wild Thing) Williams notches his third save against the Rockies. In eight days.

In Tacoma: Rehabilitating David Nied pitches four rough innings for the Sky Sox, showing little velocity (83 mph tops) and letting the Tacoma Tigers steal three bases. The Post's Pike's Peek tabs him "the first former great in the Pet Rocks' organization."

Today's milestone: S. Ehrhart and M. Nicklous announce their intentions to organize an ownership group to pursue a National League franchise for Denver (1990)

The Rockies have now ended their five-game win streak ("We'll have to start another one tomorrow," says Baylor), are 48-78 for the season, and have fallen into a last-place tie with San Diego.

The last loss to the Phillies of the season.

10:35 at Veterans Stadium
The starting pitchers: Sanford (1-0) vs. Schilling (10-6)
The W-L pitchers: Schilling (11-6) and Sanford (1-1)
The attendance: 46,448
The News Headline: Rockies' pitching woes continue
The Post Headline: Rockies' Sanford takes a Pratt fall

On the field: Fans and players dreamed of an on-the-road sweep of the league leaders, and even built a 3-2 lead in this game.

But Mo Sanford struggles, walks leadoff hitters, lets them steal, hangs curve balls, gives up a two-run lead-losing homer to backup catcher Todd Pratt, throws 98 pitches in just five innings, leaves after giving up eight hits and five runs and is charged with the loss in the year's last meeting with the playoff-bound Phillies.

Cole is easily picked off to kill a potential rally. (After stealing 21 in his first 26, he has swiped but 4 in his last 12 attempts.)

Mejia homers, then strikes out thrice.

Girardi is charged with his first passed ball of the season.

The Rockies teeter on the brink of being counted out of the NL West pennant race.

The Rox' Tragic Number—as it is cruelly called—is now down to one.

In Shea Stadium: The Mets drop their 83rd game, are mathematically eliminated from the NL East pennant race. (Meanwhile, in San Francisco, the Braves cut the Giants' lead to four and a half.)

The Rockies have now fallen back into sole possession of last place with a record of 48-79 (.378), a game behind the Padres.

In Minneapolis: Former Denver Bronco Vance Johnson says, "I needed a change of scenery."

Thursday, August 26: New York 7, Colorado 1

The first time the Rockies are eliminated from a pennant race.

5:40 at Shea Stadium
The starting pitchers: Harris (11-12) vs. Gooden (11-14)
The W-L pitchers: Gooden (12-14) and Harris (11-13)
The attendance: 20,062
The News Headline: It's official: Rockies out of pennant race
The Post Headline: Dr. K eliminates impatient Rockies

On the field: Today, the Mets officially eliminate Our Boys from the National League West race—just as the Mets were eliminated, themselves, just yesterday.

The Shea Stadium jinx continues.

When he was a Padre, the last team Greg Harris beat was the Mets. And the Mets are the only team he's beaten as a Rocky.

But not today. The NYers load the bases before Harris can get an out.

Soon, he is down by four runs.

Meanwhile, Gooden is masterful. He gives up a homer to Vinny Castilla, three other harmless hits, a walk, and that's it. (His four hitter matches his Opening Day performance against the Rox.) Only *two* Colorado players even work Gooden to a three-balls count.

The Rox spend the entire afternoon chasing balls out of the strike zone.

The result: Nine more Ks for the Doctor—three charged against Galarraga.

On the 15-day disabled list: Bruce Hurst (retroactive to August 22). His replacement is Lance Painter, recalled from the SSox.

Today's milestone: Jeff Parrett's birthday (1961)

The Rockies have now fallen deeper into last place. With a 48-80 record, they are a game and a half behind the Padres.

(Meanwhile, the Mets and Marlins are 44-83 and 53-74.)

Friday, August 27: New York 3, Colorado 2

The first Rockies game played at the same time the Broncos are playing. (And the first simultaneous losses.)

5:40 at Shea Stadium
The starting pitchers: Bottenfield (4-8) vs. Fernandez (2-4)
The W-L pitchers: Fernandez (3-4) and Bottenfield (4-9)
The attendance: 21,765
The News Headline: Rockies run way to loss
The Post Headline: Mets rocking to familiar tune

On KBCO in morning drive time: "Well, the Rockies aren't going to the World Series this year."

On the field: While the Phoenix Cardinals are crushing the Broncos 34-9 in their final preseason game, the Rockies are succumbing 3-2 in Queens. Yes, the Rox are still 0-for-Shea.

Slumping (0-11) Galarraga comes through with a homer to give Bottenfield a 1-0 lead, but the Bottman quickly gives it back to the Worst Team in Baseball by allowing a three-run blast to Ryan Thompson.

A ninth-inning baserunning goof by Cole (cut down at third) cost the Rockies an excellent opportunity to tuck this one into the W column.

In the studio: Catcher/Dittohead Danny Sheaffer left tickets for yesterday's game for Rush Limbaugh. This earned the Rockies' backstop a chance to meet his hero today—and be on Limbaugh's radio show.

Besides being a Limbaugh supporter, Sheaffer is also in the chimney sweep business back home in North Carolina.

Make up your own joke.

Today's milestone: Phillies' thirdbaseman Charlie Hayes hits his first career grand slam (1991)

The Rockies have now lost four in a row, are 38-81 and have sunk deeper into last place. They are 35.5 games out of first and 2.5 games behind San Diego. The Mets are 45-83, which means they are within 2.5 games of the Rockies—and escaping the Worst Team in Baseball appellation.

Meanwhile, Florida is strutting around with a gaudy (for an expansion team) 54-74 record.

Saturday, August 28: Colorado 7, New York 5
The first win in Shea.

5:10 at Shea Stadium
The starting pitchers: Reynoso (8-9) vs. Jones (1-1)
The W-L pitchers: Reynoso (9-9) and Jones (1-2)
The attendance: 25,238
The News Headline: Reynoso's bat helps end Shea funk
The Post Headline: Reynoso swings, Rockies sing

On the field: It's the first time Reynoso has faced the Mets.

As always, the can't-hit-worth-a-lick pitcher swings as hard as he can just in case he actually makes contact. Back in May, in Reynoso's second ML at-bat, it worked and the ball flew out of the park. Today, in the sixth inning, after the Rox have already scored a run to unsettle the Mets hurler Jones, it works again. With two men on.

Earlier, in the fourth, the Rockies had put three runs on the board with the help of as many Mets errors.

A great throw from Jerald Clark to nail Ryan Thompson at the plate chokes out a rally by the New Yorkers.

Darren Holmes pitches the ninth and records save #19 (16 in a row).

And The Curse of Shea Stadium is history.

The Rockies now have a 49-81 record (.377) and remain 2.5 games behind the Padres, who also won today.

Meanwhile, the eyes of Colorado are on Texas.
When the Rockies go on the road, a couple of their fans do likewise. They fly down to Dallas to pay a visit to Arlington Stadium (in its last season) in hopes of seeing the Ryan Express (also in its last season).

Seeing the stadium—a cozy, oft-expanded former minor league park in desperate need of immediate demolition—is a joy, but Ryan is on the DL.

Comparing the experience of watching the Texas Rangers at their home with watching Our Rox at our home is inevitable. And interesting. And a little irritating.

To wit: Their hot dogs are primo. Their seats have arms. And at no time are fans subjected to warnings by the P.A. announcer about the dire consequences of misbehavior. Nothing about flash photography being banned. Or throwing the ball back being grounds for ejection. Or arrest.

In fact, the home run balls by the opposition (Orioles) *are* thrown back. To everyone's delight.

And yes, the game *can* be heard in the men's room. A speaker brings the radio account of the game to those who are debeering.

Season ticket holders enjoy a photograph—in full color—of a Rangers player or scene on their ticket stubs. A different one each game. Tonight's is an aerial shot of the ballpark.

Their program, over a hundred pages in color with a scorecard in the middle and a four-page slip-in update sheet, costs two bucks. (In Denver, it's three.)

Instead of the stupid Coors Cutter home run ball thing on the scoreboard, they have Dot Races. Everyone in the stands is handed a red, yellow, green or blue dot. When *these* races are run on the scoreboard, something is riding on it—a free drink at Whattaburger if your dot is the winning color.

And there is live broadcast of the game on a TV at every concession stand.

So much for the plusses. Here are the bummers:

The National Anthem isn't sung live, nobody throws out the first pitch—and no dollar-or-less scorecards are available. Which may explain why not a single scorekeeping fan was spotted in two games here.

And they *do* do The Wave.

Other than when The Wave is going by, the fans are very quiet. Must be the heat.

They don't even sing "Take Me Out..." during the 7th inning stretch.

Here are two nifties the Rangers are doing re their new stadium which is nearing completion a hundred yards or so away.

They sell postcards of the new ballpark for 25¢ at the old ballpark. (Some were purchased to be sent back to Denver.)

And they are allowing people to have their names carved

into bricks that will be part of the Texas Rangers Walk of Fame outside their new stadium. Costs $100 per, which goes to "landscape and beautify the new ballpark." In addition to the brick, that hun buys you a certificate commemorating your purchase. You also get voting privileges for the selection of special players to be bricked into the Walk of Fame.

For the Rockies fans in attendance, the best part of being here wasn't seeing Juan Gonzales do something no Rocky has ever done—smash three home runs in one game. Nor was it howdying the other guy wearing a CR cap they passed on the concourse.

The best thing of all was following the course of the Mets-Rockies game on the scoreboard. Arlington Stadium has one of those boards that shows the scores of all the games being played in the majors all the time—and it tells you what inning it is, which team is at bat, and the score. Truly a baseball fan's scoreboard. (One hopes Coors Field will be so equipped.)

Watching the Rox claw their way to victory over the Mets was delicious.

Better, even, than the dogs.

Sunday, August 29: Colorado 6, New York 1
The first ML victory for Lance Painter.

1:10 at Shea Stadium
The starting pitchers: Painter (0-2) vs. Tanana (6-12)
The W-L pitchers: Painter (1-2) and Tanana (6-13)
The attendance: 25,774
The News Headline: Painter strokes a masterpiece
The Post Headline: Painter sends the Mets packing

On the field: Lance Painter, up from the minors as a surprise to everyone including himself, and visiting New York for the first time in his life, gets in trouble early by giving up a single, double and triple in the first inning and quickly falls behind 0-1.

But then he settles down and winds up throwing just 94 pitches en route to a five-hit complete game victory.

The Mets lie down and do a very convincing job of playing dead when the final 13 batters use only one or two pitches to put the ball into play—and the final stanza requires but four pitches.

All very sweet for a pitcher who was sent down to the minors on June 2 with an ERA of 11.05. Also sweet for any pitcher: Painter gets a hit, knocking in a run in the ninth.

Jerald Clark replaces the slumping Dante Bichette in right field. And responds with a three-run homer in the sixth that puts the Rox ahead for good.

The Rockies wind up splitting the season series with the Mets, 6-6. In spite of that Shea thing.

In the Post: Woody Paige knocks Phoenix's dream of getting a team and says that "We don't care about expansion, anyway, because we have a team—sort of."

In Portland: David Nied's comeback trail hits a rough stretch as the young hurler—now a Sky Sock (?)—gives up eight runs, all earned, in five innings against the Portland Beavers.

The Rockies have now won two in a row and are now 50-81, still in last place, two games behind the Padres, who split a doubleheader and finished the day at 52-79.

Monday, August 30: Montreal 6, Colorado 1
The game that broke the single-season NL attendance record.

> **7:05 at Mile High Stadium**
> **The National Anthem (Canadian):** Little London
>   Barbershop Quartet
> **The National Anthem (U.S.):** John Paul II Youth
>   Chorale
> **The first ball:** Casey Farmer, 11
> **The starting pitchers:** Sanford (1-1) and Fassero (9-3)
> **The W-L pitchers:** Fassero (10-3) and Sanford (1-2)
> **The attendance:** 47,699
> **The News Headline:** Sanford goes wild as Expos rip
>   Rockies
> **The Post Headline:** Fassero shuts down Rockies

On the field: Montreal's Jeff Fassero retires 21 in row as he cruises to a easy victory.

A low-wattage highlight for the Rockies was the career

debut of Freddie Benavides at first base. This completes his infield cycle; he's played all four infield positions.

Lowlights include Mo Sanford's first ten pitches—all balls. And Hayes trying to catch the ball in a rundown with his belly. And Galarraga whiffing and then being ejected from the game for tossing his bat in disgust after an attempted check swing was ruled strike three. (Which proves that flash photography isn't the only thing that can get you ejected from Mile High Stadium.)

Unfortunately, The Cat's outburst cost him an at-bat, a commodity he needs lots of in his pursuit of the batting title.

After the anthem: Bill Koerber, well-known National Anthem rater, says "That's a ten."

In the stands: It's Coca-Cola Lapel Pin #10 Night. Even more important, it is the night the Rockies break the '82 Dodgers' NL attendance record for a season. That year, L.A. counted 3,608,881 fans. So far, in 63 dates, the Rockies have drawn 3,617,863.

Win Bleidt, the Arvada nine-year-old who has just accompanied his dad on a visit to all 28 ML ballparks, is introduced to the crowd and waves his cap.

When told about Arlington Stadium (no threats of ejection for misbehavior) and the Texas Rangers fans (none keep scorecards), Peter Groff is appalled. "That's not a real ball game. You gotta keep score and be in danger of being thrown out."

After the Rockies' P.A. guy reads The Rules of the Ballyard before the game, Roz says "They should tell us where the firing squad is."

A Rockies fan—who *is* keeping score—notices that the Expos' base on balls production has gotten into double digits. "I bet I can guess what the headline will be in either or both of the papers tomorrow: "Expos walk over Rockies."

A couple of scorecard keepers puzzled over the proper notation to use when a player is called out for bunting foul with two strikes on him. They decide to use a K facing downward. With the K's nose ignominiously stuck in the dirt

The organist done good when Fassero becomes the first to be awarded a face-down K. The see-you-later song for the Expo was "Canadian Sunset."

Diane wonders aloud: "If Adam West married Sandy Koufax, wouldn't his name be Adam West Koufax?"

Which gets many groans and this from Alton Dillard: "That's enough cappuccino for you, Diane!"

Bob The Beer Man (vendor #001) rolls out a brand new surefire merchandising technique for selling those big overpriced boxes of Cracker Jack. "It's got a Rolex watch in it!" he yells. And, at $3.75, it oughta.

Perhaps the finest moment of the game comes in the fifth when Rockies' reliever Bruce Ruffin faces the Expos' Randy Ready. Yes, folks, it was a classic matchup: Ruffin-Ready.

Late in the game, up in the second deck down the right field line, a smoke bomb goes off. But it's nothing to get excited about. *It wasn't flash photography.*

Very late in the game, it is suggested that rally caps won't be enough to pull this one out. "What we need," Peter says, "is rally *pants.*"

Fortunately, the game ended before Peter and his pals could put their pants on backward.

In the Post: Metro State baseball coach Vince Porreco discusses Andres Galarraga's hunt for the National League batting title. "Galarraga still has to get the hits, or he'll be left in the dust by San Diego's Tony Gwynn." Indeed, The Cat hasn't had much luck at the plate of late. But even though he lacks the at-bats he needs to qualify for the championship, Galarraga is still averaging .381 to Gwynn's .360.

Rox sock it to Sox.

In the wonderful (and highly profitable) world of sports merchandising, the Rockies are the big story this year.

Rockiestuff leads the big leagues in sales, knocking the White Sox down to No. 2.

Interesting aspect to all this is that the Rockies are not making enormous dollars out of all this madness. Royalties are distributed evenly among the 28 teams, so the Rox get 3.6% of the royalties, just like the Mariners.

One exception: When they sell merchandise themselves, they get to keep the entire wholesale-retail markup just like any other retailer. Which is why the Rockies have been trying so hard to get you to buy from their store in the parking lot and in the concourse and, of course, their Dugout Store on Lincoln.

Today's milestone: M. Monus and J. Antonucci join the newly formed ownership group pursuing a NL franchise for Denver (1990)

The Rockies now have a record of 50-82 (.379) and reside in the cellar, 36 games behind San Francisco and 2.5 behind the Padres.

Tuesday, August 31: Montreal 14, Colorado 3
The first time the Rockies bat out of order.

> **7:05 at Mile High Stadium**
> **The National Anthem (Canadian):** Rockies IV
> **The National Anthem (U.S.):** Heritage Christian Center (about 110 singers)
> **The first ball:** Pastor Dennis Learned
> **The starting pitchers:** Harris (11-13) vs. Heredia (2-2)
> **The W-L pitchers:** Heredia (3-2) and Harris (11-14)
> **The attendance:** 46,288
> **The News Headline:** Rockies fall apart vs. Expos
> **The Post Headline:** Rockies bats go unidentified

In the parking lot, a carload of fans gets out of a car with a great license plate: DBLPLA.

On the field: Three pitches into the game, Grissom homers and the Expos have a lead they never give up.

Gil Heredia pretty much baffles the Rockies, dispatching them on 58 pitches through six innings while giving up just one run, an unearned one.

Confusion amongst those keeping score in the stands is resolved when it is discovered that Baylor had Bichette and Galarraga batting in that order in the three and four slots on his lineup card. But when they batted in the bottom of the first, they inadvertently switched.

Since they did no harm, Expos manager Alou said nothing. After all, you can only be so out.

When Baylor brought the out-of-order battage to the attention of the crew chief of the umpires, the ump merely instructed the batters to go back to their lineup-card order.

When the Expos bat around in the seventh inning, it is

the 31st time this season that a team has enjoyed an inning of around-battage against the Rockies.

In the stands: A fan remembers what Zephyrs manager Tony Muser once said. "In baseball, you lose about a third of the games by a lot—you're never really in them—and you win about a third of the games by a lot. It's in the other third of the games that you have a chance to win or lose. How you play those determines how your season goes."

This, clearly, is an example of the first third.

With the game careening out of control, fans find diversions where they could.

Ray Jones studies the fault line running down the steps between Sections 116 and 117.

John Ashton reads a book about child therapy, "The Healing Power of Play."

Betsy Hook examines the inside of a peanut shell and says it looks like Santa Claus. And she tries the designated driver deal wherein you sign a promise not to drink and you receive a small Coke. *Very* small. How small? The Fans' Ombudsman took the cup home and measured it. Six ounces.

Betsy, not one of your everyday fans in the stands, points to the scoreboard when Girardi comes to bat and asks a question no one has ever asked before. "Why," she wonders, "does he have a minus sign in front of the C?" No, Betsy, it doesn't mean that Girardi is below-average. "GIRARDI – C" simply means that Girardi is the catcher.

The scoreboard operator errs again when it is proclaimed that tonight is PEACE CORP NIGHT AT THE BALLPARK."

"They're privatizing *everything*!" a fan exclaims.

When the score reaches 13-1, Attorney Fleischman decides to leave. On his way out, he encounters Judge Jones and informs the magistrate that "This is cruel and unusual punishment." Well, not unusual.

Another fan: "Gotta go. The pressure's too much for me." The game? "No, the beer."

Overheard on the way out: "I'm glad the Expos scored 14. Now the sportscasters won't be making stupid cracks about missing the extra point."

Indeed, the Expos' two touchdowns *easily* beat the Rockies' field goal.

The **Rockies have now** lost two in a row, have a record of 50-83 and are in the cellar of the NL West, 2.5 games behind the Padres and 36 behind San Francisco. Atlanta is 3.5 games out.

After starting the month of August 0-7, the Rockies wind up 14-16. Fourteen victories give the Rox the expansion team record for the month of August. The Marlins were 11-17. No expansion team has ever had a winning August.

As September dawns, the Blue Jays lead the Yankees by 1.5 games, the White Sox are 5.5 games ahead of Texas, and the Phillies have a 9.5-game bulge on Montreal.

Wednesday, September 1: Montreal 11, Colorado 3
The last game with two National Anthems played in Denver in the first season.

7:05 at Mile High Stadium
The National Anthem (Canadian): Flipside
The National Anthem (U.S.): Michael Martin Murphy
    (After singing "America the Beautiful.")
The first ball: Nancy Yanak
The starting pitchers: Bottenfield (4-9) vs. Martinez (12-8)
The W-L pitchers: Martinez (13-8) and Bottenfield (4-10)
The attendance: 46,781
The News Headline: Martinez rolls over Rockies
The Post Headline: Power surge jolts Rockies 11-3

On the field: No Canadian Sunset tonight, either. Montreal takes charge from the get-go and sweeps the three-game set. This is the twelfth series the Rox have been swept in so far, half at home, half away.

Expos stars are Sean Berry (two homers), Marquis Grissom (a three-run blast), Larry Walker (4-for-5) and Dennis Martinez (who flirts with a perfect game into the fifth inning, then toys with a no-hitter into the sixth, and then dallies with a shutout until later in the sixth when Castilla scores).

Expos non-star is Rondell White. He makes his ML debut by going 0-5.

Rockies' starter Bottenfield gives up six runs in the four

innings he pitches.

Galarraga goes 0-4, drops to .369. If his current average were adjusted to meet the at-bat requirements for the batting championship, it would drop to .337, well below Tony Gwynn's .360.

In the stands: "These guys are hard to beat. I remember a time when we were 2-0 against them. Of course, back then *they* had Bottenfield."

Speaking of one of our players, a fan noted: "He's only got four hits. He's due."

Another fan: "Maybe he's due. *Or maybe he's inept.*"

In the sky: A plane goes over promoting COLO SPGS BALLOON CLASSIC. The fans in the stands are amazed. It's not an ad for a strip joint!

The Rockies have now lost three in a row, have a 50-84 record, and dwell, alone, in the cellar 37 games out of first and 3.5 out of sixth.

Thursday, September 2 is an open date, and tonight, at the Denver Buffalo Company, Rockies players, wives and kids are auctioning Rockiestuff to raise money for the Leukemia Society.

Meanwhile, the Denver media spends the day grumbling over the Montreal's sweep.

Channel 7 calls Mile High as "The Valley of the Dulls."

And the KOA morning show asks, "Can we cut off diplomatic ties with Canada?"

Meanwhile, News columnist Norm Clarke admits he wanted to see Montreal pull a 3-6-1 double play the other night "just to hear the most alliterative play-by-play call in major league history: 'Marrero to Cordero to Fassero.'" And he wishes the batter hitting into this twin killing could be Pedro Guerrero.

After all the big attendance numbers the Rockies have put up at home, they finally met their match. A three-game series that had the NL West league-leading Giants visiting the super-hot Atlanta Braves outdrew the Rockies' series with Montreal. But it's noteworthy because it is without question the only time that a series in Mile High Stadium has come in second all season.

Friday, September 3: Colorado 7, Pittsburgh 6

The game in which Baylor used the most pitchers.

7:05 at Mile High Stadium
The National Anthem: Chrissie Thompson
The first ball: Jeff Givens
The starting pitchers: Reynoso (9-9) vs. Hope (0-1)
The W-L pitchers: Holmes (2-3) and Dewey (1-1)
The attendance: 51,512
The News Headline: Sheaffer rescues Rockies in ninth
The Post Headline: Resilient Rockies top Pirates 7-6

On the field: With the spectre of a 100-loss season looming over the team, Reynoso, the Rockies' ace the first half of the season, struggles again.

Four minutes, three batters and five pitches into the game, the Pirates are ahead, 3-0, on Van Slyke's homer.

In bottom of the 8th, Rockies push across two runs to take the lead for the first time in the game.

But the Pirates retake the lead in the top of the ninth on a two-run homer by Slaught off Darren Holmes.

In the bottom of the ninth, with two outs and two men on, Danny Sheaffer doubles in the two runs the Rox needed. *Desperately*.

Baylor employs seven pitchers, a season high.

Interesting upshot: Until tonight, Holmes had notched a save in nine consecutive appearances. He blew the save when he gave up Slaught's homer—but when the Rox came back, he got a win, instead!

Galarraga breaks his longest hitless streak (0-15) of '93.

In the stands: It's Adult Cap Night #2. Which may or may not explain John Elway's presence which, when announced, elicited cheers mixed with boos in a dry martini-like 7:1 ratio.

In the TV booth: Charlie and Duane make no effort on a foul ball which sails into their booth. The ball is caught, easily, by their guest, Dan Issel.

In the News: A headline trumpets: "Gwynn closes in on Galarraga in batting war." The subhead: "Rockies first baseman's average falls from .392 to .369 since Aug. 21, while Padre hitter soars."

The Cat's average—adjusted for the lack of at-bats—has now sunk to .337. Gwynn leads the league with .357. And the article quotes Baylor: "Cat is going to hit another hot streak. Then it becomes a race."

In Las Vegas, David Nied shows good control and speed in his final rehab start for the Sky Sox, but the Las Vegas Stars get eleven hits and six runs off him in six innings.

Oh, the shame and embarrassment of it all.

Denver is still fuming of the alleged disqualification of the allegedly gang-punched ballots for Andres G. And, of course, wondering how or if the things are really counted at all.

It is irksome to think that a new rule has been made and invoked just to disqualify bushels of ballots from The Time Zone that appear to have been voted all at once by one person.

On KOA, Tim Smile has suggested that from now on this will be known as The Galarraga Rule.

How mortifying.

The Rockies now have a 51-84 record (.378) and continue to occupy the cellar of the NL West two games behind the Padres. In all of Major League baseball only the occupants of the NL East cellar have a worse record. The Mets are now 47-88.

Saturday, September 4: Colorado 10, Pittsburgh 4
The game Charlie Hayes wore his pants high.

7:05 at Mile High Stadium
The National Anthem: Richard Perkins
The first ball: Jennifer Walde, 15
The starting pitchers: Painter (1-2) vs. Wakefield (4-8)
The W-L pitchers: Painter (2-2) and Wakefield (4-9)
The attendance: 56,113
The News Headline: Rockies spot Bucs 4-0 lead, then
   roar back to win 10-4
The Post Headline: Rockies roll over Pittsburgh

In the afternoon: It is something called Season Ticket Holder Photo Day. By mail, season ticketed fans were invited to come by for a one-hour session wherein you hand your baby to Dante Bichette, snap a picture of the Rocky and your kiddie, and reclaim the kid. Then repeat for Eric Young. And Mo Sanford. And Don Baylor. And Alex Cole.

Odd infinitum.

On the field: Going in, the buzz in the stands is CAN THE ROCKIES WIN 12 MORE GAMES?

The goal, of course, is to avoid a three-digit number on the right side of the hyphen.

When the Rockies fall behind 4-0 in the third inning, it looks like this is going to be another L.

But then they score in each of the last six stanzas—a total of ten unanswered runs—to slip the L to the visiting Bucs.

Painter wasn't as masterful as he was in his last outing, but he got the job done somehow and became the first Rocky pitcher to win back-to-back starts since the All Star break.

Galarraga helped with a double and a homer.

Mejia, struggling of late, added a homer of his own.

Painter got his first ML hit, a triple.

Hayes, sarcastically dubbed "Hustling Charlie Hayes" by a Denver TV sportscaster, *is* actually hustling these days and it's paying off both offensively and defensively.

Tonight, he makes a head-first slide.

He also makes a major fashion statement.

He pulls his pant legs way up to show more of his black socks than any Rocky has heretofore shown on the field.

It's a great contrast to all the other players who belong to the pull-your-knickers-down-as-far-as-you-can school.

A fan claims Hayes is doing this to "put more sock into his hitting."

It works: Three hits in his first three at-bats.

In the stands: It's Coca-Cola Lapel Pin #11 Night. (Though most or all of the pins were all handed out to the people who came for the photo day in the afternoon.)

A number of fans are laughing about something one of the Channel 2 guys said about Bichette's fielding last night:

"If you give Bichette time, he can cover a lot of ground."

Absolutely. Time x Rate=Distance.

A strangeness tonight is a GO! (pause) ROCKIES! chant that begins with ROCKIES!

In the fifth inning, a plane flies over with this message in lights: LET'S GO ROCKIES DO IT AGAIN.

Regis to Victoria, who was about to go to the rest room: "Don't leave; you'll miss a home run." Victoria sat back down."

In New York, Jim Abbott no-hits the Yankees over the Indians. Which means that Abbott has more no-hitters to his credit than the New York Mets have had in their entire history.

As Pike's Peek says in the Post, "No hits, no runs...no handicap."

The Rockies have now won two in a row while San Diego has run up a nice little three-game losing streak. This puts the 52-84 Rox just one game behind the sixth-place Padres.

Sunday, September 5: Colorado 4, Pittsburgh 1
The game that gave the Rox a sweep of the Pirates.

> **1:05 at Mile High Stadium**
> **The National Anthem:** Prestige Barbershop Quartet
> (wearing white tails)
> **The first ball:** Sam Holt (Continental Baking)
> **The starting pitchers:** Harris (11-14) vs. Walk (12-12)
> **The W-L pitchers:** Ruffin (5-5) and Walk (12-13)
> **The attendance:** 54,034
> **The News Headline:** Rockies pass the Bucs again
> **The Post Headline:** Rockies roll Pirates for clean sweep

On the field: Greg Harris throws a strong game, sprinkling five hits over the better part of seven innings and giving up but one run. But Ruffin had replaced him by the time the Rox broke open the 1-1 game with a three-run outburst in the eighth, so it is he who gets the win.

The most memorable moment is Benavides' attempted inside-the-park homer which comes thaaat close.

The scariest moment is when Charlie Hayes, once again wearing his pant legs pulled down low like everybody else, leaves the game with an injury.

In the stands: It's Hostess/Wonder Lunch Box Day.

It's also the day 54,034 people leave their TV sets—and the Broncos' opener against the Jets on the East Coast—to come to the game. Many, of course, bring radios. Some have teeny TVs.

Interestingly, the P.A. announcer doesn't inform the crowd how the Broncos are doing until there are two minutes remaining in the football game (the bottom of the third inning).

Bill Hook on why he likes the Rockies more than the Broncos: "They win more games."

A fan speculates on a batter-umpire conversation. Player to ump: "I'm terribly sorry, sir, but I believe you misjudged the trajectory of the ball." Ump to player: "Sir, I'm afraid you are visually challenged."

Some fan in need of a life comes up with this one: "If Mariah Carey married Roberto Mejia, she'd be Mariah Mejia."

The Rockies have now won three in a row and have a 53-84 record (.387) and are tied for sixth place with San Diego, which has dropped its last four.

Monday, September 6: Montreal 4, Colorado 3
The first game in history with three Canadians in the starting lineup.

11:35 in Olympic Stadium
The starting pitchers: Bottenfield (4-10) vs. Boucher (0-0)
The W-L pitchers: Scott (5-2) and Reed (7-5)
The attendance: 40,066
The News Headline: Rockies' bullpen lets one slip away
The Post Headline: Montreal native is king for a day

On the field: Nationalism raises its maple-leafed head as the Expos put three natives of Canada into their starting lineup, a baseball first.

Making his first start with the Expos, native son Denis Boucher drew 40,066 to Olympic Stadium, where the Expos are averaging 18,759, the worst in the majors. (Although 40K is Montreal's second largest crowed of the season, it is smaller than this season's *smallest* crowd at Mile High.)

Boucher was the Rockies' final pick in the expansion

draft, was traded to the Padres for Joe Gainer and now to the Expos. He goes six innings—the first taking just five pitches—and gives up just one run—Galarraga's homer.

The other Canadian starters are catcher Joe Siddall, and rightfielder Larry Walker.

Bottenfield, the former Expo whose career has taken many strange turns, gives up only two hits in his six-inning stint. Unfortunately, both are homers.

Good news dept.: Hayes' injury wasn't serious and he's back in the lineup.

Good/bad news dept.: In the eighth, Bichette's homer gives the Rox a 3-2 lead, but—as has often been the case this season—the Rockies' relief corps gives it back. And then some. And Colorado loses to the Expos for the fifth straight time.

Still, Baylor says that "One hundred losses are not even in my vocabulary."

In the world of that funny-shaped ball: The Vance re-signs with the Broncos.

The Rockies now have a 53-85 record (.384), the same as the Padres—with whom they share sixth place in the NL West. Also the cellar.

Tuesday, September 7: Montreal 4, Colorado 3
The game the Rockies lost the services of Freddie Benavides.

> **5:35 in Olympic Stadium**
> **The starting pitchers:** Leskanic (1-5) vs. Martinez (13-8)
> **The W-L pitchers:** Martinez (14-8) and Moore (2-1)
> **The attendance:** 18,988
> **The News Headline:** Rockies let one get away
> **The Post Headline:** A big one that got away

On the field: Making his first start since July 26, Curtis Leskanic throws six scoreless innings at the Expos, leaves when his shoulder tightens up, and looks on as the world comes to an end.

The Rox had built a three-run lead for Leskanic in the top of the sixth with the help of a Benavides triple. Could have been a four-run lead except that a suicide squeeze attempt was botched. During the botchery, Benavides made a sudden stop, sprained his ankle, and is out indefinitely—maybe for the season.

With Leskanic gone, the Expos launch a four-run outburst at the expense of Muñoz, Moore, Reed and Wayne. Hayes and Clark turn in defensive efforts that are described as lackadaisical. Charlie Montoyo makes his major league debut for the Expos and it's a good one. He gets the game-winning hit.

In the Post comics, CLOSE TO HOME shows a teacher "going over a few of her rules" on the first day of school. The blackboard has 31 directives written on it, all beginning with NO. They range from NO TALKING to NO GOOFY HAIRSTYLES.

It's a joke.

In Colorado Springs, a phone rings. With Benavides out, the 1 a.m. call summons Sky Sox second baseman Nelson Liriano to the big club.

The Sky Sox season is over, and the call catches Liriano just hours before his flight back home to the Dominican Republic.

It's a game of inches. And minutes.

Today's milestone: Jerald Clark's first ML grand slam (1992)

The Rockies now have a 53-86 record and are back in sole possession of the NL West cellar, a game behind the Padres.

Wednesday, September 8: Montreal 6, Colorado 1
The first game the Rockies played before a crowd of fewer than 11,000.

> **5:35 at Olympic Stadium**
> **The starting pitchers:** Reynoso (9-9) vs. Rueter (6-0)
> **The W-L pitchers:** Rueter (7-0) and Reynoso (9-10)
> **The attendance:** 10,764
> **The News Headline:** Expos sweep past the Rockies again
> **The Post Headline:** Expos rip punchless Rockies 6-1

On the field: The Expos fuel their sweep of the Rockies (the Rox' 7th straight loss to the Montreals) with two three-run outbursts, one off Reynoso in the first and the other off Sanford in the seventh. Larry Walker homers in the Outburst A and Oreste Marero gets his first major league homer in Outburst B.

Colorado gets just six hits, three by Mejia.

In the box score, the last number—the attendance—is small. Mighty small. Smallest crowd of the season to view Our Rocks.

In Houston: The Astros' Darryl Kile throws a no-hitter against the Mets.

Projecting Galarraga.

The Big Cat is now 140 for 377. Projecting him to the end of the season with enough hitless at-bats to qualify him for the championship, he'd come in at .345 to Tony Gwynn's .358.

The Rockies have now dropped three in a row, have a 53-87 record and are in last place, two games behind San Diego. The Marlins' and Mets' records are 58-81 and 47-93.

The Rockies need to win 10 of the final 22 games to avoid 100 losses at season's end.

The Post: "They could do it, but it isn't likely."

Thursday, September 9: Colorado 10, Bucs 7 (12 innings)

The day Gary Wayne used his first big league at-bat to knock in two runs.

5:35 in Three Rivers Stadium
The starting pitchers: Painter (2-2) vs. Miller (0-0)
The W-L pitchers: Wayne (5-3) and Johnson (2-3)
The attendance: 10,016
The News Headline: Rockies blow another lead but win
     in 12th
The Post Headline: Needy Rockies get lucky

On the field: The Rocks lead. The Pirates take over the lead. The Rocks tie it up and force extra innings. Finally, in the 12th, Colorado brings in the go-ahead run. But that's not all.

There's Gary Wayne's first ML at-bat. He comes to the plate with the bases loaded—and singles in two more. [This will stand as Wayne's only AB of the season.]

Holmes shuts down the Pirates for innings #8, #9 and #10. Wayne does the same for #11 and #12.

In Boston, big league baseball's big brains vote to split the NL and AL into three divisions next year in order to add another round of playoffs.

Yes, there will now be wild-card teams.

And there will be purists claiming that the pennant races are forever changed—perhaps even ruined—and that the whole thing is motivated by cupidity.

Less cynical types would doubtless disagree, if some could be located.

In New York, where baseball fans can buy license plates with the logo of their favorite New York team on them, it is reported that the Yankees' logo is on 1,053 cars, whereas only 265 fans are willing to admit an automotive alliance with the lowly Mets.

In the box score, the final entry—the attendance—is in five figures, but just barely. Tonight's crowd is even smaller than last night's crowd.

The Rockies now have a 54-87 record, are in last place a game behind the Padres. The only team with a worse record is the Mets (47-93). The Marlins are 58-81. The Rockies must win nine of their final 21 games to avoid a 100-loss season.

Friday, September 10: Colorado 9, Pittsburgh 8
(11 innings)

The first time the Rockies played back-to-back extra-inning games.

5:35 at Three Rivers Stadium
The starting pitchers: Harris (11-14) vs. Hope (0-1)
The W-L pitchers: Moore (3-1) and Minor (7-6)
The attendance: 15,335
The News Headline: Rockies bobble big lead, win
anyway
The Post Headline: Rockies triumph in rerun

On the field: It looks like one of those rare easy wins. Harris no-hits the Pittsburghers more than halfway, has a comfy 5-1 lead going into the bottom of the sixth and a snug 6-3 edge heading into the bottom of the seventh. Galarraga is having his second four-RBI game of the season.

By the end of regulation, however, each team has an equal share of the twelvepack of runs that has been scored.

In the Rockies side of the 11th, Cole singles, is sacrificed to second, steals third, and is doubled home by Young. There's the tie-breaker. Later, Bichette adds a pair of insurance runs when he loops the ball over the keystone sack with Girardi and Young in scoring position.

This turns out to be insurance that really pays off after the Pirates scratch out a pair of runs of their own in the bottom of the stanza.

Today's milestone: The first home run is hit in Bears Stadium (by catcher Luther "Buddy" Phillips) (1948)

The Rockies now have won two in a row and have a record of 55-87 (.387). This ties them with the Padres at the bottom of the NL West standings.

Saturday, September 11: Colorado 3, Pittsburgh 2

The first 3-for-3 day at the plate for a Rockies pitcher.

5:05 at Three Rivers Stadium
The starting pitchers: Bottenfield (4-10) vs. Wakefield
  (4-9)
The W-L pitchers: Bottenfield (5-10) and Wakefield
  (4-10)
The attendance: 21,649
The News Headline: Rockies get a good Reed, quell
  Bucs 3-2
The Post Headline: Rockies set up 4-game sweep with
  3-2 victory over Pirates

On the field: The Rockies put together a mess of singles and lead 3-0 going into the bottom of the fourth. A homer by the Pirates' Martin with a man on closes it to 3-2, and that's the end of the scoring for tonight.

The big story, though, is the Pirates' end of the sixth. When Bottenfield leaves with the bases loaded and no outs, the situation looks bad. Enter Reed, who strikes out one Pirate, induces another to pop out, and gets the final out on a dribbler.

Before he left the game, Bottenfield had contributed three hits and drove in two. As it turns out, he needs them both.

Today's milestone: Larry Bearnarth's birthday (1940)

The Rockies have now won three straight, have a record of 56-87 (.392), and have sixth place all to themselves. The Padres are a game back. Atlanta leads the Giants by a game. The Blue Jays lead the Yankees by a game. Florida is 60-82.

Sunday, September 12: Pittsburgh 4, Colorado 3
Nied's first game since May 27.

11:35 at Three Rivers Stadium
The starting pitchers: Nied (3-7) vs. Walk (12-13)
The W-L pitchers: Menendez (2-0) and Muñoz (1-1)
The attendance: 21,032
The News Headline: Victory slips away in ninth
The Post Headline: Big chance for Rockies swept away

On the field: The Rockies are salivating over the prospect of another four-game sweep over an established club. And they have David Nied back on the mound for the first time in 108 days.

It starts out great when the Rocks put up three in the top of the first with a Young walk, a Girardi HP, singles by Bichette and Galarraga, and a double by Hayes. All that before their first out.

Turns out that no more runs would be scored by Colorado all evening.

Meanwhile, the Pirates methodically pick away and tie it up after six.

And then, when Mike Muñoz comes in with one out in the bottom of the ninth, Al Martin likes the look of Mike's first offering and wallops it into the right field seats. Naturally, Mike Muñoz takes the loss. [As it turns out, it's the only one he'll take all year.]

On Continental flight 1765 from Houston to Denver: Two Rockies fans find themselves sitting behind a guy wearing a black baseball cap that is sized (not adjustable) with a black button on top (not Rockies).

One cranes around to see what team's logo is on the front, discovers it is San Diego's, and reports: "It's a last place cap."

In recognition of a confection of caramel-coated popcorn and peanuts. For some reason, Cracker Jack is forever linked with The Game. And 1993 is its 100th birthday.

In that century, there have been 17 billion boxes of the stuff sold but fewer prizes. (Prizes go back only to 1912.)

It was a gent name of F.W. Rueckhem who introduced the combination of peanuts and popcorn and molasses at the 1893 Columbian Exposition in Chicago.

The Cracker Jackals proudly point out that all the prizes are made in the United States. Or, rather, printed.

The Rockies have now completed their season against NL East teams. Their best records are against Florida (7-5), Pittsburgh (8-4) and New York (6-6).

On the season, the Rox are 56-88, same as the Padres. Both share the cellar (and sixth place), 35 games behind Atlanta. (The Giants are a game back.)

Monday, September 13: Colorado and Houston (snow)

The first game that was snowed out.

7:05 at Mile High Stadium
The Post headline: A blessing from above
The News headline: Snow or not, Leskanic wanted to play

The game was called around 5:30 because a nice little snowstorm was in progress. And because it was colder'n an umpire's heart.

'Twas quite a contrast with the scene yesterday at Mile High Stadium where the Broncos played (and beat) the Chargers in Mile High in temperatures that reached 92°.

And 'twas quite a sight to Marcus Moore, who'd never seen snow before in his 22+ years on the planet, spent mostly in California.

The first day that 19 innings were played at Mile High.

3:05 at Mile High Stadium
The National Anthem (first game): Amy Carlon
The National Anthem (second game): US Air Force Quartet
The first ball: Aisha Alkayali
GAME ONE
The starting pitchers: Reynoso (9-10) and Drabek (8-15)
The W-L pitchers: Reynoso (10-10) and Drabek (8-16)
GAME TWO
The starting pitchers: Leskanic (1-5) vs. Kile (15-6)
The W-L pitchers: Holmes (3-3) and Hernandez (3-5)
The attendance: 42,657
The News Headline: Rockies have double the fun
The Post Headline: Rockies get to double pleasure

On the field: The Astros start the day with an 0-3 record at Mile High, and take an 0-5 mark to bed.

Reynoso and Ruffin split the pitching chores in the first game, with the latter shutting down the Houstons in the final four innings, during which he sets the Rockies' record for strikeouts in a single game. That's right, he punches out the record-setting nine Ks in just *four* innings.

Meanwhile, the Rocks score in most innings, with Hayes' three-run homer in the seventh pretty much putting it away. Final score: Rockies 9, Astros 4.

Five pitchers share the chores in Game Two.

Much of the Astros' scoring can be attributed to Cole miscues in the seventh. He misplays a Finley hit into an inside-the-park home run (the third in Mile High this season) and then lets another two runs score on an error.

Once again, Hayes supplies the heroics for the Rox. His double in the ninth brings in two runs to tie it up and force extra innings. In the 10th, EY singles in the winner. Rox win, 6-5.

Galarraga goes 4-for-8 on the day, propelling his average to .377.

In the stands: We have heard two national anthems sung on a single day before—the U.S. and Canadian varieties before the Expos games—but this is the first time there have been two singings of the U.S. anthem on one day, a performance before each game.

If that weren't odd enough, one of the signings is by a group called the U.S. Air Force Quartet. Which even the beer-sodden types in Section 305 can tell has *five* members. "Why five?" Someone explains: "DH."

Tonight's crowd of 42,657 is the season's smallest in Mile High, but larger than the Cubbies can stuff into Wrigley except on Midgets Day. Of course, that's the announced attendance. There are far fewer than 42 thou in the stands today.

Because of the sparseness of the attendees, there are lots of empty seats to be employed as places to set things and to put your feet on and to just stretch out. Reminds Phil D. of a Zephyrs crowd: "It's like turn-back-the-clock day at the old ballpark."

A guy asks "Think we can get The Wave started?"

"You'll be lucky to start The Trickle."

And: "This is how it'll be three years from now."

And: "There were more people at spring training."

But there's no lack of yucks. The drink vendor who does a swell impression of Stevie Wonder passes by. "Lemonade and iced tea. Help the blind. Lemonade and iced tea."

Early on, John A. wonders if, in a doubleheader, "they stop selling beer at the end of the seventh inning of the *first* game—not that I'm planning ahead or anything."

"It is odd, isn't it, that on some days you are allowed to buy beer for seven innings," a fan thinks aloud, "and today you can buy beer for *sixteen* innings."

Fans are stupefied by the news that ARA will, indeed, be the concessionaire at Coors Field.

What's this? A new song for Galarraga? He isn't welcomed to the plate with The Pink Panther theme any more? What *is* that tune? Nobody recognizes it. Better have the Fans' Ombudsman look into it.

The F.O. reports that the new ditty is a Venezuelan favorite of The Cat, "Botaste la Bola." Which translates to "hit a home run."

Hmm. The home stand opens with new signage atop he dugouts. Heretofore, there's been a listing of the six Denver-area counties which are collecting coins for Coors Field. Now, it simply says NATIONAL LEAGUE on one and COLORADO ROCKIES on the other. Both, it appears, are removable.

The Fan-O-Meter reveals itself to be -uh- not completely scientific when it hits 100 long after most people had stopped screaming and settled down.

A fan looks inside his CR cap and reads the brand. It's American Needle. And it is made in Taiwan.

Patty Calhoun had debated whether to come to the game or take a nap. After all, she'd only gotten an hour of sleep last night. Obviously, the game won. And she concludes that it was the right decision. "This is much better than a nap. It relaxes your soul. Besides, you can't drink beer while you nap."

The Rockies have moved into their thanks-for-the-patronage mode. From time to time, DiamondVisioned messages from the players salute the fans. Today's tribute by Jerald Clark to The Rockpile causes a frenzy of self-congratulatory merriment out there in Section 133.

Diane K. reports that when she bought popcorn ($3.50) and a Diet Coke ($2.00) from a concession stand, the young woman took out a calculator to determine the total.

A fan wishes he'd been keeping stats on the frequency with which Mejia rips his pants. "I think he's leading the league."

When someone says that we'll be facing the meat of the lineup in the next inning, Bob C. wonders about the rest of the batsmen. "Are they the *potatoes* of the lineup?"

Larry D. has a plan to make Bichette run faster. "We'll make his legs longer by hanging him outside down by his ankles during the off-season," he recommends. "We'll take him down in time for spring training."

Remembering that Leskanic shaves his pitching arm: "It's chilly today. Bet he wished he let the hair on his arm grow."

Mr. P.A. won't be pinned down on the time that will elapse between games. At various times, he announces that the second game will begin 20 minutes after the conclusion of the first, and 25 minutes, and 30 minutes.

But the scoreboard is certain of when it wants the crowd to react. ON YOUR FEET! it orders. Which offends those fans who prefer to schedule their own spontaneity.

Greg Akiyama wants to know how you get *your* message put up there. The Ombudsman: "Call 458-4850. It'll cost you $50 for a 15-second showing at the bottom of the fifth."

To Mascot Or Not?

"If we have a mascot, I want it to be a bear."

"I don't want one."

"Either do I, but you just *know* we're going to have a mascot and shouldn't it be a bear?"

"Well, how about an invisible bear?"

"Good idea."

On Letterman: "Last night, the Colorado Rockies game was cancelled because there were 5.3 inches of snow at Mile High Stadium. Why can't the Mets catch a break like that?"

The Rockies have now won two in a row and are 58-88 (.397). That puts them in sixth place, a game ahead of the Padres.

Wednesday, September 15: Colorado 6, Houston 4

The smallest crowd of the year: 40,814.

7:05 at Mile High Stadium

The National Anthem: Nathaniel Drinkard

The first ball: Jeff Harmes (Leaf Candies)

The starting pitchers: Harris (11-14) vs. Swindell (10-12)

The W-L pitchers: Muñoz (2-1) and Williams (4-4)

The attendance: 40,813

The News Headline: Rockies bash Astros again

The Post Headline: Rockies continue mastery of Astros

On the way in: Tonight, fans receive little bags of carrot sticks. Yes, carrots. Some suggest that it's all a stratagem by Rockies management to save money. "They are handing out carrots to everybody," a suspicious fan suggests, "so they can turn down the lights and cut their electricity bill."

On the field: Hayes, who knocked in six in yesterday's doubleheader, continues his hot batting streak with a club record three doubles. And the Astros continue to misfire in Mile High Stadium. They're now oh-for-six here.

The 'stros lead going into the Rox end of the seventh, 4-2.

Then, after Astros' starter Swindell is replaced by Brian

Williams, things start going the Rockies' way. Four pitches later, a couple of singles, one of Hayes' doubles, and an error puts Colorado up, 5-4. They add another in the next inning and smile all the way to the W column.

Galarraga smiles, too. All the time. But especially now that he has a 13-game hitting steak, the longest of any Rock.

Dante Bichette isn't smiling, though. He's gone. Left the game in the eighth after being hit by a Doug Jones pitch.

He's off to see an X-ray machine.

In the stands: The parking lot index for this game is way off— it's $7. Way too high. Today's crowd is so scanty that it can't even put together a successful "GO!" (pause) "ROCKIES!"

Still, the attendance at Mile High exceeds all but one other game being played today/night. Only the 48,825 in Atlanta beats Denver. And the Padres don't come close. Their crowd is Zephyresque—8,752.

Serious students of the umpirical side of the game discuss the apres game adventures of second base umpire Terry Tata in San Diego earlier in the season. "Wasn't he the guy I read about who took a woman to his hotel room to 'share a bottle of wine,' wound up drugged and robbed of his Rolex, several hundred bucks and two World Series rings?"

Yup.

Meanwhile, Diane K. announces that when she owns a baseball team she's going to provide the players with shelled sunflower seeds "so they don't make such a mess out in front of the dugout."

It is suggested that the organist ought to make Charlie Hayes' theme song "The Hustler."

And the fans continue to grumble every time the Rox bring in a relief pitcher. Because KOA's Call to the Bullpen always goes up on the DiamondVision accompanied by the irritating sound of a phone ringing. "That's great for when the visiting team has to bring in a pitcher because it puts their pitching down, but it shouldn't be used when the Rockies bring in somebody."

A fan happily proclaims that "We have not yet been mathematically eliminated from sixth place."

When Liriano starts a nice double play to end the eighth, then is first up when the Rockies come to bat, a Baseball Sage observes that "amazingly enough, when a guy makes a great play to end an inning, he's the first guy up in the next inning 11% of the time." Uh-huh.

More Cracker Jack jabber in the stands: "You know that the coated popcorn and peanuts product everybody calls Cracker Jacks is really Cracker Jack Singular. No ess on the end, right?" a fan asks. "But everybody says—and sings—the ess. How come?"

Nobody has the faintest. But a businessman type has another question: "By not printing the S all those years, I wonder how much money they've saved in ink."

One presumes he's the only one.

In the stands: Yesterday's crowd, the smallest of the year, isn't the smallest of the year any more. Today's is.

The Rockies have now won three in a row, are 59-88 on the season, and have a two-game lead over last-place San Diego. Florida still leads the Rockies with a 60-85 record. Baylor announces he wants his team to win 70 this year.

Thursday, September 16: Colorado 6, Houston 3

The day Art Howe called the Rockies "the best team in the league."

> **3:05 at Mile High Stadium**
> **The National Anthem:** McBride and the Ride
> **The first ball:** Paul Archer
> **The starting pitchers:** Bottenfield (5-10) vs. Portugal (15-4)
> **The W-L pitchers:** Ruffin (6-5) and Jones (1-2)
> **The attendance:** 41,847
> **The News Headline:** Astros bow to Rockies
> **The Post Headline:** Rockies a sweeping success, 6-3

On the field: The Rockies were behind, 3-2, with just five outs to go. But these days, with the Astros in town, that's no problemo. The bat of Jerald Clark soon delivers a three-run homer to break a 3-3 tie and give the Rockies a four-game sweep of the Astros. The season series ends with the Rox undefeated against the Astros in Mile High (7-0) and dominating them overall, 11-2.

Houston manager Art Howe on the Rockies: "As far as I'm concerned, that's the best team in the league."

Until today, no expansion team had ever won a pair of four-game sweeps against Real Teams.

Galarraga has a day, too. He goes 3-for-3, now has a 14-game hitting streak—a team best and a personal high—and an average of .381.

He even runs out an infield hit. His slowness was cited earlier in the season as a reason he couldn't win the batting crown. He would get no infield hits, they said.

Tom Lasorda told an ESPN audience that "Andres Galarraga is so slow, if he got in a footrace with a pregnant woman, he'd come in third."

No yucks for Dante Bichette, though.

Turns out he has a cracked bone in his left hand and will miss the remaining 14 games of the season. Bichette's final numbers: .310, 92 runs, 43 doubles (NL lead at this point), 21 HR and 89 RBI.

In the stands: The fans make a real difference. When Astro Chris Donnels fails to touch third on his way home, none of the players see it, but a group of spectators behind third do. They yell to Charlie Hayes who has Bottenfield toss the ball over to third.

Out! And give that assist to the fans.

Norm Clarke quotes one of them, John Baron: "The ump tipped his hat to the fans and gave us a little smile. It was the fans who made the call and saved the run, and even the ump acknowledged it."

The Rockies have now won four in a row, are 60-88 and are in sixth place, nine games behind the Reds and 2.5 ahead of the Padres. Florida has the same number of wins, but two fewer losses. The A's are 59-86. The Mets are 49-97.

Friday, September 17: Colorado 12, Los Angeles 3
The game that breaks the single-season attendance record.

7:05 at Mile High Stadium
The National Anthem: The Alligators
The first balls: Mark Musselman & Steve Kretzel

The starting pitchers: Nied (3-7) vs. Candiotti (8-7)
The W-L pitchers: Nied (4-7) and Candiotti (8-8)
The attendance: 56,679
The News Headline: Rockies, fans, do number on L.A.
The Post Headline: Rockies roll at the gate, rock L.A.

On the field: It was a warmup pitch that Nied nailed Bob Davidson with, but it caused a delay in getting the game under way while the ump repaired to the locker room to have his left ear repaired.

After doing harm to an ump, the Rocks turn their attention to the Dodgers.

They score in each of the first five innings and lead 12-0. Liriano's 4-for-4 day helps. As do homers by Hayes and Clark. And Boston's four RBI.

All together, it's a 17-hit day for the Rockies and one of the few laughers of the season.

Galarraga runs his hitting streak to 15 games—a team and a personal record.

Eric Wedge makes his first plate appearance for the Rox and singles.

Nied notches his first win since April 21.

And the Rockies have to win but two in their final 13 to avoid three-digit ignominy in the loss column.

In the News, Drew Litton shows a Blue Jay being trampled by footsteps heading for a turnstile. And Bob Kravitz says, "Take a bow, Denver and environs. This Coors is for you."

In the Post: Tom Gavin says that he's been to but one game, but it was enough to convince them that "they might as well go back to calling the team the Zephyrs, for that, I am sorry to tell you, is how these stiffs play. Major leaguers they aren't."

Gavin also reports that "Four people sitting ahead of me consumed, easy, $93 worth of food, semi-food, quasi-food and junk food. Also $40 worth of fluids were poured gullet-ward."

In the stands: It's Coca-Cola Lapel Pin #13 Night. A father-and-kid duo is wearing T-shirts that are obviously custom-made and one-of-a-kind. One says: FAN NO. 4,028,319. The other: FAN NO. 4,028,320. In other words, they profess themselves to be the fan who ties Toronto's 1992 attendance record—and the fan who breaks it.

Turns out, though, that the Rockies proclaim seven-year-old Jason Nicholaou of Lakewood as no. 4,000,000. And ten-year-old Tami Friend of Littleton as no. 4,028,319.

In the eighth, the entire team comes out of the dugout and doffs their caps in a salute to the fans.

Collectors of firsts note that today's was the First Game Delayed By An Umpire's Ear.

The ushers are tough.

They'll check your ticket to make sure you belong in the section you're headed for every time.

Even if your hands are full of dogs and beer. Some fans are now putting their tickets in their mouths for the ushers' inspection.

Bill H., after an intentional walk of the Dodgers' Jody Reed: "Why did Nied waste all those pitches? Why didn't he just hit him?"

And: "Yeah. Reed's from L.A. so he's used to it."

Spotted in the stands: A guy who customized his Rockies cap by gluing a bunch of stones to it.

The vendor who does the Stevie Wonder imitation has a couple of new gimmicks today. Early, he is peddling "Hot iced tea!" Later, he offers "Hot link sandwiches—fifteen dollars!"

In the top of the ninth, Scott W., a Dodger fan "when the Rockies were still a hockey team," makes a pronouncement: "Two touchdowns and we're right back in this!"

The Dodgers make an out in the fourth when Ashley passes Snyder on the base path.

Which causes much merriment in the stands.

Ray J.: "He gets the Dante Bichette Baserunning Award."

And then some guys keeping score develop some new abbreviations to use in their scorecards:

DB = ran like Dante Bichette.

APOS = amazingly preserved our shutout.

The Rockies have now won five in a row, have a record of 61-88, and remain in sixth place, 3.5 games ahead of the Padres and 8.5 behind the fifth-place Reds. Florida: 61-86. Mets: 49-98. Oakland: 59-87.

Saturday, September 18: Los Angeles 9, Colorado 0

The second shutout of the season in Mile High suffered by the Rocks.

7:05 at Mile High Stadium
The National Anthem: Christine Barnett
The first ball: Tim Darnell
The starting pitchers: Hurst (0-1) vs. Astacio (12-8)
The W-L pitchers: Astacio (13-8) and Hurst (0-2)
The attendance: 52,293
The News Headline: Rockies draw a blank
The Post Headline: Rockies find 9-0 loss is relatively
painless

Before the game: The Channel 9 weather lady, Kathy Sabine, says there's a possibility of rain, so "Take a poncho which is more fan friendly than a big old umbrella." Switching to Channel 4's Kathy Walsh brings this suggestion: "Bring your umbrella!"

Kathy's right, of course.

Umbrella etiquette at the ballpark.

When the skies opened up during Bears and Zephyrs games, it was fine to open up an umbrella. After all, people were scattered all over the place and umbrellas presented no real inconvenience to one's neighbors.

With people packed into Mile High like beer cans in a twelvepack, that isn't the case. The people sitting behind the umbrella operator almost always find the view of the field sharply curtailed. Speaking of sharply, there are all those pointy potential eye-pokers to worry about.

The only umbrellas that a somewhat fan friendly are those that are very shallow. With the typical 'brella, the user has to hold it up pretty high to see out from under same. Which does bad things to the view of the folks behind.

The best umbrella policy for a ballpark with people in it is no umbrellas.

Rain hats. Or ponchos. Or a don't-give-a-damn attitude.

On the field: The Dodgers' Pedro Astacio's seven-hitter snaps the Rox' five-game winning streak, their eight-game streak at home, their six-game streak against the Dodgers and Galarraga's 15-game hitting streak. (After going 0-for-4, The Cat is now down to .379.)

The Rockies' pitching story is Bruce Hurst, coming back from rotator-cuff surgery. Scheduled for three innings, he doesn't get into real trouble until the third, when he lets in three.

Girardi throws out two attempted base-stealers. He's now shot down six in a row.

In the stands: It's Brothers Coffee Mug Night, which is perfect for a soggy evening.

Diane K.: "My favorite player is now Dante Bichette because he can do no wrong." Bichette, of course, is out for the season with a broken bone in his hand.

The organist plays "Mack the Knife" for Mike Sharperson ("Oh, the shark bites...") and fans of dissing the members of the visiting nine mutter.

With little to cheer about, discussion turns to Brothers Coffee, which, we are told, gave away 20,000 coffee mugs. One presumes that Brothers felt that these freebies would do the company some good, and each and every one of those mugs was a good investment of their promotional dollars.

So what about the other 32,293 people in the stadium? Why wouldn't Brothers want to give *everybody* a Brothers mug?

You'd think that the Brothers brothers would have an especially well-developed sense of fair play—you can't give a gift to just one and leave the other out.

This argument can be applied to all the promotions that only reward the first X people who arrive at the ballpark—and penalize those who dally in the parking lot around tailgates.

And one fan reports that he heard that the A's have a policy that when they have a giveaway, they always make sure there's enough for everybody. Something for enlightened promo folks to ponder.

When the Dodgers' leftfielder Ashley swings and loses his bat and it winds up in the box seats near home, a guy wrestles it away from another guy who claims that, by rights, it is his.

The cops take the bat and its two claimants and assorted witnesses up on the concourse by the Taco Bell stand and hold an inquiry.

It takes quite a while to sift through the evidence—in spite of the presence of *seven* police officers—but they finally give the bat back to the original guy.

Today's Milestones: Denver's ownership group made its presentation to the National League Expansion Committee (1990) and Eric Young's first ML home run (1992)

The Rockies now have a record of 61-89 (.407) which puts them safely in sixth place, 3.5 games ahead of the Padres. Florida's record: 61-87.

Sunday, September 19: Colorado 8, Los Angeles 5

The game that gave us bragging rights over Dodger fans for the entire winter.

1:05 at Mile High Stadium
The National Anthem: United Methodist Church Choir (50 of 'em)
The first ball: Bill Shell (Bank One)
The starting pitchers: Reynoso (10-10) vs. Martinez (9-10)
The W-L pitchers: Reynoso (11-10) and Martinez (10-4)
The attendance: 61,573
The News Headline: Rockies win 8-5, notch Dodgers in their belt
The Post Headline: Rockies stay hot, burn Dodgers 8-5

On the field: The Rockies put away the Dodgers in their last meeting of the season to take the season's series, 7-6. *And the Dodgers won the first five meetings.*

Speed is today's key. There are three triples—one by Galarraga! And four stolen bases—three by Eric Young. There would've been another, but Young's attempted theft of home is just barely thwarted.

The Rox had led virtually all the way, and Baylor threw his most dependable sequence of pitchers at the L.A.ers: Reynoso, Reed, Ruffin, Holmes.

In the stands: It's Kids' Wallet Day. (But only for 15,000 of 'em.)

Spirits are high in the stands today.

Observation: "When you sit on the aisle, you have to get up when anyone goes to the rest room. Including yourself."

When Clark makes a great catch in right field: "He didn't Bichette it! He *caught* it!"

A name is given to Pat M. when she passes nachos around to everybody within arm's reach: Nacho Mama.

A name is given to the enormous new Cracker Jack box: "It's the Tommy Lasorda model."

The organist plays "Davy Crockett" for yet another opposing Dave. This time it's Dave Hansen. Grousing is heard.

An overheated vendor: "Semi-frozen yogurt!"

"The question: You know what dance Charlie Hayes never liked?" "The answer: The Hustle."

On this, most or all Rockies fans would probably agree: Our team may be comprised of rejects from real major league teams, guys who are not probably not destined for Cooperstown, but there's one thing they all *can* do.

They can hustle. Tonight, there is much tut-tutting when a baserunning Rocky fails to hustle down the line. Turns out that the bobble by the Dodgers' fielder took just long enough that a hot-footing runner would've been safe. Later, as it turns out, that moment of dawdling cost the Rockies a run.

The Rockies now have a 62-89 record and are 3.5 games ahead of the Padres (who are coming to town for a three-game series). The Rockies have a better record than the Padres, the Mets, and the A's. They're two percentage points behind the Twins and five points behind the Marlins.

Monday, September 20: San Diego 11, Colorado 7

The first time the Rockies and the Broncos scored the same number of points—and both lost.

3:05 at Mile High Stadium (rescheduled from 7:05)
The National Anthem: Jim McClung (Mitsubishi Elec.)
The first ball: Mark Sucharski (Domino's Pizza)
The starting pitchers: Harris (11-14) vs. Brocail (3-12)
The W-L pitchers: Seminara (3-2) and Harris (11-15)
The attendance: 41,531
The News Headline: Harris out of touch against former team
The Post Headline: San Diego, fans hammer Harris

Before the game: It is revealed that Coors Field will not be the site of the 1996 All-Star Game. For some reason, the Horsehide Honchos decided to hold it in Philadelphia's Cookie Cutter, instead.

And Mr. P.A. informs the assembled throng that Charlie Hayes has been named the National League Player of the Week.

At the pre-game reception, a tent filled with a couple hundred of the area's Hispanic leaders beveraged, buffeted, and *habla*ed with Rockies Galarraga, Reynoso, Castellano, Mejia, and Benavides.

Which brings up this point...

Baseball caps, south of the border.

John Mason is an architect, a baseball fan, a lover of words—and things south of the border.

Which is why he got into a conversation with a guy he works with about the *palabra, en Español*, for "baseball cap."

He says there are two words for it in Spanish. *Cuchacha* and *gorra.*

Cuchacha is what rich Mexicans call a baseball cap. Literally, it means a cloth cap. *Gorra* is what Mexican baseball fans call it.

Mason says he asked his friend what Andres Galarraga would call his cap. "He thought a minute and then he said, *'Esta rico...crea que lo llamarar una cuchacga.'"*

Yes, the Big Cat *is* rico.

On the field: Aided by the generosity of former Padre Greg Harris (who allows nine runs on six hits—and three hit batsmen—in three-plus innings), the Padres soon run off to a fine lead.

The Rockies make it look semi-respectable when Jay Gainer pinch-hits a grand slam off Padres' starter (and Lamar resident) Doug Brocail.

Boston and Mejia also homer. Sheaffer's triple is the first in his ML career.

After stealing three bases yesterday, Eric Young learns he is mortal today. With the bases loaded, he is called out on an attempted steal of home on the catcher-to-pitcher lob.

In the stands: "Boy, Harris must not like his old teammates." a fan surmises. "He hit two of the first three he faced."

Fans in Section 116 have kept an eye on Jennifer, she of Rockies management, who sits in Section 117. For every game. She has to, it's her job. One reason Jennifer's been under close scrutiny is that she's substantially prettier than Dante Bichette. Another is that she is wearing yet another outfit to today's game. Day after day, game after game, she has worn something new. She is asked if she's secretly glad those two games were weathered out. So she only has to make 79 different fashion statements instead of 81. Jennifer smiles, but has no comment.

Len B. suggests that Daryl and Alex seek out another line of work. "The ought to move to Massachusetts and open a fossil fuels business," Len says. "They could call it the Boston Cole Company."

The centerfielders' best friend: The Rockpile.

The Rockpile has been under close scrutiny of the press—and Rockies management—from the beginning.

And no wonder—it's a different world out there. *Way* out there. Until this season, it was just plain old Section 134, 43 rows of 20 seats of anonymity. Now Section 134 is both famous and infamous as The Rockpile. On days when The Rockpile overfloweth, adjacent Sections 133, 132, and 131 become More Rockpile.

The attraction, of course, is that it costs just a buck to watch the game from The Rockpile, the only general admission seats in the ballpark. And the cheapest tickets in big league baseball.

As some might say, it costs just a buck and that's what it's worth. In the News, Bob Kravitz says watching from the Rockpile is like peering down upon something that's either a dwarf baseball game or an ant colony.

During BP, many early arrivals in The Rockpile slip over toward the left field fence where the most of the pre-game home run balls land.

But when batting practice ends, 45 minutes before game time, most return to the cheap seats to do what people in The Rockpile do.

Enjoy the ballgame. Just like everybody else. And they

are like everybody else. They're a typical ballgame mix of people—single guys, packs of teenagers, young couples, families with kids, geezers.

As one Rockpile regular says, "We're just like other Rockies fans, only richer."

Indeed, with every game, they get fifteen bucks ahead of the boxseated people.

But Rockpilians aren't treated like everybody else. They are treated like residents of a Betty Ford Clinic with baseball. There are no beer vendors in The Rockpile. And when you go up to the concourse to buy a beer, that's all they'll let you buy—a beer. Just one to a customer. And they'll only sell you the small size, too.

Where did the denizens of the 'pile get their outlaw rep?

Why do most fans think of them as unwashed, no-class hoodlums?

Blame it on the press. Or on TV. The fact is, the only rough looking folks in the section are down in the front row. They're the regulars whose pictures have been oft published and broadcast. Fact is, they spend more time befriending the centerfielder than anything. And they're way too smart to spend much money on ballpark-priced beer.

Meanwhile, behind them, a sunny day like today finds your typical ballpark mix of fans.

Because they tend to be regulars, many know the words to all the commercials shown on DiamondVision. A large group loudly sings along to the Coke commercial.

Indeed, there is an aura of lighthearted fun here, a gleefulness that can only be attributed to having beat the system out of a big league ballgame for a miniscule price.

A fan tosses peanuts to a friend eight rows away. But behavior like this cannot be tolerated. It is promptly shut down by a CR Hospitality Cop. Indeed, The Rockpile is closely patrolled.

Because the seats here aren't assigned, people are free to move around. By game time, each Rockpilian has chosen between sun and shade, between low and high, between far from the game and farther still. And all have a far better idea of the position of each pitch thrown than fans in the so-called best seats behind the dugouts.

No wonder the TV camera that shows the pitches is located right there by The Rockpile.

A Rockpile dweller, part philosopher and part accountant,

suggests the best way to see a Rockies game on the cheap: "Dollar One buys you a lot of peanuts at King Soopers. Dollar Two gets you a 2-liter bottle of Diet Pepsi—you transfer that and some ice cubes to your Coleman insulated jug. Dollar Three goes for a copy of the Homestand Flyer scorecard. And then, of course, your Rockpile ticket is Dollar Four. Then just add ten bucks for parking and you've got a great day at the ballpark for less than $15!"

Tonight, in Kansas City: The Broncos lose, 15-7.

The Rockies now have a 62-90 record. This puts them in sixth place, 35 games behind Atlanta and 2.5 games ahead of San Diego. The Marlins and Twins have records of 62-88. Oakland has a 61-88 record. The Mets lost their 100th game of the season today, and are now 50-100.

Tuesday, September 21: Colorado 15, San Diego 4
The game that made sure the Rockies won't lose 100.

7:05 at Mile High Stadium
The National Anthem: South Metro Denver Chamber
of Commerce Choir (about 38 voices)
The first ball: Everett Chavez (U S West)
The starting pitchers: Bottenfield (5-10) vs. Worrell (1-6)
The W-L pitchers: Blair (6-10) and Worrell (1-7)
The attendance: 42,727
The News Headline: Rout of Padres guarantees
Rockies won't lose 100
The Post Headline: Rockies reach their magic number

On the field: This, according to the parking lot operator's sliding scale of importance, is a $7 game. This late September game is also a 74° game. And it is the game that could guarantee that the Rockies loss column will contain but two figures.

Which it does. By winning game number 63, the Rockies cannot lose game number 100.

And it's a laugher against the team the Rockies have been fighting with over sixth—and last—place all year.

The Rocks jump off to a 4-0 start in the first by virtue of five singles and a sacrifice fly. The teams exchange hits like a couple of guys at the Twentieth Street Gym until the bottom of the eighth when Colorado bats around, scores seven, and runs their lead to the final score, 15-4.

Along the way, Galarraga adds four hits to his quest.

More of a surprise, Bottenfield has gotten five hits in his last six at-bats.

In the stands: Section 115 has come up with another gimmick. Tonight it's whirly toy thingies. From time to time, a strange whirligiggy noise/sight issues from the direction of the box seats and the seats directly behind same. A plot to unravel the opposing batters' concentration, no doubt.

Evidently, it is quite effective. The Padres batsmen succumb to strikeouts seven times.

When Galarraga makes a sensational defensive play in the eighth, an admiring fan remarks that "He's just a little bit terrific, isn't he?"

The organist is really reaching when he plays "Those Were The Days" (the theme from All In The Family) when Cianfrocco comes to bat. It takes a while, but the fans decode it. The Padres' infielder's first name is Archi. Yes. Not bad.

Judge Jones is into law bigtime. And he's a fan, too. So he thinks that the Rockies' P.A. guy ought to add yet another rule to the list. "Fans will not be permitted to spill their beer." Jones explains his thinking (if any): "Spilled beer is an abomination. It can flow down and dampen the jacket that the fan in front of you has stuffed beneath the seat." So saith the Judge.

"More importantly, it is a waste of a precious resource."

It has been revealed to students of fan dynamics that The Rockpile is often the instigator of the "GO!" that soon turns into the roar of "GO!" (pause) "ROCKIES!"

Tonight, however, the 'pile fails in its attempt to launch the abovementioned chant. There is a lack of critical mass.

Speaking of such, a fan has developed a new cheer to employ when we need to encourage Eric Young to greater achievement. The organist would open with the first line of "Old McDonald Had A Farm" and everyone yells "E-Y-E-Y-Oh!"

This remains in the developmental stage.

A fan, fresh from a game in Milwaukee, reports that "I asked them when they cut off beer sales and they said after the game, of course." And? "Didn't ask about flash photography."

The scoreboard becomes a real weapon for the Rox when it greets a new pitcher with the Fan-Meter. That is one time that scoreboard-induced yelling makes sense—because it makes the new arrival on the mound wish he were *under* the mound.

When Jay Gainer comes to bat as a PH for Bottenfield in the third, a fan with a calculator announces that 17% of Gainer's major league hits have been grand slams.

The Rockies have now won 63 games and lost 90 (.412). This puts them solidly in sixth place, 3.5 games ahead of San Diego. It also puts them ahead of 62-89 Florida for the first time since April 25. The Rockies are also surprisingly close to Oakland (62-88) and Milwaukee (65-87).

Wednesday, September 22: Colorado 11, San Diego 4
The season's last Padre pummeling.

7:05 at Mile High Stadium
The National Anthem: Combined Douglas County Ponderosa Highlands Ranch String Orchestra (66 players)
The first ball: Tom Watkins (MCI Fan of the Year)
The starting pitchers: Nied (4-7) vs. Benes (15-13)
The W-L pitchers: Nied (5-7) and Benes (15-14)
The attendance: 42,061
The News Headline: Rockies just keep on rolling
The Post Headline: Galarraga's glove rescues Rockies

In the Post: A headline proclaims that "Big Cat's title is all but a lock." But nobody in The Time Zone is very inclined to count unhatched eggs.

On the field: It is close. Just two outs away from the first shutout in the history of the Colorado Rockies. And it is disappointing when it slips away. But fans take solace in an easy victory powered largely by Eric Young's four hits and Jerald Clark's career-high five RBI.

Nied hurls five innings of shutout ball. That is nice. And Wayne and Reed keep the zeroes coming until the ninth, when Muñoz gives up the shutout-breaker and some more.

Galarraga has a lot to do with Nied's success. In the fifth, Nied loads the bases and throws a pitch that Jeff Gardner nearly uses to empty them. But an unbelievable leaping catch by The Cat puts a sudden end to the rally-in-the-making.

It also helps when Padres' starter Andy Benes hits Alex Cole and is instantly thrown out of the game by the plate ump. In less than two innings, the Rox touch his replacement, Kerry Taylor, for six runs.

In the stands: The stands react to the announcement that it is Insurance Agent Appreciation Night with sparse applause.

A question is considered: Do umpires rotate counter-clockwise below the equator?

A fan is criticized for his overuse of platitudes. His response: "Cliche is my middle name."

The organist picks a good one to play for the Padres' secondbaseman, Gardner. "Tiptoe Through The Tulips."

He's also right on when he salutes the ejection of San Diego's starting pitcher and manager with "Happy Trails."

When Ray J. actually does spill his beer, all around him tut-tut and tsk-tsk. Ray defends himself: "Well, at least it's not flash photography."

Everyone is glad that Denver fans haven't adopted the annoying singsong "DAR-yl" or "JER-ald" to salute Boston and Clark.

And there was this expression of warmth from a Rockies fan to a Padres fan: "We like the Padres, too. If it weren't for them, we'd be in last place."

In Seattle: With a 3-1 count on Dave Magadan, Nolan Ryan's elbow finally gives out and the game's all-time strikeout king (5,714) is forced to retire two starts ahead of schedule.

The Rockies have now won 64 and lost 90. That 64 ties the record for a NL expansion team, set by the 1962 Houston Colt .45s. The Rox are in sixth place, 5.5 games behind the Reds and 4.5 games ahead of the Padres. Florida is 62-90. The Mets are 52-100. Oakland is 62-89.

Thursday, September 23 is an open date, but it marks the second anniversary of the naming of Bob Gebhard as GM of the Colorado Rockies.

Friday, September 24: Colorado 9, Cincinnati 2

The win that breaks the NL expansion team victory record.

7:05 at Mile High Stadium
The National Anthem: Mormon Chorale
The first ball: Eddie Shafi (senior at North High)
The starting pitchers: Hurst (0-2) vs. Ayala (6-9)
The W-L pitchers: Reed (8-5) and Ayala (6-10)
The attendance: 57,330
The News Headline: Rockies pay back the Reds
The Post Headline: Rockies going out with a bang

On the field: The victory makes the Rox the winningest NL expansion team ever, besting the '62 Houston Colt .45s' 64 victories. Today's W also gives Colorado a 15-7 record for the month. This is the first time any expansion team has enjoyed a winning September.

Galarraga doesn't do his quest for the batting crown any good—he goes 0-5—but most of the rest of the Rockies feast on Cincy pitching, scoring one run in the first, two in the second, three in the third and three more in the innings to come.

Rockies starter Hurst looks good, but only for 29 pitches, 18 of which were strikes. He is taken out of the game by shoulder tightness—and Larry Bearnarth.

Four Rockies pitchers (Hurst, Blair, Reed & Ruffin) hold the Reds to as many hits.

In the stands: Celebrity spotters spot golf pro Nancy Lopez and NBA star Danny Ainge.

A lady is wearing a CR cap that she has fixed up real nice with about an inch of lace trim hung from the bill.

A tent filled with the season's ending closeout on Rockies merchandise has gone up in the parking lot SW of the stadium. Everyone agrees that it *does* look like DIA.

An observation by Jack Hidahl: "Every time Galarraga came to bat, he got a bigger reaction from the crowd than the time before. And yet he failed to get a hit each time. In other ballparks, failure is met with boos. Here, fans just increased their support with each at-bat. The last time he came up, after going 0-for-4, a third of the crowd was on its feet. It was terrific."

On Channel 7: John Keating says that we now compare the Rockies' attendance numbers to the population of countries and "We have just passed Norway."

Today's milestone: Jim Neidlinger's birthday (1964)

The Rockies have now won three in a row, have a 65-90 record, and are in sixth place, 33.5 games out of first and 5.5 games ahead of the Padres. The Rox' record is also better than Florida's 62-91 and, of course, the Mets' 52-101.

Saturday, September 25, Cincinnati 6, Colorado 0
The speediest home game of the season.

> **7:05 at Mile High Stadium**
> **The National Anthem:** Josh Rael, 12
> **The first ball:** Andy Daly (Vail Associates)
> **The starting pitchers:** Harris (11-15) vs. Rijo (13-8)
> **The W-L pitchers:** Rijo (14-8) and Harris (11-16)
>   (1-7 with Colorado)
> **The attendance:** 61,179
> **The News Headline:** Rijo Bravo! Reds ace throttles
>   Rockies
> **The Post Headline:** Rijo tames Rockies bats

On the way in: The price of parking at the lot near Federal on Dick Connor Drive continues to be an excellent way to rate a game's drawing power. Tonight's game is a pretty fair draw; it rates a $7.

On the field: Jose Rijo throws a barely-one-hitter against the Rockies and faces just 28 as the game sails by in a minute under two hours. A fan notes with alarm that the 7th inning begins at 8:37.

It's Eric Wedge's first start. [And it will be his only.]

It's another 0-for day for Andres. It's Hayes' broken-bat single in the 2nd that keeps it from being a no-hitter for Rijo. It's the third time the Rox are shut out at home. (Although they've now suffered 13 shutouts, this is a category the Rockies do not lead. The Marlins and White Sox have each been zeroed on 14 occasions.)

Alex Cole continues to solidify his position as 1993's ML batter with the most ABs—but 0 HRs.

[The last time Cole got a HR was for Louisville four years ago. He has over 1,200 major league plate appearances, but has yet to enjoy a four-bagger.]

Rijo's masterpiece brings back mention of one of Mile High's stories out of the Old Days. Once again, we hear it:

"If I remember, the only no-no game was thrown by the Denver Bears' Ryne Duren in '57." Pause. Throat clear.

"But that was just a seven-inning game, so it doesn't really count."

In the stands: It's Ski Cap Night.

It is also grumble-about-the-organist night.

For the Reds' Reggie Sanders, he plays "Love Letters in the Sanders." It's cute, but we don't want our organist sending love letters to the opposition.

Can the fans come up with something appropriate for Sanders, something that puts him down, disses him, or distracts him from the task at hand?

No. But the consensus is that if you can't play something bad about someone, don't play anything at all.

For the Reds Juan Samuel, the fans recommend "Juan is the loneliest number."

Counters of things count seven skyboxes in use tonight. Not counting the opener, it's probably a season high. So to speak.

Already preparing for the off season, a member of a season ticket consortium decides to have a winter meeting of the members of his partnership the same time ML baseball has its winter meeting.

The swing from purple back to pink cotton candy puzzles The Fans' Ombudsman, so he makes an inquiry.

One peddler of the spun sugar confection explains it nice and simple: "Pink sells better."

But is it art?

The Rockies now have a 65-91 record and are in sixth place, six games behind the Reds and 5.5 games ahead of the Padres. The magic number for not winding up in the cellar is zero.

The Colorado Rockies have clinched sixth place!

The last home game of the first season.

1:05 at Mile High Stadium
The National Anthem: Anne Achenbach
The first ball: Steve Katzenberger (King Soopers)
The starting pitchers: Reynoso (11-10) vs. Luebbers
(2-4)
The W-L pitchers: Reynoso (12-10) and Luebbers (2-5)
The attendance: 70,069
The News Headline: Fanfare beyond compare (front
page) and Rockies make it a grand finale (sports)
The Post Headline: Attaboy, Rockies! (front page) and
Rockies home finale is Mile High (sports page)

In the air: Fall. But just a touch. Predicted for today is crummy weather, maybe even snow. But it wasn't to be.

The weather, like everything else today, is glorious.

On the field: Few said it, but many thunk it: *Wouldn't today be a great time for Eric Young to homer again!* After all, Eric was the hero of The First Home Game Ever when he led off with a homer as the First Rockies Batter Ever In Mile High Stadium— and hadn't gotten gotten another in the 80 home games since.

Naturally, he comes through. Supernaturally, he comes through *twice*. Leaving him as the hitter of the first and last homers in the inaugural season.

Baylor on Young's feat: "EY hitting two home runs in a ballgame? You might have seen it for the last time in your life."

Also sweet is Galarraga's 3-for-5 day at the plate, which makes his taking the NL batting title home to Venezuela a virtual certainty. And just as a bonus for the fans, one of those three hits is a home run. Galarraga's three RBI raise him to 97 and make him the RBI leader for an expansion player.

Reynoso's twelfth win leaves him one off the all-time record for wins by an expansion pitcher. And it closes down the last homestand of the Rockies' first season on a nifty 10-3 note.

Bichette, who hasn't been in a game since September 15, when a Doug Jones pitch broke his left hand, was installed as a pinch runner in the 8th and scored.

That's run No. 93 for Bichette, breaking the record for an expansion team set 32 years ago by the L.A. Angels' Albie Pearson. (Pearson, baseball's smallest player throughout his career, was just 5'5" and had virtually no strike zone. He drew 96 walks in '61.)

Six players started the first and last home games of Season One: Girardi, Galarraga, Hayes, Clark, Young, and Cole. Which suggests that a certain No. 25 has a sense of drama.

This is good.

In the stands: It's Colorado Lottery 1994 Schedule Holder Day. Everybody gets a schedule showing next season's tentative lineup of games. *Everybody*. To the delight of many, it's loaded with day games. Unlike this season, when the team opened and closed away from home, next season calls for the Rox to conduct both events in front of the home crowd, beginning with a tilt against the National League Champion Phillies.

Speaking of crowds, today is the day they put up the final attendance numbers. With a near-sellout crowd on hand, the home season's final turnstile click is 4,483,350—a number, all agree, that will never be threatened.

It will stand as the all-time season attendance for any team in any sport until the sun burns out.

Or until the season is extended to 262 games. Whichever comes first.

More attendance numbers to ponder in the off-season: The Rockies averaged 56,751 at home for 79 dates (two cancellations). They had 9 crowds of 70,000+, 27 crowds of 60,000+, and 63 crowds of 50,000+

Today, the most prominent sign causes a lot of head-scratching.

THANK YOU ROKIES it says, quite neatly lettered. Simply stated. Just right. But *where*, many wondered, was the comma?

Superfan Butch goes up the aisle between Sections 114 and 115 throwing out little metal crickets. They are employed when the opposition is at bat. The annoying clicking from Section 115 is credited with its first strikeout in the top of the first when Reds catcher Brian Dorsett goes down swinging.

Just as he has for game after game, Section 117's hyperfan John loudly informs the plate umpire that "MY GRANDMOTHER CAN SEE BETTER THAN YOU AND

SHE'S BEEN DEAD FOR TEN YEARS."

From across the aisle, another John asks: "Next year, will it be eleven?"

And when a woman who has called out to a vendor "One peanut, please!" yet another John informs her that "They come in a bag."

Ray Jones can't be at the home closer, so he sends a poem to be read to his seatmates. It begins: "This is the last home game of a remarkable season; I miss it sadly, but with good reason." And it contains this line: "I hope that upon rising from their beds, the Rockies resolve, as Yeltsin, to beat the Reds."

Speculation in the stands: "You know, there's a lot of talk about putting EY in the number four spot next season." "Yeah, but only for two games."

Sam Suplizio and Tillie Bishop brought two busloads of people to today's game. From Grand Junction.

Doug and Grace Fisgus are in attendance. It's their fifth game of the season—and the Rockies have won all five. "The Rockies should give us season tickets next year," Doug says. "And then, at the end of the season, they should give us World Series rings." And shares.

Lisa Trampler has a nice story along the same lines— only even longer. She went to 13 games without a loss.

When there's a pitching change, that annoying phone ringing sound is heard.

"That is so cold!" a fan says.

And another points out that "it's our guy, too."

Organist Shockney has rethunk his choice of "Love Letters in the Sanders" as a tune for welcoming Reggie Sanders.

Today, in the first inning, it's "Mr. Sandman." Another bad choice. The lyrics position the opponent as "a dream." Which turns into a bit of a nightmare for the Rockies when Sanders strokes a Reynoso offering for a triple.

Bob the Beerman is busily handing out his first annual survey. Question No. 3 asks which name you prefer for the new ballpark:

A) Bob's Field
B) The BobsterDome
C) The House That Bob Built
D) Bob's Field of Dreams
E) Bob's Soul Center of the Universe Field

On hand to witness all the wonderment of Home Game Eighty-One is NL prexy Bill White. Wearing a tie. White was last here for Game One. (EY always homers when Bill White is in the stands.) Which brings up a question: Does the NL President count? Without Bill White as a fan would the Rockies' attendance be just 4,483,348?

More on White: One wonders if he recalls visiting Bears Stadium when he was with Minneapolis in the American Association back in 1954.

The huge sign across the top of the South Stands has already been taken down. Does that mean that we're no longer THE WORLDS GREATEST BASEBALL FANS? Does that mean it's time to revert back into The World's Greatest Football Fans?

We can do that. But we've got to warn the NFL of one thing. To match the Rockies' attendance numbers, the Broncos are going to have to play more than 50 games a year.

And who's the greatest of the greatest fans? A good candidate would be J.A. (JoAn) Flower, 64, of Lillian, Alabama. Somehow, Flower attended 80 games at Mile High and 19 on the road. Yes, a move to Colorado is in the works for this fan of fans.

No hopers.

Now it can be revealed. A fan has been keeping track of Rockies' runners and keeping Yet Another Statistic.

When a ground ball is obviously going to be an out, many baserunners take it easy down the line. Which means that when the fielder fumbles an easy ball or the firstbaseman muffs the catch, the taking-it-easy runner is still out.

It is the rare player who runs just as fast as he can every time—including on no-hopers. Here's the fan's report:

"These are at-home stats: Of all the players with several no-hoper chances, two *never* ran hard: Boston and Hayes.

"These four regular players had varying running-hard percentages as follows: Cole—80%. Clark—40%. Young—38%. Bichette—33%.

"There was only one player who had several running opportunities and scored 100%. Chris Jones."

After the game: The grounds crew carefully covers up the mound with a nice tarp. One wonders why. Probably just habit.

Girardi makes a nice statement to the crowd: "If we could

only take all of you on the road—you'd have to take turns because the stadiums aren't big enough—we'd be in the World Series." Well, maybe not. Projecting the 39-42 home record to 162 games only gives us 78 wins.

And McMorris & Co. give away five cars to random fans (aren't they all?) and then, in a final emotion-packed gesture, the team walks around the perimeter of the field saluting the fans in the stands. Yes, a lot of big, bad beer-swilling umpire-bating lugs experienced glistening in the eye area, but what the hell, it'll never happen again.

In the parking lot: As two fans walk to their car, they bemoan having forgotten to do something. "Remember that great year the Denver Bears had? Remember the last game of the season when we yelled to Felipe [Alou, the manager who was coaching third base] in the top of the ninth? 'Thanks for a great season!' we yelled...and he turned to us and tipped his hat. That was great."

"What we should've done when there was one out to go in the top of the ninth was to start chanting THANKS, DON! THANKS, DON! THANKS, DON! Pretty soon, the entire stadium would've been doing it. That would've really been something!"

And it would've been the correct thing to do.

The Rockies now have a 66-91 record, which is good enough for sixth place, 6.5 games ahead of the 59-97 Padres. The Rox record is better than the fading Marlins (63-92) and faded Mets (53-102) and is enticingly close to the records of the A's and Twins (both at 66-89) and the Brewers (66-90).

Monday, September 27 is an open date, and it is welcomed throughout The Time Zone With Only One Team. After yesterday's delicious—but draining—afternoon, players and fans both need a little time to rebale their emotional hay.

From the look of his cartoon in today's News, Drew Litton has already rebaled. It shows a fan sitting alone in Mile High Stadium with a sign; ONLY 157 DAYS UNTIL OPENING DAY.

Meanwhile, the White Sox and Blue Jays clinch their divisions.

And the Rockies are off to wind up their season on the road against the two teams who are fighting to win the NL

West. There'll be a two-game set against the Giants (which has beat the Rox in 7 of 9 encounters) and three against the Braves (which has taken all ten contests with Colorado).

Joe Girardi: "That's the next step, beating the elite teams."

Ironic twist dept.: It is announced that Denver's new franchise in the International Hockey League may well be named the Denver Bears.

Toe break dept.: Tonight, Pedro Castellano fractured the little toe on his left foot as he walked from bathroom to bed in the dark.

Cleaning up after The Cat: Galarraga's exploits have brought him under intense scrutiny. Fans now litter their baseball chitchat with facts like "The Cat averages only 2.94 pitches per appearance. That's the fewest in the NL."

And "The Cat has walked only 24 times this season, 12 of them intentionally."

And "The Cat has swung at the first pitch 54% of the time and 63% of all the pitches he's seen."

And "The Cat is batting .487 when he puts the first pitch into play."

And "The Cat is batting .411 at home and .344 on the road."

And "The Cat, at 252 lbs., is the biggest man ever to win a batting title."

Tuesday, September 28: San Francisco 6, Colorado 4
The first game of the last road trip of the first season.

8:35 at Candlestick Park
The starting pitchers: Nied (5-7) vs. Hickerson (6-5)
The W-L pitchers: Hickerson (7-5) and Nied (5-8)
The attendance: 28,568
The News Headline: Giants beat Rockies, get even in West
The Post Headline: A Giant step forward

In the Post: Todd Phipers' cartoon shows a youthful (diapered, even) Rocky with his slingshot trained on a Neanderthalesque giant who says, "How about saving it for Atlanta, kid?"

On the field: Indeed, the Giants are fighting for their lives.
Their post-season lives.

By beating the Rox while Atlanta drops a 5-2 game to the Astros, the San Franciscos propel themselves into a tie with the Braves. Both now sport 100-57 records.

But should the Giants have won this encounter? If we count hits instead of runs, the Rockies would've prevailed, 14-4.

But for seven innings, the Rox waste their 11 hits, amassing nary a run for their efforts.

Finally, in the 8th, Charlie Hayes smacks homer #25 with two on. This gives him 98 ribbies.

The Rox now have 745 runs on the season. This tops the previous record for an expansion club, 744, set by the L.A. Angels in '61.

In Westword, there is disquieting news. Earlier in the year, it was reported that cities that have a major league teams have lower divorce rates.

Now Westword says that Coloradans divorced at the rate of 5.7 per thousand last year, much higher than the national rate of 4.7 a thou.

But Westword, that was *last* year.

Wait'll next year!

In front of a TV set in Wheat Ridge, a couple of beery fans recall the line Will "The Thrill" Clark is alleged to have on his answering machine: "The Thrill is gone. Please leave your message after the beep."

Whereupon they try to think up some for The Boys in the Purple Pinstripes.

Among the best were these:

For our relief ace: "Nobody's Holmes. Please leave your message..."

For Sanford: "No Mo. Please leave your message..."

And for Galarraga: "Cat's got your tongue. Please leave..."

The Rockies are now 66-92 and are safely in sixth place, six games ahead of the Padres. Colorado's record is also better than the Mets (54-103) and the Marlins (64-93), and the same as the Milwaukee Brewers.

Wednesday, September 29: Colorado 5, San Francisco 3

The first time the Rox have knocked a NL leader out of first place.

2:05 at Candlestick Park
The starting pitchers: Bottenfield (5-10) vs. Torres (3-3)
The W-L pitchers: Reed (9-5) and Torres (3-4)
The attendance: 39,377
The News Headline: Rockies put damper on Giants' party
The Post Headline: Rockies Giant killers

On the field: Going in, the Giants, riding a seven-game winning streak, were tied with the Braves at 100 wins each. During, the Giants have two bases-loaded chances which turn out to be nonproductive. Coming out, they are defeated with the help of a pair of Daryl Boston homers.

(Meanwhile, the Braves topped Houston, 6-3.)

In the News, Bob Kravitz says the Rockies have become America's Most Annoying Team.

The hero in relief is Reed, who was drafted from the Giants and hankered to do a number on the the team that left him hanging last year. Reed comes in with the bases loaded and one out to face Matt Williams and induces the slugger to bounce into a double play.

Amos Otis, the Rockies' hitting coach, is thrown out of game after he exchanges harsh pronouncements with umpire Bruce Froemming from the dugout after the second inning.

In the mail: A postcard arrives in Denver from a fan in New Hampshire, Baxter Harris:

"My my! First season and involved in the pennant race! Congrats!"

In Royals Stadium, George Brett makes his final appearance. And singles home Kansas City's winning run in the 8th.

The Rockies now have a 67-92 record, are in sixth place, 34.5 behind the Braves and 7 ahead of the Padres.

Thursday, September 30 is an open date. And a good time to relish the Rockies' record for the month. It's 17-9, the best September ever for an expansion team. Matter o' fact, it's the first time in history that an expansion team has *had* a winning record after September 1.

Amazingly, five of the NL's top six batters for September are Ours. They are Galarraga, Young, Liriano, Hayes, and Girardi. The only interloper is the Mets' Eddie Murray.

Things are really heating up in Our Division of Our League. Today, the Giants beat the Dodgers while the Astros knocked off the Braves, so the San Franciscos are once again tied with the Atlantas for the lead with identical 101-58 records.

As they head for Atlanta, the Rockies are relishing their recent success (they've won 31 of their last 49 games). And they're reportedly talking about making up for their pitiful performances of the past against the Braves. In spite of Atlanta's 10-0 domination of Colorado, the Rox are confident they'll win at least two of the three games that remain in the regular season. Darren Holmes, in fact, predicts we'll *sweep*.

Sounds good.

In the media: Much is being made of the Rockies impact on sales of caps, T-shirts, etc. throughout the country.

Not only are Rockies fans (and other lovers of Colorado, purple things, the initials CR, and God knows who else) the number-one purchasers of Rockies merchandise, this year they've accounted for 12% of the $250 million sales of baseball stuff.

Which works out to 12¢ per capita. Or T-shirtica.

Friday, October 1: Atlanta 7, Colorado 4

The game that Pendleton beat the Rockies, 5-4.

> **5:40 at Atlanta-Fulton County Stadium**
> **The starting pitchers:** Harris (11-16) vs. Avery (17-6)
> **The W-L pitchers:** Avery (18-6) and Harris (11-17)
>   (1-8 with Colorado)
> **The attendance:** 48,968
> **The News Headline:** Braves beat up on Rockies again
> **The Post Headline:** Rockies still 0 for Atlanta

Before the game, Pete Redmond, the bartender at the Elks Club in Central City, worries that the club's cable package doesn't include the channel carrying today's Rockies game—so he calls Pagosa Vision, the cable company that serves that area, and orders a package with more channels.

On the field: Harris struggles again.

As Woody Paige puts it, "they treated him worse than a rental car."

All four batters he walks in his four-inning performance wind up scoring. With the help of a pair of homers, Pendleton drives in 5.

Meanwhile, the Rockies' sole moment of glory is provided by Chris Jones in the fourth when he belts a two-run home run to pull the Rockies to within two.

But the Rockies are able to cop only one hit off Avery (8 innings pitched) and reliever McMichael (1 inning) the rest of the way.

The last time the Braves won 102 games in a season, they were the Boston Beaneaters. That was 1898. Few remember it well.

In Venezuela, fans are listening to live radio broadcasts of the last three games. For some reason.

A graphic on Channel 2: ATLATNA FULTON COUNTY STADIUM

In today's USA Today, a headline proclaims that "Marlins aiming to catch Rockies." The accompanying story points out that the best Florida can do in the battle for expansion supremacy is tie the Rockies.

But that would require 3-0 ball from the Marlins and a 0-3 performance by the Rox.

The Rockies now have a record of 67-93 (.419). They remain lodged securely in sixth place, 35 games behind Atlanta and San Francisco and 7 games ahead of San Diego.

Because the Mets knocked off the Marlins today, the Rockies are assured of finishing with a better record.

Both Milwaukee (67-93) and Oakland (68-92) are candidates for being tied or bettered by the Rockies.

The last Game of the Week.

> **1:05 at Atlanta-Fulton County Stadium (rescheduled from 5:10)**
> **The starting pitchers:** Reynoso (12-10) vs. Maddux (19-9)
> **The W-L pitchers:** Maddux (20-10) and Reynoso (12-11)
> **The attendance:** 48,899
> **The News Headline:** Braves race past Rockies again
> **The Post Headline:** Rockies crushed by Braves

On CBS TV: Baseball's Saturday Game of the Week has been around since the 1950s, but this is the last one. Televised baseball scheduling will take new fashions and forms next season. And, apparently, they won't include Saturday.

So much for the business end of baseball.

On to the game...

Braves starter Maddux tells the national TV audience that he learned from a fortune cookie that "underestimating your opponent can lead to catastrophe."

On the field: The bottom line is that the Braves smash the Rocks while the Giants slip by the Dodgers, 5-3, so the NL West is still tied with one day to go. Maybe two. (There could be a playoff on Monday.)

Here's how the Braves manhandle Colorado:

Maddux doesn't underestimate anything. He sprinkles four hits over seven innings, allowing just one lousy unearned run, before turning it over to a pair of relievers who shut the Rox down the rest of the way.

Meanwhile, the Braves strike starter Reynoso for two runs in the first inning and again in the third. Then they add three more off Leskanic and another three off Wayne. Even Maddux gets an RBI today.

And Reynoso winds up one W away from tying the expansion record for victories.

The Big Cat's big wait is over. Today, Andres Galarraga finally notches his 502nd at-bat, so when he is crowned the 1993 NL batting champ, the royal headgear will not be tarnished. He marks the milestone with a single up the middle.

Matter of fact, he collects two of the Rockies' five hits today.

Oh, and after the game he's informed that he's been named the National League Player of the Month again.

Add this factoid to the flood of Galarraga numbers that has swept over Denver and of late: 27%. That's the size of the chunk of the season Galarraga missed.

And this: He's just the fourth NLeaguer from a last-place team to win the batting title.

The Rockies now have a 67-94 record. They're in sixth, 6.5 games ahead of the Padres. Milwaukee won and Oakland lost.

Both now have 68 wins, one better than the Rox.

Sunday, October 3: Atlanta 5, Colorado 3
The last game of the first season.

11:10 at Atlanta-Fulton County Stadium
The starting pitchers: Nied (5-8) vs. Glavine (21-6)
The W-L pitchers: Glavine (22-6) and Nied (5-9)
The attendance: 48,904
The News Headline: Braves sweep Rockies to win West
The Post Headline: Braves climb Rockies to the top

On the field: Hayes and Galarraga go into the game with ribbies on their minds. Each is trying to get into three digits, but neither drives in a runner and both complete the season with 98.

But twenty-one-year-old Robert Mejia, who's described by Woody Paige as "the All-Latin American Boy," does. He bangs out a homer in the 7th inning for the Rockies' last run of 1993.

But it wasn't enough to keep the Rockies from becoming the first expansion team ever to be swept in a season series. The Braves finish the season 13-zip against the Purple. (Even the Marlins were able to win five from the chop crazies.)

It gets worse. The Rockies are the first NL team this century—expansion or not—that was swept in a season series.

The last National Leaguers to suffer this ignominy were the Cleveland Spiders. That was in 1899.

Yes, but dept.: Much is made of the fact that even the lowly Mets in their lowliest incarnation as 40-game winners in '62 won at least one game from every other team in the league.

Yes, but the league was smaller then. So each team played only nine other teams. Which meant they got several more cracks at each.

The Rockies wind up the season with a record of 67-95 (.414), which gives them sixth place, 37 games behind first-place Atlanta. (San Francisco winds up in second place, one game back.) San Diego will winter in last place, 43 games out.

The Rockies finish three games in front of the 64-98 Marlins and numerous games ahead of the 59-103 Mets (they finish with a mirror image—backwards and upside-down—of the Giants' season).

Colorado fails to finish with a better record than the hapless A's (68-94) or the feckless Brewers (69-93).

Furthermore, the Rockies have another zero to contemplate over the winter. They've never won in October.

In the American League, the White Sox and Blue Jays win their divisions by eight and seven games, respectively.

In the San Francisco Bay Guardian, a cartoon depicts two characters sitting in a bar down at the wharf. One says "Every team that beat the Giants once gets the credit for knocking them out of the World Series." The other: "Even the Colorado Rockies get credit." And hurls himself into San Francisco Bay.

Monday, October 4:
The day after the last day.

Don Baylor: "I still don't believe it."

Vince Porreco (Metro State Baseball Coach): "No other sport hurts like this one does when it comes to an end."

Gambling on God's Game.
Before the season began, 118 people put in a dollar apiece and predicted how many games the Rockies would win.

Naturally, several people would wind up picking the same number, so there was a tie-breaker: The number of victories David Nied would garner. In case there was a tie there, too, the second tie-breaker was Galarraga's batting average. (It was just chance that Galarraga was picked; who was to know that it would be his BA that was the big story of Year One?)

People picked from 23 to 103 victories for the team. Most had Nied with 10-15 wins. *And only seven of the 118 guessed the Cat would bat above .300.*

The winner of the $118 was Tom Kelsey, a photographer with the Rocky Mountain News. He nailed the wins at 67 and beat out the other three 67 guessers (Ray Imel, Jr., Sandy Sullivan and Gene Bryan) because he had the low guess for Nied victories, 7.

IRS please note.

How soon they forget dept.:

In a story about the playoffs in the October 6 Rocky Mountain News, Galarraga's legion of fans gagged on this twelvepack of words: "John Olerud, who led the majors in hitting in the regular season..."

Olerud, with a .363 BA, led the Blue Jays, the American League, and American-born batters—but not the majors.

On October 5, Michael Jordan took the mound at Comiskey Park and threw out the first pitch of the opener of the AL Champion Series between the White Sox and the Blue Jays.

The next day, Michael Jordan announced his retirement from basketball.

As Bill Gallo said, "Fans far and wide grasped the irony of the greatest basketball player of all time ending his public life with a baseball in his hand."

On October 8, Channel 4's Coors Field Cam made its debut. It will follow the progress of the future home of the Rox.

On November 18, the first fan wondered whether Howard Johnson would be the first Rock to poke 40 out.

On thinking back: In 1993, the Colorado Rockies played in eleven stadiums, one field, one park, and one dome. They didn't scare many other teams (except for the Astros and, once, the Giants), but it was one helluva year for their fans.

Like they say, it doesn't matter if it was bad or good, you never forget your first.

And the memory just keeps getting better.

Thoughts for the First Off Season Ever.

Usually, the fan goes through this progression at the ballpark:

First: Well, there goes the perfect game.

Next: Well, there goes the no-hitter.

Then: Well, there goes the shutout.

Indeed, there *have* been perfect games in baseball. But none've been truly perfect

In a truly perfect game you'd see a pitcher not just face the minimum 27 batters—but he would eradicate them with the minimum 27 pitches.

What? You say the pitcher of a truly perfect game would have to *strike out* all 27? Perhaps you're right.

But there have been well over a hundred thousand games played in the history of the big leagues and neither has occurred. Or is likely to.

There are, however, some things that haven't happened yet that may well come to pass in Season Two of the Colorado Rockies.

Here they are: Things to look forward to.

• The first shutout. *For* the Rockies.

• The first win over the Braves.

• The first win at Riverfront.

• The first win in October.

• The first triple play.

• The first pitcher to win 20 games.

• The first batter to hit for the cycle.

• The first batter to hit .371.

• The first split doubleheader. (In '93, the Rockies either won both or lost both.)

• The first Rockies' uniform with a tilde on its back. (Muñoz could use one.) (It's too late for Seañez.)

• The first appearance of Mike Shepard, the bullpen catcher in a game. Just one.

• The first expansion team to have a turnaround like the Braves had in 1991. They went to the World Series that year. But the year before, their record was 65-97.

About the author.

Raised in Denver, Lew Cady came from a family full of baseball fans. His brother, Steve, took a radio to school during World Series games (they were played during the day then), plugged in the little earphone, and told his teacher he'd become hard of hearing.

As a kid, Cady's dad took him to many Bears games, but he didn't see his first major league baseball game until he was back east in college in the mid-fifties.

The first time he stepped into a big league stadium was for a doubleheader, the Senators visiting the Yankees. Batting left-handed, Mickey Mantle blasted one of the longest hits of his career. It struck the cornice atop the second deck and was the closest anyone had come to hitting a fair ball over the roof of Yankee Stadium

Other highlights of Cady's baseball watching career:

He saw the first game played in Shea Stadium.

He caught a foul ball at a Denver Bears game on July 7, 1980. On the fly. One-handed. Without spilling a significant quantity of the beverage in his other hand.

He had the first beer—and the first hot dog—at Coors Field, moments after the groundbreaking ceremony.

He's seen at least one game in all of the 28 big league ballparks—but one.

He suggested the shade of purple (PMS 273) the Rockies adopted as one of their official colors.

Best of all, though, the highlight of his entire career of watching baseball, Lew Cady once saw Greg Luzinski steal home.